MAN AND MIND:
A Christian Theory of Personality

Edited by Thomas J. Burke

The Hillsdale College Press
Hillsdale, Michigan 49242

Books by the Hillsdale College Press include: the *Champions of Freedom* series on economics; the *Christian Vision* series; *Scorpions in a Bottle: Dangerous Ideas About the United States and the Soviet Union; Political and Economic Pluralism in the Third World; Still the Law of the Land: Essays on Changing Interpretations of the Constitution;* and other works.

General Editors: Lynne Morris and Lissa Roche

The Christian Vision Series
MAN AND MIND: A CHRISTIAN THEORY OF PERSONALITY

© 1987 by Hillsdale College Press
Hillsdale, Michigan 49242

Printed in the United States of America

All rights reserved. No part of this publication may be reproduced without the prior written permission of the publisher.

Second Printing 1989
Library of Congress Catalog Card Number 85-081263
ISBN 0-916-308-90-1

Cover illustration from Colin Blakemore, *Mechanics of the Mind* (Cambridge University Press, 1977), p. 18.

Contents

Introduction
Thomas J. Burke v

Psychology, Theology, and the Liberal Arts: Toward the Unity of Knowledge
Thomas J. Burke 1

Personality Theories: What Questions Are We Trying to Answer?
Stephen R. Briggs 19

Has Modern Psychology Secularized Religion?
Mary Vander Goot 43

Secular Personality Theories: A Critical Analysis
Paul C. Vitz 65

The Mystery of Human Nature
Charles Ransford 95

Philosophy, Faith, and Personality Theory
Merold Westphal 111

Why Secular Psychology Is Not Enough
William Kirk Kilpatrick 133

Telling the Truth: A Biblical View of Personality
John S. Reist, Jr. 149

Personality Theorizing Within a Christian World View
Mary Stewart Van Leeuwen 171

A Christian Theory of Personality: Covenant Theory
Paul C. Vitz 199

Index 223

Introduction

One uniquely human penchant is our need to have opinions about the nature and structure of the world. What is it? Where did it come from? How does it work? What is it for? These sorts of questions are characteristically human and have been asked and thought about as far back in our history as records allow us knowledge. Moreover, such questioning has not been limited to the world outside us, but has also been directed towards ourselves. Indeed, more often than not we ask such questions about the world "out there" because of the implications their answers have for us personally. We are simply incapable of functioning productively for any length of time if we are possessed of no view about ourselves and the purpose or "meaning" of our lives. It is quite natural, then, that upon having discovered a new and powerful method of learning about the world, we should eventually apply it to ourselves in order to learn just what sort of creatures we are, how we are constructed, how we think and decide, and how we can improve our lot both materially and psychologically. The rise of scientifically oriented psychology was, in retrospect, inevitable. That it took so long to develop is testimony to the power and endurance of older philosophical and religious concepts to provide personally satisfying views about ourselves. But once the idea was advanced that we could perhaps solve age-long disputes about human nature by recourse to the "scientific method," the birth and development of modern psychology was swift and its influence pervasive.

Psychology, which seeks to do more than catalog statistical

information about humans (given stimulus or environment or incentive X, Y% will respond or choose or feel, etc., Z), will properly construct theories about human nature as such. Indeed, experiment cannot take place in a vacuum, and all investigations of human behavior and thinking assume certain fundamental ideas about humans. Every influential psychology has made fundamental assumptions about human nature, explicitly or implicitly, which it develops or exploits. It has recently come to our attention, however, that these prior understandings of human nature have not been arrived at scientifically, for although science is excellent when it comes to compiling and relating data and to answering questions about how things work, it is simply incapable of answering questions about the ultimate nature of things. Even if psychology could discover all it is capable of knowing about humans, it would not thereby have been enabled to pronounce on the meaning or import of human existence. Of course, one can always rule out all such questions as misunderstanding the true nature of man, but obviously *that* view begs the question. In fact, every view of man, psychological, philosophical, or theological, gives an answer to these sorts of questions; what we are now realizing is that the answers given are *not* scientific answers but philosophical and theological. But if these questions need to be answered if we are to possess an adequate and complete view of ourselves, then science alone is not sufficient for a complete psychology; the latter will of necessity draw upon the resources of philosophy and theology in order to supply the missing ingredients. The association of a particular philosophical or theological view of man with science does not make those views any more valid than previous ones, for they will only be as good as the philosophy and theology from which they have been drawn. A fully developed view of humanity will necessitate not only the information supplied by scientific psychology and its social science sisters, but also the insights and knowledge that philosophy and theology can bring.

The inclusion of theology as a source of knowledge about what it means to be human will sound to many at best anachronistic, at worst, pitifully naive. But that is the case only if theology is false, *i.e.*, if either there is no God or there is no propositional knowledge about humanity revealed to us by God. But if God does exist and if in addition He has revealed crucial facts about mankind, then these must be considered as we attempt to formulate a total view of human nature. For those who reject theism, the current volume will be of interest only as a curiosity; but for those who do place themselves in the theistic tradition of the West, it will, we hope, be both informative and encouraging. Both psychology and theology have had much to say about man, and for the practicing Jew or Christian it is imperative that these two fields inform one another, for two fields which both deal with the same subject ought to be not only compatible in the broadly logical sense, but also mutually helpful. Psychology has for the past one hundred years been attempting to learn about personhood, and theology has for centuries assumed important ideas on the subject. While, therefore, it may be silly to imagine a "Christian physics" (for theology has never been centrally concerned with matters of natural science as it has been with foundational concepts of man), the idea of a "Christian psychology" is neither silly nor unnecessary. If one is to construct an adequate Christian world view, it is imperative.

It is to this end, the eventual development of a psychology from the perspective of a Christian theological view of persons, that the current contributions, given at CCA I (Center for Constructive Alternatives) in the fall of 1985, are presented. They by no means pretend to be definitive, but are intended to help Christian thinkers integrate psychology with Christian theology or, alternatively, to develop a psychology from a Christian perspective which will prove beneficial both to theology and psychology.

In the first paper, "Psychology, Theology, and the Liberal Arts: Toward the Unity of Knowledge," I attempt to set the stage for the conference by arguing that the integration of psychology with theology is, for the Christian, both possible and necessary. It is possible because the knowledge gained from theology is the same sort of knowledge gained from psychology, *viz.*, propositional;[1] it is necessary because only by seeing the "facts" which psychology discovers in the context of our theological understanding of man can we properly interpret those "facts," and only in light of those "facts" can our theology do justice to the biblical view of man. The Bible may be the final and authoritative verbal revelation from God to man, but in this age theology is our feeble attempt to understand and order that revelation. Consequently, it will always remain incomplete and, therefore, benefit from relevant knowledge gained through other sources. Surely, for the Christian, no ultimate irresolvable conflict between scientific knowledge and revelatory knowledge may exist, but there most certainly can be conflict with our current theology, for just as psychology utilizes philosophical ideas in both its assumptions and its conclusions, so theology employs philosophical and "scientific" (*i.e.*, currently held views about the way the world is) ideas in both its exegesis of revelation and its conceptual development. Indeed, it is the underlying unity of knowledge which allows for and makes imperative the integration of theology and psychology. I conclude that this integration is the ongoing task of the liberal arts and, therefore, part of the mandate for a liberal arts college as it seeks to educate future generations.

In "Personality Theories: What Questions Are We Trying to Answer?", Stephen Briggs continues to advance the theme that a Christian theory of man can contribute significantly to personality theory. He begins by pointing out that contemporary psychology considers itself to have learned from earlier theories of personality such as those of Freud, Rogers, and Skinner, but sees those views as basically "prescientific." The more recent approaches place much greater emphasis on empirical objectivity. One finds a variety of views which differ significantly in

---

[1]This is not to say, of course, that all theological language is propositional or that theology is an empirical science. Both of those assertions are false. But that does not rule out the possibility that both subjects make some truth claims "in the same way," *i.e.*, in the sense that if conflicting claims were deducible from them, both could not be true.

their outlook, aims, and methodology, but are at one in their desire to free psychology from lack of rigor and empirical objectivity. Briggs shows, however, that these more contemporary psychologies do in fact operate with definite assumptions about human nature, ones which usually conflict with Christian assumptions.

It is for this reason that a Christian theory of personality ought to be developed, he argues. Our understanding of human psychology will only be fully satisfactory if our basic assumptions about human nature are correct. It will make a significant difference to our interpretation of experimental results whether we believe humans to be persons created in the image of God and designed to attain a Christ-like character or hold that man is simply a complicated animal with no final end transcending this world. If humans have a spiritual nature designed for communion with their Creator, an adequate theory of human nature and human personhood will need to take this factor into consideration if it is not to present a severely distorted picture of that nature. Although he doubts Christian concepts will ever dominate secular psychological theories, Briggs concludes by noting that scientists "pay attention to results" and will be influenced by theories and ideas which are born out in tests. Thus, Christian theories of personality will doubtless influence the broader scientific community so long as they provide input which bears empirical fruit. While personality theories as such go beyond "pure science," they cannot be dispensed with, for the scientific results are ultimately unsatisfying without them. Consequently, even secular theories which desire to be free from "subjective" and "untestable" ideas nevertheless both assume them and use their experimental results to support them.

The next two articles are primarily criticisms of the ability of modern psychology and psychoanalysis to present an adequate view of human nature and, in fact, argue that they actually offer themselves as alternatives to religiously grounded views of man. If indeed that is the case, it follows that they are more intimately related to theological ideas than is admitted and can likely profit from an integration with the latter which utilize rather than rationalize them.

Mary Vander Goot investigates this theme in her very interesting paper, "Has Modern Psychology Secularized Religion?" Her thesis is that, "In modern psychology religion never was omitted, it was transformed." The personal histories of two of twentieth-century psychology's greatest theorists, Jean Piaget and Sigmund Freud, are analyzed in order to trace their personal transformations from a strong religious heritage to a completely secularized view of human nature. In the final stages of transformation, science itself becomes a "metascience" which not only deifies a particular scientific understanding of the world, but in so doing incorporates a "mythic," "religious" view of science itself. Science is thereby transformed into religion, thus dispensing with the need for traditional religious views. She points out that the process of secularization delineated in her study of Piaget and Freud is by no means unique to them, but has been trekked by a number of other exceptionally influential psychologists and psychoanalysts. Dr. Vander Goot's paper is a most interesting study of the relationship between our modern world view and religion.

In the first of two papers by Paul Vitz included in this volume, he presents a critique of modern secular psychology which sets the stage for his second paper, wherein he attempts to contribute to the positive development of a Christian psychology. In "Secular Personality Theories: A Critical Analysis," he continues the criticism of non-Christian personality theories, first by expounding the assumption upon which they are based and by which they sift data, extrapolate conclusions, and make value judgments. As Mary Vander Goot did in the specific examples of Freud and Piaget, Vitz demonstrates how in general psychology has replaced religion and become, thereby, functionally, a quasi-religion itself. In some detail he shows how modern psychology and psychotherapy (particularly of the Freudian variety) have established an entire interpretive framework which is the antithesis of a Christian world view. Specifically, he contrasts the character and acts of Jesus in redeeming the world with those of Freud's so-called "Oedipal man." He performs a similar comparison with the ideas of Jung and the humanistic psychologists, showing in both cases both the religious nature of these systems and their fundamental contrasts with Christian tenets. "The overriding religious character of so much psychology," he concludes, "is its tendency to replace God with the self."

The next three papers attempt to pinpoint some specific areas in which Christianity can contribute to a satisfactory psychology. Dr. Charles Ransford, Chairman of Hillsdale College's Psychology Department, in his "The Mystery of Human Nature," first of all provides an excellent introduction to the major psychological theories, delineating both the positive contributions and the major weaknesses of each for the development of a theory of persons. After a brief survey of Freud, Skinner, cognitive, biological, and humanistic psychology, he then argues that there is a dimension to human nature that no naturalistic psychological theory can capture. He holds that there is a "supernatural" or spiritual aspect to human nature that must be taken into account not only for the development of an adequate theory of personality, but also for truly well-balanced counseling. Trained in experimental psychology, he by no means demeans the importance of the knowledge learned through the various schools of psychology and the methods employed by each; indeed, he holds that each school he discusses has in fact contributed to our knowledge of human nature. By leaving out the spiritual dimension, however, these schools fall short of a fully adequate understanding of human thinking, feeling, and action. While the physical, mental, and spiritual aspects all affect the total person, they each have their own input and importance, and the elimination or reduction of one or the other to some other realm can only result in a distorted and incomplete theory of man. The Bible and Christian tradition supplies, then, some vital information about human nature which, through the development of a Christian psychology, can lead to a richer and more accurate understanding of man. His conclusion presents an excellent thesis statement for the papers which follow and which attempt to depict the sorts of contributions to psychology which Christianity can make. "I suggest that Biblical revelation combined with rational, scientific, and intuitive exploration will give us the best understanding of human nature possible in this life."

In "Philosophy, Faith, and Personality Theory," Merold Westphal uses current philosophical concepts to demonstrate both the shortcomings of a psychology which neglects these dimensions and the contribution which philosophy and theology can make to psychology. He too begins by pointing out that despite its claims, psychology has not managed to capture all that human nature involves. He notes that philosophical existentialism, not for the most part known for its Christian leanings, has argued forcefully against "naturalistic, objectivistic, reductionistic theories of the human self." Westphal develops two insights which nineteenth- and twentieth-century philosophy have uncovered about human personhood, insights which any adequate theory of human nature must take into consideration: self-knowledge and intersubjectivity. While the secular construals of these characteristics of human personhood are inadequate from the perspective of Christian theology, nevertheless they are important aspects the neglect of which, he argues, stems from an overconfident Cartesianism and results in a distorted, reductionist view of persons. Consequently, he argues, Christian theology can contribute to personality theory by offering a balanced biblical view of persons which recognizes the negative elements so forcefully portrayed by existentialism and Freud and the positive elements stressed by humanism and humanistic psychology, both of which, according to traditional theology, comprise essential aspects of our human selves. In addition, he argues, Christianity can provide unique contributions to theories of personality, provocatively suggesting that courage, as a necessary quality for building a self, is one such concept which can be profitably analyzed from a Christian perspective. He concludes that a Christian theory of personality must be sought, one which has the balance and openness to do justice to the multifariousness and complexity of personhood.

The selection by William Kirk Kilpatrick, "Why Secular Psychology is Not Enough," continues the theme that psychology is not a sufficient tool for an adequate understanding of human nature and argues that the key ingredient missing in its various theories is "meaning" or "purpose." He argues forcefully that human life transcends the categories and concepts by which psychology and sociology, as sciences, must operate. Moreover, these categories are employed in such a way that all other explanations are reduced to them and thereby explained away. Consequently, while giving plausible explanations of human behavior, they are unable to tell a truly human story about each of our lives. But without a "story," a "plot" by which our lives can be integrated and meaning discovered, human life is reduced to unimportance and triviality. Thus, while we may be enabled in one sense to "understand" our lives and feelings, we are not given any reason to live them, any motive for aspiring to do something with our lives, to hope, to dream, or to strive. For that our lives need a story.

Kilpatrick is not denigrating the accomplishments of psychology—he himself is a psychologist—but simply arguing that secular psychology does not have the conceptual possibilities to tell the whole truth about human life; there needs to be reference to another dimension of our existence, the dimension of meaning or purpose which comes to light when we use the logic of narrative to understand our situation and our purpose, and not merely the logic of the social sciences. Psychology is perhaps necessary, but by no means sufficient for a fully adequate and satisfying understanding of human life. Here, he argues, is an area where Christian thought can bring a real contribution to psychology, for "Christian psychology" which remains true to its origin will of necessity include the dimension of story in its approach to the study of human behavior.

In order to obtain a general view of the person as portrayed in Scripture and to provide a general biblical background for attempts to actually begin the construction of a Christian psychology, Dr. John Reist, Director of Hillsdale College's Christian Studies Program, has contributed "Telling the Truth: A

Biblical View of Personality." As Reist points out, the view of personality one finds in the Bible is not packaged in a clearly defined and outlined system. But a sustained examination of Scripture reveals a concept of human nature which neither deifies nor trivializes humanity. Reist uses the story in Mark 5:25–34 of Jesus' encounter with a woman having an issue of blood in order to explore the breadth and the depth of the biblical understanding of what it means to be a human being. The conclusion of his analysis is that to "tell the truth" about what it means to be human demands that we see human beings created in the image of God.

This, of course, raises a number of long-standing, difficult, yet important, questions such as the nature of this "image," the relationship between "flesh" and "spirit," and both the social and individual aspects of "mirroring" the God in whose image man has been created. Reist weaves his discussion of these and other important issues into a tapestry which clearly, but not simplistically, affirms the essentially irreducible, mysterious, nonetheless knowable fact of human nature, *viz.*, that we are creatures whose life is fundamentally undermined unless we see both ourselves and our lives in vital relationship with God. In essence, he affirms the insight which is the cornerstone of Calvin's *Institutes*, that we are fully ourselves only when we know ourselves as known by God, for without the knowledge of ourselves which a knowledge of God reveals, we see, experience, and become only a mirage.

Our last two papers actually attempt to outline the foundations for a Christian theory of personality. The first of these, "Personality Theorizing Within a Christian World View," by Mary Stewart Van Leeuwen, utilizes the metatheory of Salvatore Maddi in order to present the broad structure of a Christian theory of personality. Her exposition of Maddi's metatheory is quite helpful and provides an excellent framework for analyzing and contrasting competing theories. The final section of the paper utilizes the categories provided by Maddi in order to present the core characteristics of a Christian theory of man. Her discussion of the image of God and the many long-standing difficulties surrounding that concept is penetrating and stimulating. Moreover, she shows how core Christian beliefs can be integrated with concepts in personality theory in order to build a Christian theory of personality which remains Christian without simply rejecting current theories outright and beginning *de novo*. This paper contains a number of riches well worth mining.

In the concluding paper, "A Christian Theory of Personality: Covenant Theory," Paul Vitz develops a theory of human personhood which aims to correct and expand our notion of person by drawing from the biblical and Christian theological traditions. The core of Vitz's position rests upon the concept of personhood as it developed in Judaism and Christianity. Central to the biblical view of man, Vitz argues, is his covenantal relationship with God. The covenant establishes man's interpersonal relations as fundamental to his nature. It is by means of these relationships with others, characterized by caring, commitment, and love, that personality develops. Our character, for example, develops the particular traits that come to define us as individual persons through our interactions with others. Consequently, we realize our nature as beings created in the image of God through our "covenantal" relationships with others. The biblical covenants, of course, stress the community's and individual's relationship with God as well as with other humans and see the former as vital to the proper alignment and functioning of the latter. Vitz sees this notion of personhood as in stark contrast with the secular theories prominent today, witnessed by the latter's stress on individuality, rights, and self-fulfillment in contrast with the former's stress on person, love, and responsibility. Indeed, the contrasts he draws between the two concepts of human personhood are striking. He makes it clear that he does not reject twentieth-century psychology *in toto*, but it is also evident that he believes its underlying assumptions greatly reduce both its correctness and its adequacy.

The values inherent in the biblical view of man as created in the image of God will bring, Vitz argues, a revolution in our conception of what a human being is and how a human being needs to think, act, and relate if he or she is to fulfill his or her purpose as a child of God. He holds that a model based on Christian assumptions about human nature will lead to a much more satisfactory understanding of humanness and much more powerful and effective counseling techniques.

It is hoped that these essays will provide both a rationale for the development of psychological theories based on Christian assumptions about man and fruitful explorations for the beginnings of what we perceive as an important, even vital, endeavor for both the Christian church at large and scientific psychology. The church is in need of a comprehensive world view, and certainly such will not materialize unless the psychological dimension is included in such a way that the knowledge gained through contemporary psychology is neither ignored nor rejected out of hand, but rather appropriately incorporated into that world view. Psychology is in need of more comprehensive and accurate assumptions about the nature of human beings, and here, we believe, Christian theology can play a helpful and creative role.

Thomas J. Burke
Hillsdale College

Psychology, Theology, and the Liberal Arts: Toward the Unity of Knowledge

Thomas J. Burke, Jr.

Dr. Thomas J. Burke is a faculty member of Hillsdale College with teaching responsibilities in the philosophy of religion, historical theology, epistemology, and biblical studies. He earlier taught at the Sacred Heart School of Theology, Hales Corner, Wisconsin. Burke received his bachelor of arts degree from Baylor University and went on to earn the M. Div. from Trinity Evangelical Divinity School and his Ph.D. from Northwestern University. Dr. Burke has also earned a master's in philosophy from Michigan State University where he is in the final stages of completing his second doctorate. He is the editor of Volume II, *Man and Morality*, and Volume III, *Man and Mind: A Christian Theory of Personality*, of *The Christian Vision* series.

The twentieth century has seen an accentuation of the partitioning of knowledge into disparate and disjointed fields which began with the decline of Scholasticism after the inception of the "scientific revolution." It is significant that in the centuries following the rise of modern science, both rationalists and empiricists appealed to the "new science" in support of their particular epistemological predilections. The success of science in developing a steady and progressively superior series of theories, each new theory encompassing and surpassing its predecessor both in theoretical explanatory power and in the extent of the data with which it was able to deal, gave rise to the belief that scientific method provides a solution to the traditional epistemological questions raised in philosophy. Consequently, analyses of scientific method were made, each seeking to uncover the secret of its epistemological success.

In the meantime, other, more traditional disciplines such as history and theology were considered valid means of acquiring knowledge only to the degree they conformed to the particular analysis of scientific method under consideration. Hume's famous exhortation at the end of the *Enquiry* to scour the libraries, examining each work to see if it contained anything of either relations of ideas or matters of fact, keeping only those and burning the rest,[1] gave expression to an attitude which was to become more and more dominant as science became more and more successful and traditional disciplines failed to resolve age-long disputes and, indeed, became even more diversified and fragmented than previously. Science, in particular the natural sciences, became both the paradigm and the criterion of knowledge. Eventually, the view that only science gives us cognitive knowledge became dominant and other fields such as metaphysics, theology, and literature were viewed at best as merely art forms, valuable and perhaps even necessary for the well-rounded life, but unable to give us knowledge of the world; indeed, misunderstood if thought so to do. At worst, they were spurned as pseudo-disciplines masking much nonsense in the guise of normally meaningful grammatical structures.[2] During the heyday of Logical Positivism, even subjects like history were highly suspect because of the impossibility of extricating the interpretive bias of the historian from the finished product. Fields that seemed amenable to empirical methods soon adopted them with the hope of becoming as quantifiable and objectively "verifiable" as physics or chemistry. Philosophy

---

[1]David Hume, *An Enquiry Concerning Human Understanding* (New York: Washington Square Press, 1963), p. 158.

[2]See, for example, Rudolf Carnap, *Philosophy and Logical Syntax* (London: Kegan Paul, Trench, Trubner & Co., Ltd., 1935; New York: HMS Press, 1979) for a brief explanation; Carnap, *Logical Syntax and Language* (London: Kegan Paul; New York: Harcourt, Brace & World, Inc., 1937) for a more complete exposition. Also, A. J. Ayer, *Language, Truth and Logic* (London: Gollancz, 1936; 2nd edition, 1946).

reduced itself to linguistics, psychology to behavioral observations or quasi-empirical theories like those of Freud and Jung, and in some quarters it was imagined that sociology would provide the ultimate explanations of human behavior and existence, and ought, therefore, to accept the mantel of "queen of the sciences."

The quite natural reaction to this epistemological deification of science often tends to the opposite extreme. Science is looked upon as the corrupter of all that is good and virtuous in life, the destroyer of beauty, feeling, sentiment, and the truly human. Those on the counterattack take comfort in the now well-recognized limitations of scientific method and consequent incompleteness of scientific knowledge. Its facility with relations, it has been stressed, entails a corresponding inability to deal with traditional questions of essence and intentionality.[3] Its limitation to the quantifiable, measurable, and physical prevents it from giving satisfactory answers to those questions which are most vital to genuine human existence. Consequently, its reduction of the universe to a purposeless mass of stuff moving unthinkingly but determinately through aeons of time and space, its elimination of rational order and meaning from human community through statistical generalizations, and its apparent inability to deal with the individual as other than a highly evolved and organized complex nervous system is seen as disqualifying it from the truly rational and nobler levels of discourse on which alone intellectual satisfaction and ultimate truth are to be found. Natural science and its poor sisters in the social sciences are viewed as *techne*, skill which is helpful for getting around in the world, but not a source from which we can gather information about the truly vital questions facing mankind.

This separation of knowledge into disparate and at times warring camps, the scientific and the humanistic, has been an unfortunate turn of events, and although recent analyses of

---

[3]See Henry Veatch, *Two Logics: The Conflict Between Classical and Neo-Analytical Philosophy* (Evanston, IL: Northwestern University Press, 1969).

science have revealed rather severe misjudgments in earlier beliefs about its objectivity and the certainty of its conclusions,[4] it should be noted that the epistemological shortcomings of science do not argue for the epistemological superiority of the humanities. The failure of science to provide a panacea for all philosophical questions does not justify the conclusion that the humanities do. It is the thesis of this paper that this bifurcation of knowledge into the scientific and the humanistic is fundamentally mistaken.

This is not to say that humanistic disciplines such as philosophy, literature, history, and theology need mimic science, nor that they must await the latest scientific information before they can go about their business. On the other hand, no view which seeks somehow to deduce the fundamental principles of the sciences from humanistic disciplines or to set their limits by rationalistic construction alone is intended either. Rather, it will be argued that the hubristic tendencies of both science and the humanities need to be overcome, that both have a proper place in developing a satisfactory understanding of humanity and its place in nature, and that each actually assumes and uses the other in its own work. Further, it will be argued that while there are indeed important distinctions between the humanities and the sciences in both the nature of the objects considered and the methods employed in studying them, these distinctions are not fundamental, and both give us knowledge of the world which is ultimately compatible and consistent, and that failure to heed the results of either sorts of study will lead to lopsided and fundamentally disfigured and distorted views of reality. The philosophically naive scientist who blithely believes that mind is merely a living brain and man only an intelligent primate is as pathetic as a humanist who spins fine webs of opaque and pretentious prose about man's immaterial essence, existential

---

[4]The best known of these is Thomas S. Kuhn, *The Structure of Scientific Revolutions*, 2nd edition (Chicago: University of Chicago Press, 1970), but consider also the popularity of nonrealist philosophies of science. See, for example, Bas Van Fraasen, *The Scientific Image* (Oxford: Clarendon Press, 1980).

angst, and transcendent reason seeking oneness with the Being beyond all being, the Ground of being, or Being Itself.

This topic is important to Hillsdale College not only because it is a liberal arts institution, but also because it has begun in earnest a program in Christian Studies which seeks to integrate the college's curriculum from a theological perspective. Consequently, the relationship between the humanities and the sciences confronts those of us involved in that program in a particularly poignant manner. If the knowledge gleaned by the natural sciences and the social sciences on the one hand, and the humanities and theology on the other are not capable of achieving some sort of unity and cohesiveness, the enterprise is an exercise in futility. Because our interests transcend the concerns of theology and psychology in particular and are relevant to a broad spectrum of problems facing theology and science in general, we will first look at the problem in its general form and then turn to the interrelationship between theology and psychology. Consequently, after a brief discussion about the sort of knowledge relevant to academic education, we shall examine the nature of the relationship between science and theology and psychology. Hopefully, this study will result in an appreciation for the need of scholarship to seek integration, and thereby demonstrate the vital importance of a liberal arts education. In addition, it is hoped that the cognitive contribution theology can make to our knowledge of the universe and our purpose within it will also be made clear.

If it is the case that these very different disciplines each contribute to a comprehensive view of the world, what we mean by knowledge must be the same for each of them. There is a long-standing distinction between knowledge that, knowledge how, and knowledge by acquaintance. While philosophers have frequently attempted to prove that one of these is fundamental and the others reducible to it, these attempts have on the whole failed. But that does not mean these three types of knowledge are three subdivisions of some super concept, "Knowledge," but only that there are three sorts of human states which we designate by the word "knowledge." Our concern, however, will be only with the first category, knowledge that, or propositional knowledge, for it is this sort of knowledge which forms a world view and which any academic discipline worth pursuing gives us. If we do not acquire propositional knowledge of some sort from a subject, we simply do not acquire rational knowledge from it at all.[5]

The mention of propositional knowledge in the same breath with theology is bound to raise questions, if not knowing smiles. How, it might be asked, given the advance of science, can it be asserted by any informed and rational human being that theology has anything to do with propositions? Surely, in our enlightened age we know that such a view has been destroyed forever by the advance not only of science, but of theology itself. Indeed, it has become axiomatic in theological circles that theology is rational reflection on "faith." What that really means is unclear, but one thing it certainly is meant to entail is that theology does not give us objective, propositional knowledge of anything—the world, God, man, or even faith for that matter.

But such irrationalistic tendencies were not always current dogma. Traditional Christian theology begins with Scripture. Until recently, Scripture has been held to be a revelation from God in which truth is taught. In the twentieth century, a plethora of theologies of revelation have sought to make sense of the concept in a world which has been increasingly viewed as a self-explanatory causal system which, despite the upsetting results of quantum mechanics for deterministic and mechanistic philosophies, is still not open to the occasional meddlings of the Deity. For some reason, rarely clearly and unambiguously, and never cogently, articulated "modern, scientific views of the world" are supposedly incompatible with supernaturalism. For

---

[5]It could be mentioned here that even if theology, ethics, and other "nonempirical" subjects do not give us propositions about God, moral truth, etc., they certainly do consist of propositions *about* theology, morality, etc. If nothing else, the proposition that these subjects do not give us real propositions about their supposed subject matter is debatable, but it would be a strange course that offered the student no propositions at all.

some it is merely the immensity of the universe. God would just have to be too infinite to have much to do directly with us if indeed he created a 15-billion-year-old universe trillions upon trillions of miles in extent. For others, religion was simply the best primitive and superstitious ancients could do to explain the world to themselves and their children. Now we know better, and any reliance upon or reference to transcendent causes is simply incompatible with scientific method. For still others, the discovery of supposed discrepancies between the Bible and science rules out any belief in the former as a reliable source of information. Regardless, a supposedly supernatural impartation of knowledge, *i.e.*, propositional revelation, has been deemed indefensible. Revelation must, it is argued, be something else.[6] The standard view which has arisen is that it is the personal revelation of God to individuals or redemptive communities such as Israel and the Church.[7] Disputes over the manner in which this revelation has been imparted, whether through personal, existential encounter or historical events, or some combination thereof[8] have not deterred theologians from the general consensus that divinely authenticated propositions about God, man or anything else have decidedly not been revealed. The propositions of theology are the humanly created and thoroughly fallible, albeit to some extent divinely approved, opinions derived by men from their experience of God.

The total inability of such views to provide theology with a foundation from which to develop a rational discipline, and the consequent inability of theology to sustain itself as any sort of

---

[6]See John Baille, *The Idea of Revelation in Recent Thought* (New York: Columbia University Press, 1956) for an excellent exposition of these views.
[7]*Ibid.*
[8]See, for example, Wolfhart Pannenberg, ed., *Revelation as History*, trans. by David Granskov (New York: The Macmillan Company, 1968) as an alternative to Barth and Boltmann who emphasize existential encounter. Also, Oscar Cullmann, *Salvation in History*, trans. by Sidney Sowers (New York: Harper & Row, 1967), particularly pp. 122 ff. For an excellent exposition and critique of these views, see Carl F. H. Henry, *God Revelation and Authority*, 6 vols. (Waco, TX: Word Books, 1976-83), particularly Vols. II and III.

independent discipline whatsoever, has still not become evident to a great many who teach and write in this area. After experimenting with the death of God in the 1960s,[9] theology has settled down to find its niche as either the religious wing of leftist political agendas or story telling.[10] Thus, the theologian has become a combination of political-economical prophet on the one hand, and literary critic on the other. The more traditionally minded opt for pop-psychology and/or sociology. Ironically, in matters traditionally thought to be the domain of theology such as the nature of God, salvation, the Person and Work of Christ and man's relationship to God, the Bible becomes no more authoritative than Homer, Vergil, or Shakespeare, while on matters commonly thought far removed from the concerns of priest and minister, not only biblical teachings, but biblical examples become absolutely authoritative. The Exodus becomes rationale for political revolution, and the denunciation of the prophets on the evil rich of ancient Israel becomes justification, indeed, mandate, for economic policies which have failed miserably to bring either justice or humanity to the societies in which they have been most vigorously pursued. Yet biblical pronouncements on the Deity of Christ, the Spirituality of God, the depravity of man, or the purposes of God are viewed as grossly misunderstood if taken in any fashion as literally true or as the basis for the rational development of dogma. Obviously, there is a lack of coherence in modern theology, but after all, theologians must do something, and if the propositional nature of revelation is denied, politics, economics, psychology, and story telling are as good substitutes for theology as any. But of course, without propositional revelation, there is simply nothing that theology can contribute to our

---

[9]See, for example, Thomas J. J. Altizer and William Hamilton, *Radical Theology and the Death of God* (New York: Bobbs-Merrill Company, Inc., 1966).

[10]See Gustavo Gutierrez, *A Theology of Liberation: History, Politics, and Salvation*, ed. and trans. by Sister Caridad Inda and John Eagleson (Maryknoll, NY: Orbis Books, 1973) as an example of the former and *Interpretation*, XXXVII (October, 1983), No. 4, of the latter.

understanding of man that the political philosopher, the economist, the psychologist or the literary critic cannot say equally as well and with far better reasons and style. The fact is, if this is what theology is, there is no need for theologians, and any lingering curiosity over what was once called "theology" can be adequately handled by the history of theology.

For theology to be a legitimate discipline, it must have its own arena of investigation, its own data source, if you will. And if it is to give us verifiable truth about reality, it must have a reliable, trustworthy source. For Christian theology, the Bible has been that source, and if it really were shown that it is completely unreliable, theology would be a dead discipline. That such an eventuality is a logical possibility is obvious; but that it has occurred is certainly not the case. In fact, the very vulnerability of Christian theology to empirical falsification is its strength. By claiming to be based on historical events and to deliver factual truths about the nature of man and the universe, Christian theology demands the investigation of the world. Outright falsification of any theory is extremely difficult, even in science. Usually, it is not so much a theory's explicit falsification that results in its rejection, but the arrival of a more powerful theory. Indeed, if stubborn enough, a bullheaded believer in any theory can make sufficient adjustments to accommodate whatever data come his way. But surely, such is not the honorable path for either science or theology, and if enough data contrary to fundamental Christian teachings were discovered, Christianity would have to be given up. But while falsification of Christian teachings in these areas is possible, from the Christian perspective, the experience to date should be seen as heartening and enlightening.

Properly understood, there is a symbiotic relationship between theology and the sciences. The dependence of theology on science occurs on two levels, that of propositional content and that of theoretical conceptual meaning.

Assuming with traditional theology that Scripture is a propositional revelation from God does not give us immediate and unambiguous entrée to truth. A naive fundamentalism which uncritically accepts Bible verses at face value and strings them together by topics is wholly inadequate for a constructive and viable theology, and no theologian of note has ever used such a methodology. The difficulty lies not merely in deciding what the text says, but more problematically, in what it teaches. Granted verse x expresses proposition y, what judgment do we now make as to whether or not this proposition is actually being taught? Similarly, granting that proposition y is being taught, what extension of its possible implications can properly be deduced from it and incorporated into a theological structure? Joshua commands the sun to stand still. Can we legitimately deduce a geocentric view of the solar system? Given our current state of knowledge, no. Any standard commentary written from even the most conservative viewpoint will point out that Joshua 10:12-14 is an accommodation to our normal ways of speaking, paralleled in our own day by our talk of "sunsets" and "sunrises." But such glosses are post-Copernican, and during the Ptolemaic days which preceded Copernicus, Joshua was considered confirmation of the earth's physical centrality in the universe.

The above is a rather simple and obvious example, but its relevance derives from a much deeper relationship between cognitive disciplines and the words we use to form and communicate our propositions. The meaning of our words derives from their place in our theories about the world. "Theories" is meant broadly and is not to be limited to formal or axiomitized systems. As intended here, they include our common sense, everyday theories, which not only spill over into each other, but often are taken up into more sophisticated theories. "Conceptual frameworks" would, perhaps, be a good gloss. The point is that concepts cannot be analyzed independently from whole systems of thought covering ranges of beliefs which often do not follow traditional lines of demarcation. Consequently, the meanings of concepts are notoriously difficult to determine in any satisfactory manner. Plato's discussions of justice, beauty, religion and knowledge in the early and middle dialogues show just how difficult this can be. But note that when Plato finally does get around to offering us what he feels are acceptable answers to such questions, he does so in the context of full-blown metaphysical, ethical, and epistemological theories. At least part of the difficulty in the earlier attempts derived from the assumption that one can analyze such extremely complex concepts individually and arrive at satisfactory results. But if concepts derive their meaning from theories implicitly as well as explicitly assumed, then they cannot be adequately understood apart from those theories.

The importance of this for theology lies in the fact that even foundational concepts found in the Bible itself cannot be fully understood in isolation from theories which include them. It would, of course, be nice if God had given us a completely articulated system of thought, with all terms explicitly or implicitly defined and in need of no further explication. In His wisdom, he did not, and consequently, theologians have work, indeed, very important work to do. Moreover, this work must be carried on at many levels. First of all, the meanings of terms used in Scripture must be determined. Not only does this require study of the internal relationships established in biblical usage itself, it also demands the historical and literary investigation of the languages and ideational contexts in which these words were employed. After all, even commonly used words such as "redemption," "God," "believe," "righteousness," "justification," etc., were taken from languages in which they had previously determined meanings which themselves resulted from their place in ancient theories, *i.e.*, conceptual frameworks. Biblical usage often molded these concepts in new ways, but a full understanding of those new uses and twists of meaning depends upon an understanding of their previous meanings within the cultures from which they were borrowed.

Moreover, if Scripture truly is a propositional revelation from God, then the ultimate meaning of the concepts and theories found in Scripture cannot be limited to a purely grammatical and historical investigation of the text. A more fundamental and pervasive manner in which science can influence theology is on the theoretical, conceptual level. For example, consider the traditional view of man as created in the Image of God. The exact meaning of this concept is never completely articulated in Scripture. Traditionally, man's reason has been taken as the locus of the Image, but rationality itself is not fully understood. The increasing ability of machines to simulate certain human thought processes, particularly some which have been thought paradigms of rationality,[11] may cause us to revise our concepts of rationality and, accordingly, of the precise nature of the *imago Dei* itself. As our concepts or rationality become more refined, our concept of the Image of God will become correspondingly more refined. Similarly, Christianity has affirmed the existence of the mind and its distinction from the body. But the precise relationship between them or the ultimate nature of the mind are questions which are not given any explicit theoretical development in the Bible. Consequently, as we uncover more about the brain and its cognitive functions, it is possible that a great deal of light will be shed upon these matters.

If truth is a totally coherent and consistent whole, as indeed it must be, then truth that we discover now can illuminate concepts, ideas, and principles found in the Bible. Ethical reflection can bring deeper and clearer understanding of the *Ten Commandments* and the Law of Christ; scientific investigation can reveal truths which help explicate the biblical dogma of creation; and psychology can deepen our understanding of the biblical view of man.

This does not mean that theologians must await the latest results of scientific, philosophical, or historical scholarship any more than the latter need master theology to make sense of their own disciplines and carry on their own work. Nor does it mean that these long-standing philosophical and theological problems are capable of scientific resolution. That, I believe, is clearly not the case, although neither is scientific information totally irrelevant to proposed philosophical and theological solutions; and it may well be that information from science will help bring about a conceptual breakthrough. What it does mean, however,

---

[11]Such as the ability to calculate or to follow deductive lines of reasoning.

is that scholars cannot remain completely ignorant of current knowledge without running the danger not only of misunderstanding the broader implications of their own fields, but also on occasion even acquiring distorted ideas within them. The theologian who lives in a pre-Copernican, pre-Einsteinian universe may still have a great deal to say; but far less of value than he would were he to be a better-read scholar. Augustine, Aquinas, and Calvin have, because of their brilliance and seminal theological insights, developed theologies which will never be irrelevant, but the next theologian of their stature will need to know a lot more than they did. It should, of course, be noted that they themselves were aware of the most recent developments in the scholarship of their own day.

In short, if theology is to function properly, it must be continually interacting with the knowledge being discovered in other fields, continually seeking to develop a coherent and consistent view of the world. Because theology deals with the world as a whole and man in particular, there is virtually no field which is completely irrelevant to it. Of course, it does have its own areas of specialization in which it is essentially independent of other disciplines. But theology cannot and ought not limit itself to them, and to the extent it does, it will be the poorer for it.

The relationship between theology and science works in both directions. It is not merely theology which is dependent upon other fields for its continued development; science itself is dependent upon certain philosophical and theological views. This point has been recently urged by Willis B. Glover in *Biblical Origins of Modern Secular Culture*, where he argues that modern science is ultimately indebted to the biblical doctrine of creation *ex nihilo*.[12] It was, he holds, the Nominalists who saw for the first time in the history of Christian theology the radical implications of the doctrine and removed the necessitarianism which Aristotelian essentialism had imposed on the high-

---

[12]Willis B. Glover, *Biblical Origins of Modern Culture* (Macon, GA: Mercer University Press, 1984), pp. 79 ff.

scholastic conception of God and creation. He quotes an earlier article by A. R. Hall who had written,

> No Christian could ultimately escape the implications of the fact that Aristotle's cosmos knew no Jehovah. Christianity taught him to see it as a divine artifact rather than as a self-contained organism. The universe was subject to God's laws; its regularities and harmonies were . . . a result of providential design. The ultimate mystery resided in God rather than in Nature. . . . The only sort of explanation science could give must be in terms of descriptions of processes, mechanisms, interconnections or parts. Greek animism was dead. . . . The universe of classical physics, in which the only realities were matter and motion, could begin to take shape.[13]

Later, Glover points out the tremendous difference Christian theology made in the concept of the "laws of nature." He writes,

> The concept of the laws of nature as it was understood in seventeenth-century science had not been known in the ancient world. Natural law in ancient classical thought had been law imminent in nature and in particular natural objects; natural law as it was conceived by seventeenth-century *virtuosi*, on the other hand, was a law imposed on nature by a law-giver who was beyond and outside of nature.[14]

Glover is careful to emphasize that he is not contending that Christian theology—in particular, its voluntaristic stream—necessitated such developments, only that they allowed them.[15] It must also be emphasized that the validity of the view that theology has significantly influenced science is not dependent on Glover's or Hall's views. Other theses regarding its influence have also been propounded. Stanley Jaki, for example, has contended that it was the Nicene–Chalcedonian doctrine of the

---
[13]*Ibid.*, pp. 82-83.
[14]*Ibid.*, p. 91.
[15]*Ibid.*

logos which made Western science possible.[16] The point is that whatever the influence of theology on science, there has been an influence. Theological views of the world do impact on scientific views, and modern naturalism is to a great degree ignorant of the extent to which it has absorbed and adopted metaphysical views which originated in theology.

There is, then, an interdependence between our "scientific" understanding of the world and our "humanistic" understanding. This is what one would, of course, expect if indeed there are both quantitative and nonquantitative dimensions to reality, and if the best means of acquiring information about these respective dimensions is at least approximated by the present *modus operandi* in science and in the humanities. A philosophy of whatever subject matter which fails to take cognizance of what experience tells us is bound to mislead us, and an empiricism which attempts to eliminate either all *a priori* assumptions or the information acquired through other than rigorous scientific method will lead to attenuated and incomplete views of man and the world. If such were consistently attempted, science could not even get started. But neither is it necessary to hold some assumptions "come what may." An imaginative theoretical scientist may question some of the most fundamental assumptions of a theory, thereby either modifying it significantly or, if drastic enough, actually creating a new theory. If a truly viable theory, this modified or new theory can be tested by whatever means are appropriate in the field. As is well known, this is what Einstein did when, questioning the Newtonian idea of simultaneity, he developed the theory of relativity. No presupposition, no matter how fundamental, is logically ever beyond any questioning whatsoever in either science or the humanities, so the fact that science draws upon and utilizes ideas which do not originate in science itself does not mean that the presence of such somehow destroys the experimental and provisional nature of science. What it does mean is that all of

---

[16]Stanley Jaki, *The Road of Science and the Ways to God* (Chicago: University of Chicago Press, 1978).

our ideas in whatever discipline are subject to confirmation or falsification. But this "testing" is not accomplished entirely through empirical science. Certain assumptions in science also need to be critically evaluated by the tools available to the humanistic disciplines. Neither science nor the humanities are sufficient unto themselves; there are regions of reality which are closed to the methods of one or the other, and only the utilization of each in their proper domain and mutual respect for the knowledge attained by each will keep us from distorted and at times dangerous misunderstandings of ourselves and our world.

If the interdependence of the humanities and science as outlined above is true in general, it is even more pronounced in areas such as psychology which seek an understanding of man and propose to do so by empirical methods. If man were only a physical organism and his mind only his brain performing algorithms like a computer, then of course a discipline such as psychology could be wholly empirical and eventually as quantifiable as physics. On such assumptions, bizarre psychological theories such as behaviorism have developed and, for a time at least, thrived. The philosophical weaknesses of behaviorism are legion, but it should also be noted that behaviorism cannot even get off the ground unless all that theology has taught about man is simply rejected. There are few scientific theories that are totally incompatible with theology, but behaviorism is one of them. But then behaviorism is contrary to both common sense and our own experience of our own individual consciousness as well, and that did not daunt the true believers who in blind faith tallied forth to win the world to the truth of stimulus–response explanations of human behavior. The irony is not in the fact that experimentation as practiced by these researchers was attempted. Indeed, much valuable information has been acquired through such efforts. What is ironic was the belief that they revealed to us *all* there is to man's *psyche*, for we then have the absurd situation of a scientist trying to demonstrate a rationally derived theory by means of rationally constructed experiments the results of which are to be rationally evaluated, and all of this to be accomplished by a human mind which, if the theory were correct, has a mental life in no way qualitatively different from that of a platyhelminth (*i.e.*, a flatworm). The psychologist's own theory and his efforts in behalf of that theory are incompatible with the truth of the theory itself. Obviously, blind, irrational faith is not the sole possession of religious adherents.

The difficulties inherent in behaviorism make it clear that their root lies not in the scientific or experimental methods themselves, but in the philosophical assumptions that determine not only how they are employed, but also what they mean. Indeed, it is a straightforward and strong assumption that they can be legitimately and meaningfully employed at all. In the case of psychology, the logical priority of philosophical and theological—or more properly, antitheological—*a priori* is more evident than in other sciences because the nature of the subject matter is so unamenable to the methods and procedures of empirical investigation. Consequently, failure to recognize the metaphysical assumptions underlying the discipline is even more disastrous than elsewhere. *Qua* physicist, the physicist is unlikely to have a distorted view of physical theories if he remains ignorant of the intellectual inheritance to which he is heir—although, of course, his understanding would be deepened the more knowledgeable he became in these matters. But a wrong-headed view of humankind, and in particular, man's mind, is bound to lead to erroneous psychological theories. If man is not a mere naturalistic phenomenon the depths of whose being can be ferreted out by quantitative data collecting, experimental psychology of any persuasion can never give us a complete account of man. As mentioned above, information it provides may be illuminating, helpful, and occasionally interesting, but never adequate for the construction of a moral, social, political, or religious understanding of man. Indeed, if overestimated, it can be counterproductive to our attempts to understand human nature. The failure and the danger of physicalistic reductionism is nowhere more evident than in psychology.

Of course, these criticisms and cautions become even more important when considering secular metaphysical views of man which mask as scientific theories. Freudianism, for example, is no more scientifically testable than absolute idealism and considerably less so than Christian theology.[17] Its pretensions have not gone undetected, but it continues to enjoy the honorific status of a scientific theory. If the thesis of this paper is correct, it should be noted, its proper classification as "philosophical" rather than "scientific" should not detract at all from its intellectual significance or result in abandoning any and all research aimed at developing its implications.

Knowledge, I would suggest, is on a continuum from that which is almost completely invulnerable to experiential judgment to that which is highly vulnerable. Or, to borrow an analogy from W. V. Quine, our human knowledge is like a net, each part connected to all the others through the webbing, with those parts of the web closer to the edge more directly affected by experience than those on the interior, but nevertheless, no part completely immune from all experience whatsoever.[18] The fact that it is a continuum and not a series of isolable levels means that our human efforts to understand the world and ourselves is properly a joint effort. Conversation, interaction, and openness to the implications for one's own field of theories outside one's own area of specialization ought, then, to be a normal, ongoing part of man's intellectual endeavors. But then, is not this what the liberal arts has traditionally envisioned as the proper nature of human learning? I would only add that such a vision makes conversations between theology and psychology such as those included in this volume not only possible, but also obligatory.

---

[17]As has been argued on numerous occasions, Freudian interpretations of behavior are compatible with every conceivable case and, therefore, are impossible to refute; Christianity is at least theoretically refutable, *i.e.*, it could be proved that (a) Christ never existed, or (b) he never rose from the dead. That would at least disprove that any sort of traditional Christianity was true, or so its earliest proponents thought (see I Corinthians 15:17-19; I John 1:1; 4:2-3; II Peter 1:16).

[18]Willard VanOrman Quine, "Two Dogmas of Empiricism," in *From a Logical Point of View* (New York: Harper Torch Books, 1961), pp. 42-46.

Personality Theories: What Questions Are We Trying to Answer?

Stephen R. Briggs

Stephen R. Briggs is assistant professor of psychology at the University of Tulsa. He earned his Ph.D. in personality psychology from the University of Texas at Austin. An editor for *Personality Forum*, the *Journal of Personality and Social Psychology*, and *Contemporary Psychology*, Dr. Briggs is also an occasional reviewer for a number of psychology journals. Additionally, he is a co-author of *A Sourcebook on Shyness: Research and Treatment* and a dozen articles on personality psychology. He has written chapters in several psychology books and presented papers on such topics as obesity, social anxiety, older adults and the experience of unemployment, and shyness.

If a Christian theory of personality is to be articulated, we must be clear about two things: what we mean by the term "*Christian*," and what we mean by a "*theory of personality*." Obviously, a comprehensive treatment of either issue is well beyond the scope of this brief essay, so in the space available I want to concentrate primarily on the second of these issues—what it is we mean by a theory of personality. Specifically, I intend to clarify something about the nature of theory and research in the field of personality psychology today. Toward the end of my talk, however, the first issue will reemerge as I attempt to specify the extent to which current thinking in the field of personality is consistent with a Christian view of man. At that point, I will be as explicit as possible about how I will use the term "Christian."

A theory ought to be able to explain something, and so it seems reasonable to begin by asking what it is that personality theories are attempting to explain. Although this question seems straightforward enough, the answer turns out to be rather elusive because it hinges on the meaning of the word "personality." Defining it is no mean feat. In his remarkable text on personality, Gordon Allport carefully recorded 50 different definitions of the term taken from a variety of academic disciplines (*e.g.*, philosophy, sociology, law, and theology as well as psychology).[1] Although a subsequent paper by Donald MacKinnon suggested that this plethora of meanings could be summarized in terms of two major themes, MacKinnon also pointed out that "two meanings could hardly be more antithetical."[2]

One meaning of personality originates with the perspective of an observer. It involves an individual's public presence and social reputation, a meaning which is consistent with the term's etymological origins. Personality derives from the Latin word *persona* for the mask worn by ancient actors to signify their roles in a theatrical performance. In its original form, *persona* meant pretense, a fiction. Later, however, the term was used to describe the role or part which an actor assumes in a drama, and then still later to the distinctive personal qualities of an individual. Personality in this first sense, then, describes an individual's social-stimulus value, the distinctive impression one makes on others.

Conversely, personality in its second sense refers to the inner self—the vital, inward, and essential nature of an individual. This meaning of the term apparently dates back to the writings of early Christian theologians. In describing the attributes of God, the Church Fathers expounded the distinct personalities of the Trinity, each of whom was said to possess—in purest and

---

[1] Gordon W. Allport, *Personality: A Psychological Interpretation* (New York: Holt, 1937).
[2] Donald W. MacKinnon, "The Structure of Personality," in *Personality and the Behavior Disorders*, Vol. I, J. McV. Hunt, ed. (New York: Ronald Press, 1944), p. 3.

most infinite form—intellect, sensibility, and will. More recently personality in this second sense has come to mean the deep and enduring structures of an individual that comprise the central attributes of the self.

The first point I want to emphasize, then, is that the term personality can mean two apparently opposite things. It can mean outer mask or it can mean inner substance, surface, or depth. These two meanings have different histories and they lead to the study of different issues. Therefore, as we consider various approaches to the study of personality, it will prove useful to keep this distinction in mind. Although it may be unfortunate for a word so significant to have two meanings that are at such cross-purposes, perhaps the contradiction is partly inherent in the concept. This is the issue that the French psychiatrist Paul Tournier describes as he struggles to differentiate the outer, visible *personage* from the inner, invisible *person*. He writes:

> In a manner of speaking I occupy a privileged observation post. The majority of those who have come to see me have made up their minds to reveal themselves more openly than they have ever revealed themselves before. . . . And yet, however privileged my observation post, I become increasingly aware that the person, pure and unvarnished, will always escape us. Doubtless God knows it. I can never grasp the true reality, of myself or anybody else, but only an image; a fragmentary and deformed image, an appearance: the "personage". . . . There is thus a strange relationship between the personage and the person; they are linked together, and yet they remain distinct. I can approach the person only through that image which at one and the same time allows me glimpses of it and also tends to hide it from me, reveals as well as conceals it.[3]

Perhaps then it is more accurate to say that the two meanings of the word personality are somehow complementary rather than contradictory. Although inward and outward approaches to the

---

[3] Paul Tournier, *The Meaning of Persons* (New York: Harper & Row, 1957), p. 9.

study of personality often seem to conflict, any convincing theory of personality will have to encompass both aspects of human nature.[4]

In the next section, I want to identify the kinds of research activities that currently occupy the limelight in personality psychology. Before proceeding to that topic directly, however, I feel compelled to warn the reader that personality research is often quite different from what the uninitiated observer expects. Let me illustrate this point in several ways. First, if you pick up a typical text on personality theories you will find individual chapters covering the work of various theorists representing several broad traditions. The best known of these theorists, of course, are Sigmund Freud, B. F. Skinner, and Carl Rogers, and they represent, respectively, the schools of psychoanalysis, behaviorism, and humanism (which are sometimes called the three forces of personality). However, if you pick up a recent copy of a major journal (*e.g.*, *Journal of Personality and Social Psychology*), you are not likely to find more than an occasional, isolated reference to any of the theorists from these three schools. For example, of the 16 articles in the September 1985 issue of the *Journal of Personality and Social Psychology*, only three articles referenced Freud, just one referenced Rogers, and there were no references at all to B. F. Skinner. Frankly, I think the references for this particular issue are apt to be an overestimate rather than an underestimate of the contemporary literature as a whole, and I would not be surprised if you had to examine a whole year of issues to find even a single reference to Skinner. The point here is that although these figures are major theorists in some sense, their theories do not provide a major impetus for the research currently being conducted in the field of personality. Furthermore, of the three schools, only psychoanalysis (and Freud in particular) seems to

---

[4]R. Hogan and J. M. Cheek, "Identity, Authenticity, and Maturity," in *Studies in Social Identity*, T. R. Sarbin and K. E. Scheibe, eds. (New York: Praeger Publishers, 1983).

have had any lasting impact on the academic research community.

This point is evident from a survey recently conducted of some 80 personality psychologists. This group included many well-known scholars, recognized leaders in the field. When asked to identify the psychologist having the most impact on their thinking, three names emerged from the pack: Sigmund Freud, Gordon Allport, and Henry Murray. Runners-up included Erik Erikson, George Kelly, Robert White, Hans Eysenck, and Carl Jung. (Only a couple of participants listed Rogers or Skinner.) When asked to list the classic works in the field of personality, again the obvious winners were Freud, Murray, and Allport.

Even with Freud, however, it is important to recognize that his influence has more to do with the issues that he identified than with his particular solutions to those issues. As one recent author comments: "The suggestions that people inevitably deceive themselves about social motives, that there are fixed limits to human nature that are impervious to social change, and that man is naturally aggressive as well as loving seem far more important than the question of where the ego gets its energy or how the meaning of dream symbolism is acquired."[5] Many current researchers find Freud's ideas insightful, but few adhere to his theoretical accounts of those ideas. In fact, couching one's research in the jargon of Freudian psychoanalytic theory is almost a sure way to chart it into obscurity in the empirical literature.

The point I want to make here is that many personality psychologists do not identify themselves with the psychoanalytic, behavioristic, or humanistic traditions; in fact, most of those who do research in the field of personality today represent a somewhat different intellectual tradition altogether. In part, this distinction has to do with a focus on "normal" people and competent performance or ordinary problems rather than on

---

[5]R. Hogan, *Personality Theory: The Personological Tradition* (Englewood Cliffs, NJ: Prentice-Hall Inc., 1976), p. 54.

clinical populations and psychopathology, and in part it derives from an emphasis on basic research rather than therapeutic applications. Most of the research in the field of personality is conducted by individuals who are not practicing therapists and whose primary interest is not in treatment issues. This brings us back to our original question. What is it that modern personality psychologists do and what is it they are trying to explain?

In attempting to provide an answer to these questions, I want to return to the distinction between the two meanings of personality, between an outer and an inner orientation. As I suggested previously, these approaches differ not only in terms of their history, but also in terms of their focus.

Personality from the Outer Orientation

For those interested in the outer orientation, the central issue in the study of personality involves how to assign meaning to the behavior of others. Why do we perceive other people as we do? Why do we attribute certain characteristics to others and use particular labels to describe them? How is information about others processed and stored, and how do we use this information to make decisions? What purpose does it serve? Let me briefly describe three lines of research that fall into this tradition: the sociological perspective, the perspective of social cognition or person perception, and the summary-trait point of view.

The sociological approach to personality asserts that the individual exists only in relation to society. Identity and status is bestowed socially, maintained socially, and transformed socially. Peter Berger's chapter "Society in Man" in his *Introduction to Sociology* provides an elegant statement of this position. He writes:

> Looked at sociologically, the self is no longer a solid, given entity that moves from one situation to another. It is rather a process, continuously created and re-created in each social situa-

tion that one enters, held together by the slender thread of memory. . . . If one wants to ask who an individual "really" is in this kaleidoscope of roles and identities, one can answer only by enumerating the situations in which he is one thing and those in which he is another.[6]

Thus, for the sociologist personality is the concatenation of one's roles; it derives from one's precise location in a social matrix that is societally defined and regulated.

The second line of research—that of social cognition or person perception—studies the processes by which we make attributions about others (and about ourselves). Researchers in this area are particularly interested in perceptual biases that lead us to make incorrect inferences given the information available. Perhaps the best known of these biases is the "fundamental attribution error"[7] wherein observers tend to underestimate the power of situations in shaping an individual's behavior and tend to overestimate the importance of personal traits and dispositions.

Recent research in this area has focused on the nature of the cognitive processes and schemata by which we categorize other people.[8] From this perspective, personality that is ascribed to others reflects as much on the person doing the observing (and that person's mental structures) as on the person being observed. To quote an influential article by Jones and Nisbett: "Traits exist more in the eye of the beholder than in the psyche of the actor."[9]

---

[6]Peter Berger, *An Invitation to Sociology* (New York: Doubleday, 1963), p. 106.

[7]L. Ross, "The Intuitive Psychologist and His Shortcomings: Distortions in the Attribution Process," in *Advances in Experimental Social Psychology*, Vol. 10, L. Berkowitz, ed. (New York: Academic Press, Inc., 1977).

[8]See, for example, N. Cantor and J. F. Kihlstrom, eds., *Personality, Cognition, and Social Interaction* (Hillsdale, NJ: Erlbaum, 1981).

[9]E. E. Jones and R. Nisbett, "The Actor and the Observer: Divergent Perceptions on the Causes of Behavior," in *Attribution: Perceiving the Causes of Behavior*, E. E. Jones et al., eds. (Morristown, NJ: General Learning Press, 1972), p. 89.

The third line of research takes up where the second leaves off. The summary-trait approach to personality focuses on the content of the adjectives or trait words used to describe others rather than on the processes which govern these content categories. Research in this tradition has generally employed the statistical technique of factor analysis to reduce the lexicon of trait terms to its primary dimensions. In recent years there has been a growing consensus that we typically describe others in terms of five or six core dimensions: surgency (which sometimes breaks into sociability and ambition), agreeableness or likeability, conscientiousness or self-control, emotional stability or adjustment, and cultural or intellectual interests.[10] However, it is important to distinguish between the investigation of the trait lexicon as it is used to describe others (which is an outer orientation), and the investigation of traits as explanatory constructs (which assumes more of an inner orientation). Traits in the descriptive sense imply only social consensus—how individuals agree to define and use adjectives—whereas traits as explanations imply something enduring inside a person, some underlying "neuropsychic entity" or "bona fide mental structure."[11]

Perhaps it is clear from the discussion so far that none of these lines of research requires any assumptions about the individual who is the target of our observations. Nothing is said specifically about the nature of the person being observed. How is it, then, that we assign meaning to the behavior of others?

---

[10] J. M. Digman and J. Inouye, "Further Specification of the Five Robust Factors of Personality," *Journal of Personality and Social Psychology* (in press); R. Hogan, "A Socioanalytic Theory of Personality," in *Nebraska Symposium on Motivation*, M. Page, ed. (Lincoln, NE: University of Nebraska Press, 1983); L. R. Goldberg, "Language and Individual Differences: The Search for Universals in Personality Lexicons," in *Personality and Social Psychology Review*, Vol. 2, L. Wheeler, ed. (Beverly Hills: Sage Publications, Inc., 1981); R. R. McCrae and P. T. Costa, Jr., "Updating Norman's 'Adequate Taxonomy': Intelligence and Personality Dimensions in Natural Language and in Questionnaires," *Journal of Personality and Social Psychology*, 49 (1985), 710–721.

[11] Allport, *Personality*; S. R. Briggs, "A Trait Account of Social Shyness," in *Review of Personality and Social Psychology*, Vol. 6, P. Shaver, ed. (Beverly Hills: Sage Publications Inc., 1985).

From the sociological perspective, meaning resides in the roles enacted, not in the individual actor; thus the focus of study is on the nature or roles rather than on the individual. From the vantage point of social cognition, meaning is in the eyes (and cognitive structures) of the beholder; research focuses on how the observer acquires, processes, stores, and uses information. And from the summary-trait perspective, meaning derives from the structure and use of language; the trait terms used to describe others do not necessarily correspond to anything real and enduring about those people.

Gordon Allport labelled all approaches of this sort *biosocial* and deliberately excluded them from his use of the word personality. Although he acknowledged that our knowing is limited to the observable, stimulus properties of individuals, he emphatically stated that "Our errors of judgment and perception do not change their personalities any more than a star becomes a savory because it is misperceived by the scientist who has a taste for cheese."[12] For Allport, personality is as objective as any other event in nature, and the study of personality ought to focus on the properties of the individual rather than on the properties of the observer.

Conversely, in a fascinating book entitled *Appearance and Realities*, Gustav Ichheiser argues that "Any adequate theory of personality and interpersonal relations has to deal not only with how personalities 'really are' but, in addition and equally important, with how they appear to other people." He goes on to add that "the way we see, interpret, and evaluate each other constitutes a set of facts and problems actually fundamental in any realistic science of personality and interpersonal relations."[13] Although there are disagreements about whether research rooted in the outer orientation ought to be included in the domain of personality, it seems clear enough that many who label themselves personality researchers are from this tradition.

---

[12]Allport, *Personality*, p. 42.

[13]Gustav Ichheiser, *Appearances and Realities: Misunderstandings in Human Relations* (San Francisco: Jossey-Bass, 1970).

Personality from the Inner Orientation

An inner orientation to personality leads to a different type of research agenda. A typical definition of personality from this point of view would refer to "more or less stable internal factors that make one person's behavior consistent from one time to another, and different from the behavior other people would manifest in comparable situations."[14] The key assumptions here are the words stable, internal, consistent, different, and comparable.[15] Not all researchers have believed such assumptions are warranted (for instance, some of those who adopt an outer orientation), and the doubts they voiced resulted in a heated debate that spanned the decade of the 1970s and that lingers on even today. The issue: should an individual's behavior be described primarily in terms of enduring regularities (behavioral traits), or should the emphasis be on the situational specificity of behavior? The answer, of course, is that both positions should be emphasized. Behavior is the product of these complementary forces. Individuals who ignore environmental demands and respond without regard to the appropriateness of their behavior are acting abnormally. But so also are chameleons who are at the mercy of situational vagaries. The inner orientation to personality attempts to understand the enduring regularities that characterize the behavior of individuals without ignoring the fact that behavior always occurs in context.

Researchers interested in internal and enduring characteristics—in what a person brings to a situation—have generally focused on the following kinds of issues:

1. How can we best describe an individual's personality?
2. How are personality traits acquired?
3. How are personality traits encoded and preserved?

---

[14]I. L. Child, "Personality in Culture," in *Handbook of Personality Theory and Research*, E. F. Borgatta and W. W. Lambet, eds. (Chicago: Rand McNally & Co., 1968), p. 83.

[15]S. E. Hampson, *The Construction of Personality: An Introduction* (London: Routledge & Kegan Paul, 1982).

4. How are various characteristics integrated; how do they fit together to comprise a unique individual?

In the remainder of this section, I will look briefly at how these questions have been approached.

To answer the first question, researchers have generally assumed that all individuals can be described in terms of a limited number of personality traits. Although a few theorists (notably, Gordon Allport) have argued that traits are ultimately individual and that common traits are not true traits at all, most researchers have sought to identify the fundamental dimensions of personality by analyzing people's responses to lengthy questionnaires. They again use the statistical technique of factor analysis to reduce a large pool of items to a small number of nonredundant dimensions. However, this approach differs from the summary-trait approach described previously in two ways: (1) it typically relies on what individuals say about themselves (self-reports) rather than on what they say about others (peer ratings); and (2) it assumes that the information obtained from self-reports, although flawed, nevertheless offers insights that are unavailable from any other vantage point. Studies using self-report inventories generally yield a more differentiated set of dimensions than the five or six factors that characterize the summary-trait approach. For example, Cattell argues for 16 primary personality factors[16] and Guilford for 13.[17] However, other theorists (*e.g.*, Eysenck and Tellegen) believe that these longer factor lists can be subsumed under two or three superfactors which they argue can be linked to underlying brain structures and biological processes.

That brings us to the second question: how are enduring personality characteristics acquired? There are three general approaches to this issue: the biological, environmental, and cognitive approaches. The biological approach suggests that our individuality derives in part from our genetic and constitutional

---

[16] R. B. Cattell, *Personality and Mood by Questionnaire* (San Francisco: Jossey-Bass, 1973).

[17] J. P. Guilford, *Personality* (New York: McGraw-Hill, 1959).

makeup. Just as we inherit certain genes from our parents which influence whether we are tall or short, musically gifted or tone deaf, athletically talented or uncoordinated, so also do we inherit genes that *predispose* us to be bright or dull, outgoing or shy, and schizophrenic or "normal." Please notice the verb that I chose: predispose. Genetic influences on personality (and human behavior more generally) are not fixed and immutable like eye color or gender. Rather, genetic influences provide a range of potential. Our talents do not ensure success, and our weaknesses do not ensure failure. But our talents and weaknesses establish the range within which we can expect to move. My favorite analogy here is that of a card game. Each player is dealt a hand of cards, and the players have no choice as to the cards they are dealt. They have considerable latitude, however, in deciding how to play out their particular hand. Do they hold their cards or attempt to trade for something better? Do they bluff or try to shoot the moon? The long-term success of any player will depend on his or her ability to develop the potential inherent in the hand of cards that has been dealt.

The second approach emphasizes not what we start with, but what we acquire. This approach suggests that what we are is due largely to the environment in which we are raised. It correctly points to the important ways in which our personal characteristics are molded by parents and family, friends, and culture. The fact that many of our enduring tendencies have been learned does not imply, however, that these tendencies are easily changed. Quite to the contrary. Try changing a well-ingrained but incorrect tennis stroke. Ask a chain smoker to quit. Habits or dominant response tendencies as a rule are enormously resistant to change, and learned personality traits are no exception.

Here then are two pervasive influences on personality—things inherited and things learned. The question is often asked: which is more important, nature or nurture? But this is not a useful question. The issue is not nature *versus* nurture, but rather how these processes work together to produce regularities in the behavior of individuals.

A third approach—which is popular today—explains behavioral regularities in terms of how we think about ourselves. One variant of this approach holds that individuals are concerned about how others evaluate them and that they therefore actively attempt to manage their social performances so that others will evaluate them positively. Specifically, an individual attempts to convince others to adopt an image that is consistent with his or her own self-image. Enduring dispositions, therefore, reflect an individual's attempt to convey to others how he or she wants to be perceived. This attempt may be quite deliberate or it may be largely nonconscious, but in either case it revolves around a relatively stable self-image.

The kind of explanation one prefers—biological, environmental, or cognitive—will also influence how one visualizes the mechanisms that lead to regularity in a person's actions, thoughts, and feelings. Thus, answers to the third question—how are personality traits encoded and preserved?—will differ depending on the type of explanation offered. Cognitive scientists prefer computer metaphors: programs, hardware and software, feedback loops, and internal processing algorithms. Biological theorists explain regularity in terms of the brain's electrochemical pathways and point to the role of neurotransmitters in governing brain action. Perhaps the important point here is that the model selected will influence one's views about the stability of behavior and the intervention strategies that are likely to result in change. By choosing to pinpoint regularity either in terms of mental structures or neuropsychic entities, we imply that there is something inside a person which persists and which produces some regularity in the way that individual thinks, feels, and acts.

The questions I have posed thus far are the ones that dominate the field of personality today. I have suggested that there are two distinct and somewhat complementary research traditions. One focuses on the outward manifestations of personality, the other on inner structures and processes. The first examines how individuals perceive, interpret, and evaluate one another. The second inquires as to the internal characteristics that lead to regularity in an individual's personality from one time and place to the next, and that also result in differences among people. Both traditions attempt to explain the regularities or tendencies that individuals observe in one another. Both traditions typically look for laws or processes that generalize across individuals. In some cases, the laws are thought to apply to all people—to be typical of the species. Examples would include general laws of perception, learning, information processing, and inheritance, and the basic stages of attachment or cognitive maturation, as well as the primary dimensions of emotion and personality. In other cases, the laws are directed toward specific groups or classes of people: women, adolescents, leaders, people who are depressed or ambitious, and so forth.

But what does all this research tell us about individuals—specific people? In terms of the questions I posed earlier, how do personality characteristics fit together to comprise a unique individual? Critics of the "science" of personality correctly point out that in searching for the general laws of personality (what is called the nomothetic approach), we have learned surprisingly little about individuals *qua* individuals. Our ability to analyze and dissect has exceeded our ability to put the pieces back together again. As Sir Arthur Eddington once said: "We often think when we have completed our study of *one*, we know all about *two*, because "two" is "one and one." We forget that we still have to make a study of "and." Runyon argues that "the goal of understanding individual persons is one of the important objectives of personality psychology, that universal and group knowledge are often insufficient in themselves for obtaining this goal, and that there is a need for developing idiographic methods of inquiry in order to attain an in-depth understanding of individual lives."[18] This idiographic approach focuses on laws that apply to the particular case in order to generalize about, describe, explain, predict, and intentionally

---

[18] W. M. Runyon, "Idiographic Goals and Methods in the Study of Lives," *Journal of Personality*, 51 (1983), 417.

alter the behavior of specific individuals. This is the point at which personality theory becomes relevant for the practicing clinician who deals not with individuals in the abstract, but with real individuals and their very real hopes, fears, questions, and problems.

Summary

Up to this point I have tried to make three general points. Let me summarize them briefly. The first point is that the theories of Freud, Skinner, and Rogers no longer represent the mainstream of thought in the field of personality psychology. These theories have all played a role in shaping the field, but most contemporary personality psychologists would not label themselves as Freudian, Skinnerian, or Rogerian, and would endorse these theories only with marked reservations. The typical academic would probably describe Freud as insightful but prescientific and lacking in rigor, Skinner as scientific and rigorous but simplistic to the point of being irrelevant, and Rogers as unscientific and "soft."

The orientation of the field today would be more properly labeled scientific or empirical. My second point has to do with this "science of personality." The emphasis is on objectivity. Researchers strive to translate their ideas into testable hypotheses, their concepts into quantifiable measures, and their proofs into statements of statistical probability. Within this framework there are several distinct research traditions (inner and outer orientations, nomothetic and idiographic approaches), but the common goals involve describing and explaining the regularities that exist in the way people think, feel, and behave.

Finally, let me point out that the contemporary approaches, although explicitly scientific, still begin with certain assumptions about the nature of human nature. In this regard, I agree with Paul Vitz when he asserts that personality theorizing is fundamentally religious in nature. At the same time, I would add that contemporary personality theories are fundamentally irreligious in that they begin by assuming (at least implicitly) that there is no God or at least no reason to talk about God. Instead, the view of human nature that dominates the social and natural sciences today originates in evolutionary theory. The dominant view is that *homo sapiens* currently represents the most advanced form of animal life, having achieved this pinnacle by way of natural selection. The features that make us uniquely human bestowed on our ancestors a greater degree of success in becoming progenitors, and these features therefore survived the passing of generations better than other features which were also once part of our gene pool. Although there is not room here to detail the view of human nature that evolutionary theory implies, or to describe alternate views such as the essentially mechanistic view of the cognitive sciences, it is important to recognize that these scientific perspectives begin with definite assumptions about human nature and that these assumptions are fundamentally at odds with a Christian view of man. With these three points in mind, we can now turn to the final section of the paper.

A Christian Theory of Personality

In this section I want to focus on a series of questions: (1) How should we define the term "Christian"? (2) How should we define a Christian view of man? (3) Why do we need a Christian theory of personality? (4) What can Christians borrow from psychology? and (5) Will psychology want to borrow from Christians?

I promised at the outset of the paper that I would define my terms as clearly as possible. Unfortunately, the term Christian—much like the term personality—has been used to represent such a plurality of positions that it has lost much of its significance. In its most general sense, the adjective has come to mean nothing more than humane, respectable, and tolerant. However, using the term in this fashion denudes it of historical significance and theological relevance. My preference is to employ the term in its restricted and more traditional sense, and to ground the Christian viewpoint in the teachings of the Old and New Testaments. I specifically hold to an evangelical or reformed interpretation of the Bible as articulated, for instance, in the Westminster Confession of Faith.

This definition provides the basis for articulating a Christian view of man. The Bible takes a definite stance on the nature of human nature. Although there is much worth discussing here, the basics were ably specified by James Packer in an earlier volume of this series. He identifies four double-barrelled attributes: dignity and dependence (based on our creation in God's image); delight and development (what we were created for); design and deformity (why we seek meaning to life but cannot find it); and delivering and deprogramming (God's solution).[19] As I suggested earlier, the Christian view of man is fundamentally at odds with the view of man espoused by most natural and behavioral scientists. This leads us to our third question.

Why do we need a Christian theory of personality? To answer this question we need to think back once more to what we mean by "a theory of personality." If we develop such a theory in order to describe and explain the regularities that exist in the way people think, feel, and behave, then it is not immediately clear how a Christian theory of personality would differ from its secular counterpart. However, as soon as we look at how secular theories are applied and at the value and belief systems that are inherent to these theories, the need for a theory of personality that is fundamentally Christian becomes painfully obvious. Christianity comes with a morality and value system that is radical and unambiguous because it is rooted in the nature of the relationship between the Creator God and created beings. We cannot expect a theory that begins by denying (or ignoring) the existence of God to lead to applications that are in harmony with the teachings of God.

We can ask, then, whether current research in personality is

---

[19]J. Packer, "A Christian View of Man," in *The Christian Vision: Man in Society*, Lynne Morris, ed. (Hillsdale, MI: Hillsdale College Press, 1984).

relevant for a Christian view of man. Or, to paraphrase one early theologian, what does Athens have to do with Jerusalem? I believe there is much that Christian personality theorists can learn from their non-Christian colleagues, just as Christian physicians, philosophers, and businessmen can learn from non-Christians in their fields. Science is a method, a set of procedures that enables us to study the world (and ourselves) systematically and effectively. Science refines our powers of observation, deduction, testing, and generalization.

Many of the facts and principles emerging from current research on personality are consistent with a Christian view of man, or at least in no way inconsistent. Let me give two examples of the kinds of research from which I believe we can learn. Recent research suggests that cognitive processes and structures function largely outside conscious awareness. What we attend to, what we remember, what we say and feel, the way we interpret events, all of this and much more is in part the product of nonconscious information processing. The things that we let into our minds affect us just as pervasively and just as surreptitiously as the things we let into our stomachs. The ideas and images we dwell on become the building blocks of our thought lives just as the food we ingest provides the elements for our body. In both cases, we can choose to feed on nutrients or poisons. In this light, we can better appreciate the wisdom of meditating on and memorizing the Scriptures so that, as King Solomon taught, "when you walk, they will guide; when you sleep, they will watch over you; when you awake, they will speak to you" (Proverbs 6:23).

My second example involves personality characteristics that seem to have an inherited or biological component. These genetically influenced traits are called temperaments. Although some find this idea troublesome, we now have fairly clear evidence of these temperaments from studies of identical and fraternal twins, studies of adopted children and their biological and adoptive parents, and most recently from studies of identical twins raised apart. Characteristics that have an inherited component would include such traits as emotionality (fearfulness and shyness), activity level (tempo and vigor), and sociability,[20] as well as intelligence, depression, and schizophrenia.[21] Although the Bible does not speak to this issue directly, these findings are compatible with the biblical notion that different individuals are by the grace of God given different gifts and talents. Similarly, in the Church different individuals function as different parts of the Body. God creates and uses us differently. Does this mean we are not all created equal in God's sight? Yes and no. The Bible teaches that God loves each one of us, and that Christ died for each one of us; in this sense, we are all of equal worth. But we are not equal in physical appearance or ability, and no two individuals are created with the same personality.

I give these examples to make a point. I believe that the Bible is the revealed and trustworthy Word of God, but that is not to say it is an exhaustive textbook on human psychology. Thus, God left many things for us to explore and discover on our own. He provided us with certain fundamental truths from which we should always start and to which we must always appeal. God also imbued us with curiosity and intelligence. Science is a method, a set of procedures which enables us to study the world around us more effectively. Used properly it can also help us to understand ourselves. At the same time, however, the truths that are learned from secular thinkers must be carefully scrutinized and extracted from their original systems of belief. Although secular science is increasingly true, it is always rooted in falseness. A Christian theory of personality will always be incompatible with secular theories because it must begin with the existence of God. Therefore, although Christians can discern nuggets of truth in secular thought, we cannot simply adopt and thereby baptize secular systems of

---

[20]A. H. Buss and R. Plomin, *Temperament: Early Developing Personality Traits* (Hillsdale, NJ: Erlbaum, 1984).

[21]S. Scarr and K. K. Kidd, "Developmental Behavior Genetics," in *Handbook of Child Psychology: Vol. II—Infancy and Developmental Psychobiology*, M. M. Haith and J. J. Campos, eds. (New York: John Wiley and Sons Inc., 1983).

belief. The initial assumptions, the presuppositions, of such systems will, by definition, reject or make irrelevant the existence of God.

The science of personality can provide insights into the enduring characteristics of an individual: what those characteristics are, how they came to be there, and how they might be altered. But what is missing? From a Christian perspective, two areas of omission stand out: character, and the uniqueness and value of the individual.

Character is traditionally defined as moral constitution. It involves the application of the labels "good" and "bad" or "correct" and "incorrect" to an individual's behavior. All of us think morally; we evaluate ourselves and others according to a moral code. Character is one of the features that makes us distinctly human. However, in its zeal to be objective, the science of personality has largely ignored the issue of character. Some researchers have studied types or levels of moral reasoning, but the issue of character traits has been left alone. Gordon Allport provided the following scenario:

> The layman asks the psychologist, "How ought I bring up my child?" And the psychologist is presumptuous enough to tell him; although no psychologist *qua* psychologist can tell how a child ought to be brought up. The most he can do is to disclose human nature as it is, and then, *after a moral code has been chosen*, find out means of incentive and training that will achieve the end desired.[22]

Thus, the science of personality has very little to say about how to implant the virtues espoused in the New Testament: humility, contentment, thankfulness, joy, holiness, self-control, faithfulness, peace, patience, gentleness, kindness, and love. It is quiet also concerning the concepts of immorality and sin. But by ruling out the issues of character and morality, has it not excluded something fundamental about our nature?

Similarly, the science of personality has never quite known

---

[22]Allport, *Personality*, p. 52.

what to do about the uniqueness and worth of human life. The value of human life is problematic from a secular viewpoint because any design one perceives in the world is ultimately illusory, and the final meaning and purpose of life is reduced to one's ability to produce viable offspring. Conversely, from a Christian standpoint, the value and uniqueness of human life emanates directly from God.

Three fundamental truths form the theological base for the uniqueness and worth of the individual life in the Christian faith. (1) Men and women were created in the image of God, but this image was tarnished and distorted by willful rebellion. (2) Men and women can be restored to fellowship with God by the redemptive work of Christ Jesus—who was God incarnate, the living expression of God—and by the transforming power of the in-dwelling Holy Spirit. (3) Presently, God reproduces and lives out his image in the corporate Body we call the Church. Each member of the body is essential to the well-being of the whole.

I believe these truths provide a framework from which to develop a Christian theory of personality. These truths focus our attention on a number of important issues. What does it mean to be created in the image of God? What are the implications of the fall? These questions ask about our essential humanness, and our answers as Christians must take into account God's special revelations (the Word of God and the Word made flesh) as well as God's general revelation (the world around us and we ourselves). In part, we must answer how we are distinct from nonhuman life, but we must also consider the ways in which we are not different from other primates and mammals, a topic that Christian theorists have often ignored.

A second set of issues involves the process of redemption. What does it mean for a person to be redeemed? What changes when an individual becomes a believer in the gospel of Christ? In what sense does that person now have a new nature and a renewed mind? Conversely, in what ways is an individual left struggling with the limitations of the old nature? What are the psychological implications of Romans 7?

Finally, we may ask how human responsibility enters into the process of redemption. What is required of the individual, and what role is played by the corporate body of believers? Let me digress briefly here to say that I do not believe we are instructed to change our basic personality when we become Christians. The Bible calls us to be obedient in two ways: we are to be God-centered, and we are to be Christ-like. We are called to keep our minds on God (by praying without ceasing and meditating on the Word of God day and night), and we are called to walk like Christ—to take on his moral and spiritual attributes. Notice that I did not say we should take on Christ's personality. Certainly, the apostles differed markedly in terms of their personalities (consider, for example, John and Peter). When the apostle Paul told his readers to imitate him, he did not mean for them to imitate his personality style (his demanding, scholarly, confrontive nature), but rather his God-centeredness and Christ-likeness. This is a liberating distinction. One personality type is not more spiritual than another. God can transform whatever personality we have and enable us to live a life of holiness as exemplified by the virtues (fruits of the Spirit) listed earlier. God may choose to change our basic personality, but that is not what we are called to do. We are to be obedient and Christ-like in character.

To summarize, a Christian theory of personality moves beyond the secular science of personality in its willingness to deal with issues such as character and the value of the individual. It deals with issues that science rules out of bounds. Interestingly, however, secular theories of personality (both traditional and contemporary) often stray from "pure objectivity" by attempting to deal with these issues also. For instance, the human potential movement emphasizes the value and uniqueness of the individual, and behaviorism sometimes speaks to how we should raise our children. Even many evolutionists hold to a naïve optimism that the human race is improving with age and offer strategies by which it might improve more rapidly. In this regard, I again agree with Professor Vitz when he argues that personality theories are often more religious than scientific.

Their presuppositions require at least as great a leap of faith as Christianity. In this sense also I agree that Christianity offers a viable alternative to secular theories because it starts with presuppositions that accurately and authoritatively describe the human condition.

Is it likely, then, that secular theories will one day adopt a Christian viewpoint? Personally, I doubt whether a Christian theory of personality can ever achieve broad support in the secular, academic community. The metatheoretical and metaphysical assumptions that differentiate these two positions are simply too discrepant. Although it is true that personality psychologists are becoming increasingly aware of the ubiquitousness of such presuppositions, this awareness has not often lead to a serious consideration of the Christian perspective. More typically, the result is an acceptance of the "modern philosophy": that all facts are interpreted facts.

However, I am optimistic that Christian ideas and principles will continue to influence secular theories of personality. Scientists are pragmatic; they pay attention to results and they incorporate what works. Christianity has worked in the past, it works today, and it will work in the future because God is the author of truth.

Has Modern Psychology Secularized Religion?

Mary Vander Goot

> Dr. Mary Vander Goot is professor of psychology at Calvin College in Grand Rapids, Michigan. She received her M.A. and Ph.D. degrees from Princeton University and has taught in Canada. Since the late seventies, she has been a consulting editor for the Edwin Mellen Press as well as a contributing editor to the *Reformed Journal*. She is the author of two books, *A Life Planning Guide for Women* (1982) and *Piaget as a Visionary Thinker* (1985) as well as a number of articles. A registered psychologist in the state of Michigan, her interests include the history of psychology, its philosophical foundations, and "alternative methods" in the human sciences such as feminist criticism, neo-Marxism and phenomenology.

About fifty years ago, religious concerns were exiled officially from the fair land of science where the discipline of psychology—at least academic psychology in America—took up its residence. It had not always been the case that religion was barred from the domain of psychological inquiry. We only need to look back to sixty-five years ago when William James wrote *The Varieties of Religious Experience*.[1] It was a well-received statement by a prestigious psychologist who was intensely concerned with religion, and who was convinced that religion and psychology were each necessary for the other.

> Let me propose as an hypothesis, that whatever it may be on its *farther* side, the "more" with which in religious experience we

---

[1] William James, *The Varieties of Religious Experience* (New York: Longmans, Green & Co., 1919).

feel ourselves connected is on its *hither* side the subconscious continuation of our conscious life. Starting thus with a recognized psychological fact as our basis, we seem to preserve a contact with "science" which the ordinary theologian lacks.[2]

Those of us who have been trained in the discipline of psychology in the last fifty years know that times have changed. William James, were he our contemporary, would be reminded politely (or perhaps even impolitely) that religion and psychology really should not be muddled together. Psychology has become proudly secular, confidently secular, I would even venture to say, dogmatically secular.

The hands-off policy of separation between psychology and religion has not been reciprocal, however, because the science of psychology is allowed to make comment on religion, but religion, both on the level of institutions and ideas, is not allowed to interfere with, comment on, or stand in judgment of science. The best statement of this attitude, a classic statement because it is a milemarker of the shift from a religiously respectful to a secular science of psychology, was made by S. S. Stevens in 1939 in an article entitled "Psychology and the Science of Science."[3] In this article he proposes that the proper method for psychology is operationism because this method offers the hope that persons of reason might find common agreement in science. He then goes on to say:

> It [operationism] is not opposed to hypotheses, theories, or speculation. It seeks merely to discover criteria by which these things may be detected and labeled. It is not opposed to poetry, art, or religion. It wants only to know the difference between these things and science. It wants to know under what conditions the consorting of science with metaphysics breeds pseudo problems. Scientists as people may be opposed to pseudo problems,

---

[2]*Ibid.*, p. 512.
[3]S. S. Stevens, "Psychology and the Science of Science," *Psychology Review*, 36 (1939), 221-263.

but operationism's business, as a principle of criticism, is to discover them.⁴

We who study and construct the science of psychology in the 1980s work in a context in which the ideal of operationism is held by the majority of persons who participate in the discipline. At the same time, this ideal is being challenged by a strong minority which insists that science must recognize the interdependence of science and ideology (consider Marxist psychology), of science and political interest (consider the justifications given for government support of research), of science and personal identity (consider feminist scholarship). In Stevens's terms these would all be examples of science consorting with metaphysics. Although it is interesting that some consorting of science and other human concerns is now being reintroduced, it is even more interesting that the "consorting"⁵ of science and religion is still not tolerated.

Those of us who have been trained to keep the standard of operational science, but who are not willing to exile religion, find difficulties on two sides. As if it is not enough that we feel unwelcomed by many of our colleagues in the hallowed halls of the academy, we also face the additional embarrassment that, even if we will to do so and are given the opportunity to do so, reintegrating science and religion turns out to be far more difficult than we first anticipated.

We are caught in a double bind. In the academy we feel like a disenfranchised minority—a group of zealots who are treated as if they are asking for an exception clause that will allow them to be a little less scientific than the rest so that they may be a little more devoutly religious than the rest.⁶ But, in the company of

---

⁴*Ibid.*, p. 230.

⁵It is helpful to consider the various meanings of the word "consort." "To consort" means to associate with, agree with, or join; however, the noun "consort" refers to a spouse, especially that of a reigning monarch.

⁶It is interesting that the division in the American Psychological Association is designated as the division for psychologists interested in religion, *i.e.*, religion is the object of study, not the point of view from which an object is studied.

fellow Christians who tell us, "Yes, we are listening; tell us how to integrate faith and psychology," we find it hard to get beyond *post facto* moralism about the uses of science or platitudes about the sacred truth that knowledge is.

I would like to invite you to explore with me why the reintegration of science and faith is so difficult, by considering this thesis: *In modern psychology religion never was omitted, it was transformed.* If religion had been omitted and not revised we might expect that there would be a void to fill. In that case those of us who are concerned with the integration of faith and science could reinstate religious concerns where they obviously are lacking in the deliberations of our disciplines. But, religious concerns do not easily find a place in secular disciplines because they have been replaced by surrogates and there is no obvious void. Extra-scientific concerns which were once obvious, for example when James talked about God and faith, are still operative in science. There are deep commitments in science which have the force of religious faith, but they do not seem or sound religious anymore because in the process of secularization they were transformed and thus masked.

The best way to identify secularized religious themes in psychology is to look at specific cases of the process of secularization. This requires that we look back in time to an important generation of psychologists who were founders in our discipline, *i.e.*, those psychologists who developed major schools of thought. I believe that by studying the process of their intellectual metamorphosis we can trace lines of development and thus come to see clearly the secular ideas which have come to hold the space for what were previously religious concerns. In addition, I think we can begin to discern that there is a design to the process as it has occurred in several key figures. By identifying the structural similarity, we can train our intellectual eyes to see what is and has been there all along in our discipline, *i.e*, religion in secular form.

In the course of our explorations we will move through three steps. As a first step I invite you to consider with me the work and life of Jean Piaget, a psychologist with a striking religious odyssey. Although some facts of his work are well known, the very intense religious struggle of his early years is a closely kept secret. As a second step I would like to consider with you whether there is a discernible pattern — a design — in the process Piaget went through from being a self-consciously religious thinker to being a secular scientist.

Perhaps I am getting ahead of my story by telling you that I believe there is a discernible structure. Furthermore, I believe that it is a structure not unique to Piaget, but which can be found in other thinkers as well — thinkers who were founders, in the sense that they developed their own views of the discipline beginning with basic assumptions.[7] As a third step in our reflections here we will consider an additional figure: Sigmund Freud.[8]

Jean Piaget

Jean Piaget was born on August 6, 1896 in Neuchatel, Switzerland. A well-known feature of his intellectual biography is his precocious achievement in biology. He wrote his first professional article at age ten, by eighteen had written eight more, and by age twenty-two had completed a doctorate.[9]

In addition to the well-known story of Piaget's intellectual achievement there is another less well-known sequence of events in his life that has to do with his religious odyssey. Piaget was raised as a Calvinist. Especially after the time he was catechized he struggled with faith and doubt. He could not find sufficient reason for faith, but he also did not want to let go of it because

---

[7]In contrast to "founders" we should recognize that by far the majority of psychologists are "extenders" of theories founded by others, *i.e.*, they accept a set of assumptions uncritically, and they work to elaborate or refine theory within the boundaries set by these assumptions.

[8]Jean Piaget and Sigmund Freud are chosen here as cases for study because they are among the most familiar figures in the discipline. Roughly speaking, we might say, "Everyone knows who they are."

[9]"Jean Piaget," in *History of Psychology in Autobiography*, E. G. Boring, ed. (New York: Russell and Russell, 1968).

it seemed to him that without faith reason was barren and amoral.

During the era when Piaget was struggling with issues of faith and doubt, he read a theological treatise that was very helpful to him. Its title was *Outlines of a Philosophy of Religion Based on Psychology and History*, and its author was Auguste Sabatier. The preface of the book could have been addressed to Piaget personally. It read:

> Our young people, it seems to me, are pushing bravely forward, marching between two high walls; on the one side modern science with its rigorous methods which it is no longer possible to ignore or to avoid; on the other, the dogmas and the customs of the religious institutions in which they were reared, and to which they would, but cannot, sincerely return. . . . Must we then choose between pious ignorance and bare knowledge?[10]

Sabatier's argument so impressed Piaget that he wrote an article about it which he submitted to *Revue chrétienne*, a prestigious theological journal published in Paris. The article appeared in 1914, at which time Piaget was eighteen years old.[11]

Piaget's interest in theology was by no means unrelated to his studies of biology, nor was it purely an intellect interest for Piaget. Europe was becoming embroiled in World War I, and Piaget, like many intellectuals of the time, saw the war as painful testimony that with all of its gains in science and technology civilization still had not answered basic questions of morality. Biologists responded to the tragedy of war by crediting it to survival of the fittest and natural selection. The amorality of this response distressed Piaget. He was also bitterly disillusioned that the church was unable to offer counsel and showed no courage or moral leadership, but instead only flat-

---

[10] Auguste Sabatier, *Outlines of a Philosophy of Religion and History* (New York: James Pott & Company, 1902), p. xiv.

[11] Jean Piaget, "Bergon and Sabatier," *Revue chrétienne*, 61 (Paris, 1914), 192-200.

tered the political powers upon whom it depended for its own prosperity.[12]

Convinced of the need for religiously based morality and reasonably founded science, Piaget concluded that science and religion needed each other. Many years later as he recalled these times he wrote in his autobiography:

> I recall one evening of profound revelation. The identification of God with life itself was an idea that stirred me almost to ecstasy because it now enabled me to see in biology the explanation of all things and of the mind itself. . . . It made me decide to consecrate my life to the biological explanation of knowledge.[13]

For several years Piaget struggled with how he might go about consecrating his life to the biological explanation of knowledge. By the time he was twenty years old, Piaget had written a book called *La Mission de l'idée* (*The Mission of the Idea*).[14] It introduces the concept of "the idea" with a hymn to the idea which is very religious in its tone. Then follows an explication of "the idea" through which is woven themes of creation, fall, redemption, and eschaton.

"The idea" is "life." "Life is a force, an elan, a stream of consciousness which penetrates and organizes matter, thus introducing harmony or love to it."[15] But, the original harmony of all forms was disrupted by human egoism. The original human act of egoism was possible because intellect can conceive both the good and the evil. It can choose to act altruistically by seeking harmony or give in to evil by putting selfish pursuits before the good of all. The disruption by evil can be overcome if persons are willing to follow the selfless example of Jesus. Piaget writes:

---

[12]Jean Piaget, "La biologie et la guerre," *Feuille centrale de la Société Suisse de Zofingue* 58 (Zentralblatt des schweizerischen ZofingerVereins, 1918), 374–380.
[13]Piaget, *History*, p. 240.
[14]Jean Piaget, *La Mission de l'idée* (Lausanne: Edition la Concorde, 1916).
[15]*Ibid.*, p. 17.

50   The Christian Vision: Man and Mind

> Let us respect the ultimate reality of Christianity; let us believe in Christ, in his salvation, in his work in us, in man's sin, in conversion, in life. Let us follow Jesus in everything he established. . . .[16]

Soon after completing *The Mission of the Idea*, Piaget seems to have had an emotional collapse and was sent to the Alps to recuperate. While there he wrote a novel entitled *Recherche* (*The Quest*).[17] He chose a novel format to give himself freedom to express his own views without needing to justify them at every point.

The novel's only character is a young man, Sebastian, who goes to the mountains to think. From his place high above everything he looks out over the world and contemplates God, faith, science, war, the church, social organization, morality, and aesthetics. As he considers all of these other matters he searches for a vision of his own vocation as a scholar. Distressed by the state of the world and distressed by his own lack of understanding, Sebastian is convulsed with sobbing and begs God to help him. In return for the divine help he seeks, he promises to fulfill a divine mission.

After a night of incessant prayer, Sebastian enters a state of "exquisite communion in which all his Being finds life and strength. He converses with the God of science and faith . . ."[18] In this moment of revelation, Sebastian understands that he must devise a synthetic view of the sciences and at the same time clarify the absolute value which is life itself.

By coming to a new understanding of the basis of knowledge, Sebastian also comes to a new view of the nature of God. He determines to seek the basis of knowledge in biology, thus he also seeks in biology the knowledge of God. "God" becomes for Sebastian (who clearly speaks for Piaget himself) a symbol of the ideal equilibrium, or the perfect state in which all the parts of the grand totality are in balance with each other. Thus he

---

[16]*Ibid.*, pp. 36-37.

[17]Jean Piaget, *Recherche* (Lausanne: Edition la Concorde, 1918).

[18]*Ibid.*, p. 112.

concludes that God is transcendent because the ideal is never actual; it is always beyond the real state of things. On the other hand God is also immanent because the absolute value of life which God represents is everywhere and in everything. In reaching this conclusion, Sebastian believes that finally he harmonized faith and science.

Recherche was published in the same year that Piaget finished his doctoral work in molluscology. Instead of going on to work in biology or philosophy, Piaget determined to study psychology. This decision was not a change of career plans but rather a fulfillment of the commitment he had made earlier. Through the study of intelligence he hoped to gain understanding of how the structures of mind and intellect emerge from biological functions. It was this very process of the emergence of intelligence from biological structures that he outlined in his now-famous theory of the stages of cognitive development.[19] By uncovering the basics of a biological explanation of knowledge, Piaget believed that he could further his view of the synthesis of the sciences and could verify that even in the formation of knowledge the fundamental value is life itself.

For the ten years after which he wrote *Recherche*, Piaget studied psychology intensely and published nothing in the area of theology or religion. Then in 1928 he published a book entitled: *Deux types d' attitudes religieuses: immanence et transcendance* (*Two Types of Religious Attitude: Immanence and Transcendence.*)[20] This work presents Piaget's conclusion that the divine is not personal or supernatural, but rather is a quality which exists within persons. He justifies this view by drawing on quasi-scientific notions drawn from sociology and psychology.

In constructing the sociological view, Piaget suggests that at

---

[19]The place of Piaget's stage theory in the larger context of his understanding of the sciences is clarified in Jean Piaget, *Structuralism* (New York: Harper & Row, 1970), Chapters 1 and 14.

[20]Jean Piaget and J. de la Harpe, *Deux types d'attitude religieuse: immanence et transcendance* (Geneva: Editions de l'Association chrétienne d'étudiants de Suisse romande, 1928).

certain stages in the evolution of civilization a view of divine transcendence serves a useful purpose, because survival requires social organization, social organization in turn depends on rules, and where the origin of rules is not well understood their power is shored up by ascribing them to a divine source. With the evolution of reason, continues Piaget, persons see that the rules which support organization are worth keeping because it is reasonable to do so. The source of these rules is an interior conscience. Thus, according to Piaget, with reason one comes to see that the source of order, God, is immanent.

The second major portion of Piaget's argument in defense of divine immanence borrows from Freud's argument that religious feelings originate in the relation of children and parents. Children believe that parents are all-powerful, all-knowing, and morally perfect, but as they grow up and realize their parents' shortcomings they undergo great disillusionment. In order to cushion the blow of this disillusionment they ascribe the power and perfection they once believed a parent had to an overparent, a divine being.

Although there is a deep psychological need to respect an ideal, with the evolution of reason one comes to see that this does not require that a weak being admire the ideal of a stronger being. The ideal of mutual respect can be based on reciprocity and equality, and this ideal resides in the person who holds it. Thus, belief in a transcendent god is not necessary, and it is sufficient to recognize the divine within. In conclusion Piaget writes:

> I believe therefore that the transcendent God, a spiritual substance, creator of the world, source of miracle . . . is nothing but a symbol which can be attributed to mythological and infantile imagination. It has no relation to the God in spirit and in truth which the consciousness postulates.[21]

Not only does *Deux types d'attitude religieuses* summarize where Piaget's religious odyssey had led him, but it also reveals

---

[21]*Ibid.*, pp. 27-28.

how he had resolved the basic issues of faith and science with which he had begun to struggle as a young man almost fifteen years before. By turning inward to scrutinize the process of thought he had found an immanent god, a god within. This god, he assumed, is just as real as a transcendent and personal god because *thinking* is real. The conditions of thought are best exemplified in scientific thinking, and the more science progresses, the better the norms for thought are understood. In other words, Piaget's immanent God is evolving, just as thought and rationality are evolving, and just as the objects of thought are evolving. They are all evolving because they are parts of a rationally structured universe. As Piaget himself expressed it:

> In the measure that science conquers the universe, thought interiorizes itself. Only at the limits do scientific realism (of method) and critical idealism recover themselves completely. Meanwhile there is simply a circle. Thanks to positive science, thought explicates itself in the universe; thanks to rational norms the universe explicates itself through thought.[22]

The circularity which appears in Piaget's final view is curious. The forward movement of thought in the course of evolution leads us to change our views of God, Piaget is suggesting. But thought is God, and God is thought. Thus, the evolution of thought is the process of the divine changing itself.[23]

The Emerging Pattern: A Hermeneutical Shift

Is it possible, as we review Jean Piaget's spiritual odyssey, to detect some major elements or steps which mark the course of it? I would like to suggest that there are three major steps in the course of his understanding of religion and science, and these

---

[22]*Ibid.*, p. 22.
[23]For a more thorough discussion of Piaget's religious thought, see Mary Vander Goot, *Piaget as a Visionary Thinker* (Bristol, IN; Wyndham Press, 1985).

stages represent a "hermeneutical shift," *i.e.*, a transformation in the structures of authority which operate in his thinking.

Stage One: The Crisis. During the formative years when Piaget was gaining expertise in both the traditions of science and theology, he encountered events which threatened his secure notions about the world. Faced with the disturbing reality of World War I, Piaget was sure that the two arenas in which he had deeply invested himself should offer a solution, but when he was unable to see his way to the needed solution, he became disillusioned with both science and faith. In the disillusionment engendered by this crisis Piaget took a first major step toward skepticism, *i.e.*, he determined never again to accept anything as true merely on the claim of authority.

Stage Two: The Elevation of Science. Because Piaget could no longer accept religion on the basis of authority or for the sake of tradition, he needed a new standard of justification for those elements of religion which he wanted to retain for the purpose of answering his own questions about morality and basic values. He identified "life" as the basic value and found the foundations of religion in biology. However, this step denied religion its distinctive claim. Rather than allowing it to rest on an authority other than science, religion was made an object *dependent on* the authority of science. While religion required an external authority, science did not because it was allowed to be its own means of justification.

Stage Three: The Reassimilation of Religious Thinking in Metascience. Once Piaget had elevated science to the status of an exclusive authority he also developed a new and highly idealistic rhetoric to account for the origin and future of science. This rhetoric had a mythic character. It referred to the past in terms of archetypal events rather than in terms of historically specified events. And, it referred to the future in such a way that the unfolding of the future depended on the guidance of science developing itself.

Basic to Piaget's metascience was his conviction that intellect, both as manifest in the *operations* and the *products* of the reasonable mind, was the most powerful and hopeful development in human history. Eventually he came to see this power as a divine presence, *i.e.*, intellect was as godlike as anything could be, and religious accounts of the divine were no longer necessary. Thus, traditional religious thinking could be consigned to the category of primitive and outdated thinking. It could be explained, discounted, and replaced by scientific thinking. Intellect had become for Piaget an absolute authority with its own myth of origin and its own promise for the future. The metascience which Piaget developed is, in its structure, religious.

We have traced religious themes in Piaget's thought, and have considered steps or stages in his thinking. We will now take our outline of these steps and examine whether they can also be seen in the thought of another major founder in the discipline. The case chosen is Sigmund Freud.

Sigmund Freud

Sigmund Freud is one of the most widely studied figures in the history of psychology. It is not the intention of the discussion which follows to summarize Freud's work or judge its significance, but to trace Freud's religious development and the relation of religion and psychoanalysis.

Sigmund Freud was born on May 6, 1856 in Freiburg (in Moravia). A few years prior to his birth his family had moved to Freiburg from Tysmenica (in Galicia); however, they did not remain long in Moravia. Sometime within a few years after Sigmund's birth the family moved first to Leipzig and then on to Vienna, which was not only the capital of the Austro-Hungarian empire, but also the city in which its diversity was most represented.

The various locations in which the Freud family lived may very well have had some important implications for their identity as Jews. Tysmenica was a small town with a well-established community of observant Jews. Freiburg was somewhat less orthodox, and Vienna was a center in which many branches of Judaism were forced to coexist cooperatively, the strongest of which was the Reform movement. In Vienna all persons of the Jewish faith were members of the *Israelitische Kultusgemeinde* (Israelite Confessional Community) to which they were required by law to pay a special tax. The *Kultusgemeinde* kept essential family records and provided religious education for Jewish children.[24]

Among the leaders of the Viennese Jewish community were several influential rabbis whose efforts seemed to be directed toward maintaining a strong sense of Jewish identity among its members while also removing as many obstacles as possible to their modernization and assimilation into the activities of gentile Vienna. Among other things, efforts at assimilation involved a relaxing of dietary laws and ritual observance, as well as an increased emphasis on prosocial concerns such as freedom, charity, justice, and good citizenship.

In all likelihood Reform Judaism set the tone for Freud's religious education. It is not clear how much his family involved itself in his formal religious training, but it is known that all Viennese school children, including Jewish children, were required to have religious education. During his first school years, Freud attended a Jewish school, but later transferred to a public school. In both schools he received the religious education approved by the *Kultusgemeinde*.

Sigmund's religious education was in marked contrast to the Judaism of his father, Jakob. The father's home town, Tysmenica, was a center of Chassidism, a form of mystic Judaism especially prevalent in the Eastern provinces of the Austro-Hungarian empire. Important among the mystics was the Kabbala, the tradition. While certain documents such as the *Zohar* were important in the tradition, its most important secrets were

---

[24]A helpful summary of this material appears in Reuben M. Rainey, *Freud as Student of Religion: Perspectives on the Background and Development of His Thought* (American Academy, Religion and Scholars Press, Dissertation Series No. 7, 1975).

conveyed by word of mouth from leaders to initiates. The respected Kabbalistic leader was a person who understood that mystical wisdom could be hinted at but never captured in its entirety. Indirect forms of discourse, instruction by paradox, and tolerance for obscurity were all acceptable. This was the tradition of Sigmund Freud's father who, although not strict in practice, continued as an old man to study the Talmud and the writings of the mystical tradition.

As Sigmund grew to an age of self-consciousness, the Jews of the provinces were an embarrassment to him. For example, in a letter which he wrote when he was sixteen years old he tells of being stuck near a Jewish family on a train. They reminded him of a "thousand" he had met before in Freiburg where he was born. With disdain he relates how the father and son discussed religion, and what a disgusting fellow the younger man was. In the course of observing them, Freud discovered that they were from Meseritsch, which is a town in Moravia, and he concludes that it is "the proper compost heap for this sort of weed."[25]

Freud detested the peculiarities of dress and habit, the ritual observances, and the separatism of the orthodox. He thought of himself as an enlightened Jew. In practice this meant that he had determined that neither his Judaism nor his Jewishness should impede his personal ambitions. Nevertheless the problem of being a Jew in a gentile world was a great personal crisis for Freud, and it remained a point of great sensitivity with him throughout his entire life. This tension marks the first stage in Freud's religious odyssey.

It seems that the best solution Freud could reach in dealing with his own identity crisis was to become a scientist. Gentile Vienna certainly held the scientist in high regard. In fact, science was a significant way in which a Jew could climb the social ladder. The assimilated Jews of Vienna also supported the venture of science. What better way to prove that one is enlightened than to be trained in the skills of rational inquiry? And, last but not least, even orthodox Jews and those raised in a

---

[25]*Ibid.*, p. 21.

Chassidic tradition could respect science, because scholarship had long been considered an important balance to mysticism.

It is quite clear that Sigmund became a scientist with his father's blessing. On Sigmund's thirty-fifth birthday, Jakob presented him the family bible with the following inscription:

> It was in the seventh year of your age that the spirit of God began to move you to learning. I would say the spirit of God speaketh to you: "Read in My book; there will be opened to thee sources of knowledge and of the intellect." It is the Book of Books; it is the well that wise men have digged and from which lawgivers have drawn the waters of their knowledge.
>
> Thou hast seen in this Book the vision of the Almighty, thou hast heard willingly, thou hast done and hast tried to fly high upon the wings of the Holy Spirit. Since then I have preserved the same Bible. Now, on your thirty-fifth birthday I have brought it out from its retirement and I send it to you as a token of love from your old father.[26]

The course that Freud took once he had decided to be a scientist was heavily influenced by his teacher and mentor, the renowned physiologist, Ernst Brucke. In Brucke's view of the world there was no place for mysteries, gods, or nonmaterial principles or forces. Brucke was a radical materialist. He believed the real world was a world of atoms moved by forces of attraction and repulsion.

Brucke, along with Carl Ludwig, Emil du Bois-Reymond, and Hermann von Helmholtz, had been a student of the famous Johannes Mueller. Just as in his day Mueller had been one of the deans of the science of physiology, so this quartet of his students represented the greatest minds in physiology in the next generation, and they held the most esteemed posts in Europe. They all had in common their radical materialist views and their determination to fight against vitalism — the view that in living things there are forces in addition to those found in

---

[26]Max Schur, *Freud: Living and Dying* (New York: International Universities Press, 1972), p. 24.

inorganic bodies. Brucke and Du Bois had even pledged an oath never to swerve from the materialist position and never to give up the fight against vitalism.[27]

Brucke's laboratory was the setting for Freud's first training as a scientist, and it seems that for a time Freud was thoroughly convinced by Brucke's view.[28] The story is told that at a meeting of a student fraternity to which Freud belonged he defended the materialist position in a debate, and the debate became so heated that it threatened to end in a duel.[29]

By the time Freud was a young adult he had set aside Judaism. In fact he was so determined to be separated from it that he ran into conflict with the family of his future wife, the granddaughter of one of Germany's most prominent rabbis, because Freud did not want to have a traditional Jewish wedding ceremony. However, the debate was finally concluded in favor of Martha's family because at the time a religious ceremony was required for any marriage that was to be recognized before the law.

Although Freud was committed to scientific research, practical forces drove him out of the laboratory and into the practice of medicine. Brucke had made it clear to Freud that in the university certain doors would be closed to him because he was a Jew. He was also struggling to become financially self-sufficient so that he could marry. For these reasons, Freud began a private practice in the treatment of nervous diseases.

The cases which Freud encountered in his practice required a different set of techniques and interpretations than those he had learned in the course of his training for medicine. It was in response to this challenge that Freud began to develop his psychoanalytic method. There is much to suggest that Freud's interpretations were not welcomed by the medical establishment. Freud tells in his autobiography that soon after presenting his

---

[27]Edwin Boring, *A History of Experimental Psychology* (New York: Appleton-Century-Crofts, 1929), pp. 299, 708.
[28]*Ibid.*, p. 709.
[29]*Ibid.*, p. 101.

ideas on hysteria he was excluded from the laboratory and no longer had anywhere to give his lectures. Consequently, he withdrew from academic life.[30]

It is significant that Freud's withdrawal from academic life pushed him into a flurry of other activities that could give his psychoanalytic approach public respectability. He began to write at a steady pace and began looking for sympathizers among other practitioners. The turning point seemed to come in 1892 when Freud was thirty-six years old.[31] This turning point marked his shift from natural science to analysis, and from a concern with psychoanalysis as a form of treatment to psychoanalysis as a metascience, a general theory of knowledge including scientific knowledge. Thus it is perhaps significant that it was also at this stage that Freud began to show a renewed interest in religious traditions and rhetoric.

The method of analysis which Freud developed had striking similarity to that method of interpretation in which the Kabbalists were skilled. Furthermore, even the themes that he pursued, though foreign and unacceptable to the medical community of Vienna, were familiar in the discussions of the Jewish mystics: notions such as libido, bisexuality, incest taboos, the origin of perversity in childhood, the interpretation of dreams, and many other "Freudian" concepts are to be found in the writings of the Jewish mystics.[32]

Many of the matters taken up in a thorough psychoanalysis are related to guilt in one way or another. The analysand is one who feels that he or she has not lived up to the expectation of civilization and is therefore unacceptable. In the past these problems of failure, inadequacy, or evil inclination were dealt with in the context of religion with such concepts as sin, forgiveness, and grace. In Freud's view it was this function of religion that was being replaced by science:

---

[30]David Bakan, *Sigmund Freud and the Jewish Mystical Tradition* (Princeton: Van Nostrand, 1958), p. 198.
[31]*Ibid.*, pp. 199-200.
[32]Bakan, *Sigmund Freud*.

> Those historical residues have helped us to view religious teaching, as it were, as neurotic relics, and we may now argue that the time has probably come, as it does in an analytic treatment, for replacing the effects of repression by the results of the rational operation of the intellect.[33]

In the process of an analysis the analysand was encouraged to see that fear and guilt were leftovers of misunderstanding. They were childish thoughts that needed to be replaced.

In the last decade of his life, Freud returned to general questions of religion and tradition. He had insisted all along that religion was a form of obsessional neurosis, and he admitted quite freely that he was prone to such obsessional neurosis himself. As a therapist he had dealt with these conflicts on an individual level, but as an aging man, it seems, he needed to deal with them as more universal patterns of human nature. In his writings he presented a view which, he believed, would transform religion. For example, in 1936 he wrote in a postscript to his autobiography:

> My interest after making a long *detour* through the natural sciences, medicine and psychotherapy, returned to the cultural problems which had fascinated me long before, when I was a youth scarcely old enough for thinking.[34]

Freud's efforts at revising religion focused on the figure of Moses, the Israelite leader who had brought the tables of the law down from the mountain top where he had met God.[35] These laws Freud identified as the strictures that had twisted persons in civilization, and the transgression of these laws, or even the wish to or fear of transgressing them, was the source of guilt and neurosis which persons brought to the analyst for cure. In his study of Moses, Freud rewrote the myth. He

---

[33] Sigmund Freud, *The Future of an Illusion* (New York: Norton, 1961; originally published in 1927), p. 44.
[34] Sigmund Freud, "Autobiography," *Standard Edition* 21 (1935), 72.
[35] Sigmund Freud, "Moses and Monotheism," *Standard Edition* 23 (1939), 3–137.

claimed that Moses was a Gentile, son of the pharaoh, and that Moses had been an imposter in Israel. The Jews had been deceived into believing that Moses was one of them, and the laws he forced upon them had been the source of their misery.

Because the Jews had bequeathed the Mosaic laws to Christians, they too were its victims. In addition, Freud suggested the Jews were for Christians the origin of their bad conscience, as well as the scapegoat for relieving it. Freud believed this was the origin of anti-Semitism. But, he asserted, it is not the Jews, but Moses who is responsible for anti-Semitism.

Believing that he had exposed the deception, Freud also believed that he could lift the burden of the law from the shoulders of men and women in modern civilization. In the process of psychoanalytic insight, the weight of the law is lifted, and the analysand comes to see that guilt is unnecessary. In a very helpful study of the religious significance of Freud's preoccupation with Moses, David Bakan goes so far as to suggest that Freud saw himself as a new sort of religious figure:

> If the Jews represent the authority of the Law, only a Jew can declare the Law is dead. . . . Such a role can be accomplished by Freud only through his full identification of himself as a Jew who is, moreover, dissociated from the figure of Moses. In this presumptive position of authority he can *rescind* the Law, declare the Law invalid. Thus Freud plays the role of a new Moses who comes down with a new Law dedicated to personal psychological liberty.[36]

Here we have seen in Freud, just as earlier we saw in Piaget, the transformation of religion by science and of science by religion. Freud was a child of two traditions. He was a child who had learned to see the world through Jewish eyes, and he was an assimilated Jew who had supposedly altered his vision with the lenses of science. This was the stage of crisis for him, and this was the occasion for his first step into skepticism.

---

[36]David Bakan, *Sigmund Freud and the Jewish Mystical Tradition* (Princeton: Van Nostrand, 1958), pp. 159–160.

As Freud immersed himself in scientific training, religion was subordinated to the scrutiny of science. It became an object for science, and a source of knowledge without authority of its own. This was Freud's second stage.

Finally, after Freud had refined his approach in science and developed his own methods of analysis, he needed also to validate them with a metascience. The methods he used took him back to the rhetoric of religion. He constructed his own Mosaic myth and extended it to include his own science of psychoanalysis. Having thus been validated, Freud believed psychoanalysis held promise for the future.

In Conclusion

Freud and Piaget are not the only major thinkers in modern psychology in whom the process of secularization and the hermeneutical shift may be recognized. It has happened time and again: Wilhelm Wundt, Franz Brentano, William James, G. Stanley Hall, and J. B. Watson, to name just a few. I might add that I believe the process of secularization is at least in its second stage in those who believe that science ought not to consort with religion.

How can we come to an understanding of how science can be seen in the light of religion, can be energized by the power of religion, can be made to harmonize with the religious life lived, if we convince ourselves that religion is now absent from science and waiting for us to fill in what is missing? There is religion operating in science. It is religion in disguised form, it is religion which already several stages ago was made to bend the knee to science, religion whose distinctive claim was preempted, religion whose tradition was severed, but religion enough to block the way of religion informed by the gospel, unless it is understood to be religion in secular form.

Finally, how can we begin to gain the insights necessary for understanding religion and science for what they are unless it becomes permissible to talk about religion in intelligent company? When will we discard those taboos against talking about religion in the academy? When will the rules of scholarship change enough to let Christian scientists out of the catacombs and on with their work? And, when all of this happens, will we be ready?

Secular Personality Theories: A Critical Analysis
Paul C. Vitz

Dr. Paul C. Vitz, professor of psychology at New York University, attended the University of Michigan where he earned Phi Beta Kappa honors. He received his Ph.D. from Stanford University. He is currently the director of New York University's newly established graduate program in the psychology of art. He is on the board of directors of the Fellowship of Catholic Scholars and the executive committee of the Catholic Commission on Intellectual and Cultural Affairs. Dr. Vitz is the author of *Psychology as Religion: The Cult of Self-Worship*, *Sigmund Freud's Christian Unconscious*, and many articles. His recent book, *Modern Art and Modern Science: The Parallel Analysis of Vision*, reflects his interest in the relationships between contemporary aesthetics and science. Other interests include Christian thought and the topics of personality theory, moral development, psychoanalysis, and counseling.

To many people, especially psychologists, the very concept of a Christian theory of personality would seem impossible, strange and even offensive. Yet that is what is being proposed here. But, before getting to the concrete nature of such a project it is necessary to present a context within which such a proposal makes sense. Unless this is done, many readers might assume that the contemporary psychology of personality is some kind of objective science and thus there could not be such a thing as a Christian theory of personality. This paper will be devoted to context, to a critical analysis of secular theory, so as to set the intellectual stage for my second paper in this volume focused on the Christian theory itself.

Antireligious Assumptions of Secular Psychology

We begin by looking, rather briefly, at some of the methodological and philosophical assumptions that characterize much of today's psychological theory. Taken together, these assumptions represent in a general way the essential foundations of modern secular psychology. These foundational assumptions are rarely understood or acknowledged either by psychologists or Christians, but since they constitute the ground rules or underlying intellectual control mechanisms, they heavily determine, in advance, how human nature will be seen and valued. It is therefore necessary for Christians to become aware of them and keep in mind that they are assumptions and not part of the data, or part of objective science — whatever that might mean.

Assumption 1: Atheism or Agnosticism

It is unfortunate but true that all the major theories of personality and counseling are either explicitly or implicitly based on atheism. Freud, of course, is well known for his attacks on religious belief as an illusion, but all the other major theories are implicitly antireligious as well, as shown by the fact that genuine religious motivation is ignored or treated negatively when it occasionally comes up. In no theory of personality does spiritual life figure as essential or even as important. The only partial exception to this is Jung's psychology. Even Jung, however, is far from reliable on this issue, and my own experience with Jungian Christians is that Jungian categories have commonly overshadowed their Christianity. In short, psychological theory is either explicitly atheistic or it is simply functionally atheistic in that it completely ignores God, religious motivation, and spiritual life. Christians should always keep this "functional atheism" in mind and should do everything possible to correct for it.

Assumption 2: Naturalism

Closely related to atheism is Assumption 2: Naturalism. In psychology this assumption means that all mental events are assumed to be either ultimately physical or that the mind considered on its own is a purely natural thing—and that it can be completely understood by reason and observation. Most especially the assumption of naturalism means that nothing "supernatural" actually exists. For example, Abraham Maslow, sometimes thought a friend of religion, is rather well known for a concept he described as the "peak" experience. Christians might think Maslow has therefore accepted religious experience. This is not the case, for Maslow writes:

> It is quite important to dissociate this [peak] experience from any theological or supernatural reference, even though for thousands of years they have been linked. Because this experience is a natural experience, well within the jurisdiction of science.[1]

For these bald assertions, he offers no defense at all.

Assumption 3: Reductionism

The secular modernist assumes that all so-called "higher" things, especially religious experience and related ideals, are to be understood as really caused by underlying lower phenomena. Examples: Love is reduced to sex and sex is reduced to physiology, as in Kinsey and in Masters and Johnson. Spiritual life is reduced to sublimated sex, as in Freud. Even the ego is reduced to underlying ego states, as in Transactional Analysis. In contrast, the Christian is typically a constructionist who sees higher meaning and divine significance in psychological experiences. Sex is seen as love, love as sacred; marriage as divinely supported, and by some Christians as a sacrament.

---

[1] A. Maslow, *Toward a Psychology of Being*, 2nd edition (New York: Van Nostrand Reinhold, 1968), p. 164.

As an example of reductionism I would like to look briefly at the psychological treatment of sex as represented by Masters and Johnson—and the kind of sex therapy which they have "spawned," as it were. In this summary of what might be called the "Masters and Johnson understanding," I will draw heavily on the work of Hogan and Schroeder, two secular psychologists who are part of a recent critical stance toward modern social science which is growing in the secular world, at the time many Christians are still trying to catch up with secular sexology. Somehow the Christian world is always buying into secular ideas at the top of their influence, and selling out Christian ideas just when they have no place to go but up! This is the classic "buy high and sell low" behavior of the stock market victim. (As an example, secular psychologists have recently discovered such ideas as character, virtue, chastity, celibacy, and even virginity. Soon these will be hot topics in the secular marketplace—just as these ideas and values have almost totally dropped out of Christian use.) To return to Masters and Johnson, in their *Human Sexual Response*[2] they deal almost entirely with anatomy and physiology. More recently, Masters and Johnson state that they do not purport to cover the emotional and social aspects of sex, much less religious aspects. In spite of their disclaimer, they nevertheless explicitly criticize traditional cultural teachings:

> The omnipresent religious orthodoxies, social intolerances and ignorance of sexual matters by health-care professionals, contributed immeasureably to our culture's lack of comprehension of sexual response as a natural physiological process, a process comparable to other natural functions such as respiratory, bowel or bladder function.[3]

---

[2] W. H. Masters and V. A. Johnson, *Human Sexual Response* (Boston: Little, Brown & Co., Inc. 1966).

[3] W. H. Masters and V. A. Johnson, *The Pleasure Bond* (Boston: Little, Brown & Co., Inc., 1975), pp. 4-5.

Thus, they reject the cultural teaching of the past and view sex in a purely biological light. The effect of this position has been to amplify Kinsey's implied message: sex can be regarded perfectly objectively, as morally neutral, and one need not feel the socially bestowed compunctions about sexual activity. Although Masters and Johnson did not intend to encourage sex without responsibility, they have contributed significantly to that effect.

Often Masters and Johnson discuss clinical difficulties in sexual functioning. They use a concrete, reductionistic approach emphasizing overt behavior, anatomy, and physiology. They explicitly do not view sexual functioning as symptomatic of deeper or broader psychological factors. Hogan and Schroeder describe this attitude very lucidly:

> A major theme (in Masters and Johnson, *The Pleasure Bond*) is how individuals have been overburdened with the responsibility to meet their partner's needs. For Masters and Johnson, individuals are responsible primarily for their own gratification.[4]

Of course this is a complete reversal of the Christian injunction that the body of the husband is for his wife and vice versa. Hogan and Schroeder come to a similar conclusion when they comment that the Masters and Johnson position "would seem to turn the entire sexual process back on itself. What is generally construed as an expression of affection for another becomes an expression of interest for one's self."[5]

Somehow the reductionist strategy of focusing first on the individual and then only on the physiology of sex has resulted not only in losing sight of the many higher meanings of sex; it has led to an active rejection of such meanings. As a result, at the end we see how interwound and mutually supportive are the

---

[4]R. Hogan and D. Schroeder, "The Joy of Sex for Children and Other Modern Fables," in *Character Policy*, E. A. Wynne, ed. (Washington: University Press of America, 1980), p. 96.

[5]*Ibid.*

reductionist and individualist assumptions. We turn next to this latter assumption—individualism.

Assumption 4: Individualism

Secular psychology assumes that the isolated, autonomous, self-preoccupied individual is the only significant social and psychological reality. Specifically, the modernist is devoted to what he considers to be independence, while the Christian is aware of and cultivates interdependence, and indeed dependence on God and obedience to Him.

Modern psychology emphasizes the isolated individual while the Christian is focused on others—family and community. Secular psychology emphasizes self-will and its decisions in a life of calculated self-advancement, unconcerned with others, while the Christian is concerned with following God's will and living a life of Christian love and holiness. It is most revealing that there is not one major psychological theory of personality which does not assume the isolated individual as the central unit and primary concern of its theory. Likewise it is rare to find influential psychological theory which has any major positive theoretical terms for the important fact of human interdependence, even less, of course, for such concepts as obedience, or humility. Yet, the only time Jesus referred to himself in what might be called psychological terms he said: "learn from me; for I am meek and lowly of heart" (Matthew 11:29).

Assumption 5: Relativism

The secular modernist assumes that all values are relative to the individual or to the culture. In spite of this assumption, secularists take an absolute position toward relativism and, in flat contradiction to their philosophy, they often take an absolute position on certain modern, secular values, *e.g.*, egalitarianism. In contrast, the Christian assumption is one of absolute values across all cultures and times—values revealed in Scripture, expressed in the church's tradition and values always mediated through the absolute of absolutes, namely the love of god and of neighbor.

Assumption 6: Subjectivism

Much of modern psychology is based on the assumption that all we really know are states of the mind or the kind of knowledge found in the physical sciences. As a result, it assumes that psychological, moral, and spiritual truth is intrinsically nonobjective, nonrational. Closely related to this assumption is the idea that the important thing is to express, understand, and communicate one's thoughts and feelings, and to be open to this same thing in others. Again we find a kind of emphasis on the self, on feelings, rather than on others, God, and religious, moral, and social truths which exist independent of and outside of ourselves. One of the reasons for the popularity of psychotherapy is undoubtedly its ability to focus on and cultivate the subjective world of the patient and to attribute great worth to a person's feelings and opinions. A common expression of this in psychology is found in encounter groups and related therapies where the emphasis is on getting in touch with your feelings. For example, primal therapy, or the vogue for touchie-feelie groups in the early 1970s, had an extreme emphasis on catharsis. No doubt there is a place for catharsis in psychotherapy—at least up to a point. But, persistently delving into your personal emotions in private or expressing your feelings in extreme ways in public has no basis in Scripture or in church tradition. In particular, public, *i.e.*, group, expression can often lead to deep divisions between the person "catharting" and the person being "catharted about." The Christian emphasis is always on the outside reality, of God and others—there is no basis for today's almost blatantly narcissistic preoccupation with getting in touch with feelings at the expense of getting in touch with God through prayer, or getting in touch with others through charity.

72   The Christian Vision: Man and Mind

Assumption 7: Gnosticism (Knowledgism)

This assumption, which is very closely related to subjectivism, is commonly made by all contemporary psychology; it involves the belief that if there is any truly better state, *i.e.*, if there is any kind of "salvation," then it comes by intellectual insight, by knowledge. In the older, rational atheism, the better state could come through science and reason. Today, however, the gnostic way is primarily psychological with an emphasis on self-knowledge. As an example of this category consider Jung's psychology which is described as follows by one of his foremost students, Jolande Jacobi:

> Jungian psychotherapy is . . . a *Heilsweg*, in the twofold sense of the German word: a way of healing and a way of salvation. It has the power to cure . . . in addition it knows the way and has the means to lead the individual to his "salvation," to the knowledge and fulfillment of his personality, which have always been the aim of spiritual striving. . . . Jung's system of thought can be explained theoretically only up to a certain point; to understand it fully one must have experienced or better still, "suffered" its living action in oneself . . .
>
> Apart from its medical aspect, Jungian psychotherapy is thus a system of education and spiritual guidance.[6]

The process of Jungian movement on this path is, Jacobi continues, "both ethically and intellectually an extremely difficult task, which can be successfully performed only by the fortunate few, those elected and favored by grace."[7] The last stage on the Jungian path, the goal stage of individuation—the salvation—is called by Jung *self-realization*.

I suppose this says it all in a nutshell. But, the Jungian gnostic goal is widely found throughout all the psychology which places the achievement of self-realization or psychological wholeness as the highest aim of life. In every case the com-

---
[6]J. Jacobi, *The Psychology of C. G. Jung*, 8th edition (New Haven, CT: Yale University Press, 1973), p. 60.
[7]*Ibid.*, p. 127.

mand, "seek to know thyself," replaces "seek to love God and others." Many years ago it was noted with approval by the liberal Protestant Harry Emerson Fosdick that psychological integration had replaced salvation.[8] Today integration is called wholeness. In general wherever you find a preoccupation with wholeness and self-actualization, God and Jesus have been put aside for the goal of self-enhancement and self-salvation through self-knowledge.

As Christians we have good reason to understand why gnosticism cannot work. One is that salvation comes from putting down the very self—the old man or the old woman—that the gnostics think can be repaired and made whole. The very will, the very desire, which drives people to find wholeness of self is the same self-will that is at the center of our sin. We should never forget that the search for self-esteem is driven by our pride, and it is this which must be laid aside in order to do God's will. Furthermore, the way of knowledge is a terribly elitist way since it is restricted to the small number of people with the intellectual ability, the time, and the education to take up the gnostic disciplines. The gnostic way is not open to the poor of the world, to the uneducated, or to many, many others. The gnostic way, for example, is just another way of saying you need a high IQ to find salvation.

Now of course we may become whole by putting down our old self and putting on Jesus, but this is not certain; what *is* certain is that we must accept Jesus to be saved. And even if we do become whole (whatever that means) we know we are not to *search* for wholeness; we are to search for God and then many other good things, perhaps including wholeness, will be added as well.

It will be instructive, I believe, to observe how the preceding seven assumptions operate in the case of abortion—a major challenge to Christianity. Although it is possible to be an atheist and philosophical naturalist and still be against abortion, the

---

[8]H. E. Fosdick, *On Being a Real Person* (New York: Harper & Row Publishers, Inc., 1943), Chap. 2.

odds are very small. Without a doubt one of the major bulwarks against atheism and for the value of life is belief in a transcendent God in whose image all humans are made, and the related beliefs of a revealed morality and of judgment after death. Take these away and abortion almost always becomes an acceptable act with no deeply spiritual significance. The assumption of reductionism aids the pro-abortion position by allowing a human to be reduced to a strictly natural phenomenon and the fetus to just biological tissue. Individualism favors abortion by assuming that only the autonomous individual counts in a moral decision and that neither the unborn baby, nor society, much less the father, have any acceptable moral basis for affecting the decision to abort. Relativism has much the same effect by making all claims to an absolute moral law no longer acceptable — indeed they are made intolerable. In the case of a decision to abort, subjectivism has much the same effect as individualism. The last assumption of gnosticism makes moral knowledge the private discovery for the few. Furthermore, gnosticism rejects the authoritative status of Scripture and tradition. All this, of course, favors abortion.

In short even this one example shows how modern secular psychology *through its assumptions* creates an interpretive framework of human nature with profound anti-Christian consequences.

General Religious Characteristics of Modern Psychology[9]

The many similarities to religion on the part of modern psychological theories of mental pathology and psychotherapy were noticed from the time these approaches emerged early in this century. Each theory was a kind of general psychological interpretation of the meaning of personal existence, complete with an explanation of what facilitates and what blocks the

---

[9]For more on this and on related topics, see P. C. Vitz, "Psychology as Religion," in *Baker Encyclopedia of Psychology*, D. G. Benner, ed. (Grand Rapids, MI: Baker, 1985), pp. 932-938.

development of a healthy or ideal personality. Since all of these psychologies were based on secular philosophy and values, they were explicitly or implicitly hostile to traditional religion, especially Christianity.

Initially these psychologies functioned as alternative world views or secular religions primarily in the lives of the psychotherapists, most of whom were drawn to modern psychology because they were already alienated from traditional Christianity or Judaism and were looking for an alternative understanding of life that could be interpreted as scientific and as compatible with life in the increasingly secular world. Even those who started training in psychology with a religious commitment often abandoned their faith or greatly reduced its importance. This replacement of religion by psychology was a common consequence of the immersion in a secular mental framework which assumed that religion and religious experience were psychological phenomena, and that the supernatural did not truly exist. Religion was interpreted as an illusion, at best, or as some kind of pathology, at worst. This rejection of religion was largely a result of the assumptions (a point we have already noted). That psychology per se did not—and does not—logically or empirically require that one lose his religion, is clear in the lives of such prominent psychologists and Christians as Stern, Tournier, Zilboorg, Pfister, and others.[10]

Psychology often came to serve the same religion-replacing function in the lives of the patients who entered therapy at a time of mental anguish in which they were actively looking for answers. It was a common occurrence for the patient to accept

---

[10]K. Stern, *The Pillar of Fire* (New York: Harcourt, Brace, 1951); K. Stern, *The Third Revolution* (New York: Harcourt, Brace, 1954); P. Tournier, *The Meaning of Persons*, trans. by E. Hudson (New York: Harper & Row, 1957); P. Tournier, *The Healing of Persons*, trans. by E. Hudson (New York: Harper & Row, 1965); G. Zilboorg, *Psychoanalysis and Religion* (New York: Farrar, Straus, & Cudahy, 1962); S. Freud and O. Pfister, *Psychoanalysis and Faith: The Letters of Sigmund Freud and Oskar Pfister*, H. Meng and E. L. Freud, eds., trans. by E. Mosbacher (New York: Basic Books, 1963); E. M. Stern, *The Other Side of the Couch* (New York: Pilgrim, 1981).

the theoretical framework of his therapist—to be "converted" to psychology. Such a change was facilitated by the frequency of the therapy sessions and by the reinforcing effect of any cures or benefits caused by, or attributed to, the therapist. Any negative experiences with religion that the patient might have had would also support the exchange of psychology for religion. Furthermore, in many respects the psychotherapist/patient interaction had something of the character of the religious relationship of master/disciple, confessor/penitent as well as being similar to traditional pastoral counseling.

A fundamental way in which psychotherapy functions as a religion is that (at its best) it heals. The healing or cure aspect of psychotherapy is its primary justification, and one should not forget that healing, both psychological and physical, is a major concern of Christianity. It is probably no accident that the secular psychotherapies first developed in a period when healing was much neglected in the major Christian churches—especially those which ministered to the more educated and sophisticated.

Another important characteristic of psychology has been the serious personal involvement with religion and religious issues on the part of many psychological theorists and innovators. This was the case for the founders of psychotherapy, Freud, Jung (see below), and Adler, who converted to a somewhat liberal Protestantism from a Jewish background. The following psychologists either started with a serious religious concern or clearly expressed such in their professional life (or both): William James, G. Stanley Hall, Carl Rogers, Erich Fromm, Rollo May, Karl Menninger, Gardner Murphy, Michael Murphy (Esalen founder). This list is by no means complete. Such examples strongly imply an affinity between the religious and the psychological mentality.

One interesting sociological feature of psychology has been its religious "denominational" character. Christopher Lasch has pointed out the presence of a "Catholic–Protestant" split in psychology.[11] Freud and much of psychiatry stand for Catholicism—that is, for orthodoxy and excommunication, doctrine, priestly mediation between the "sacred texts" and the patient, formality and distance between therapist and patient. Adler and his followers—the humanistic-self psychologies such as Rogers—created a psychological "Reformation." This involved taking psychology out of a special vocabulary and putting it into the vernacular. It also meant reducing the distinction between therapist and client, emphasizing empathy and emotion and the client's own interpretations. All of this resulted in a kind of psychological equivalent to the priesthood of all believers. This "protestantized" version of psychology has tended to follow many of the paths taken by historical Protestantism: a gradual simplifying and watering down of theory (doctrine); increasing optimism about human nature among "mainline" psychologists; the splitting of the rest of "Protestant" psychology into various sects and movements. For example, encounter group psychology is much like revivalism;[12] Fromm's psychology is close to the social gospel; self-help psychology is an expression of positive-thinking Protestantism, such as that espoused by N. V. Peale; transpersonal psychology and related types are analogous to Mind Cure and aspects of Christian Science.

One psychologist not really discussed by Lasch is Jung. A denominational interpretation, nevertheless, suggests itself. Jung is a mixture of "Catholic" psychoanalytic-psychiatric psychology and the "Protestant," less formal, counseling psychology. Hence, Jung should appeal to those who identify with aspects of both Catholicism and Protestantism, to those who seek "Catholic" intellectuality plus "Protestant" freedom of choice—a kind of "Episcopalian" psychological mentality. According to this rationale, Jung should be popular with the

---

[11]C. Lasch, "Sacrificing Freud," *New York Times Magazine* (February 22, 1976), pp. 11, 70–72.

[12]T. C. Oden, *The Intensive Group Experience—The New Pietism* (Philadelphia: The Westminster Press, 1972).

especially educated and those with an interest in symbolism, ritual, and aesthetics. This seems, indeed, to be the case, as Jung is well received in Episcopal seminaries; note also the Jungian religious writers Morton Kelsey and John A. Sanford, both Episcopalians.

With the growth of psychotherapy and the increasing secularization of society, psychological ideas began to spread throughout the culture at large. Colleges and universities with their many psychology courses, plus such phenomena as newspaper advice columns, contributed greatly to the disseminating of psychology. An important consequence has been that today the public discourse concerning people who are facing life crises — that is, emotional, moral, and interpersonal problems — is almost entirely dominated by secular psychological theory. The older religious understanding of these issues is restricted to private life and, indeed, is no longer even understood by many secularized Westerners. There has been a "triumph of the therapeutic" over the theological.[13]

Specific Religious Characteristics of Modern Psychology

Psychoanalysis: Freud

The connections of Freud's thought and life with both Judaism and Christianity are deep and complex; only the most easily observed religious characteristics of psychoanalysis will be noted here.

Freud directly acknowledged the essential similarity between psychoanalytic therapy and religious counseling by describing psychoanalysis as "pastoral work in the best sense of the

---

[13]P. Rieff, *The Triumph of the Therapeutic* (New York: Harper & Row, 1965); E. Becker, *The Denial of Death* (New York: Free Press, 1973); E. Becker, *Escape from Evil* (New York: Free Press, 1975); C. Lasch, *The Culture of Narcissism* (New York: W. W. Norton & Co., Inc., 1979); W. K. Kilpatrick, *Psychological Seduction* (Nashville, TN: Thomas Nelson Publishers, 1983).

words."[14] Freud thus recognized in psychoanalysis what is true of all secular psychotherapy and counseling, namely that it is similar, and indeed a rival, to the long Christian tradition of confession and counseling.

In addition there were specific cultic characteristics of early psychoanalysis. Freud often functioned like the founder of a religion: he was surrounded by disciples who formed a kind of inner sanctum; the best and most loyal of these were given rings to designate their special status; a deep allegiance to Freud's ideas, especially the "dogma" of his sexual theories, was expected of any true follower. Freud likened himself to Moses, and Jung (before the schism) to Joshua. Many of Freud's students broke from his ideas and were treated rather like heretics. The psychoanalytic establishment that emerged after Freud's death has often been compared to an orthodox religious organization which "excommunicated" deviants.[15]

Freud was personally involved in religious issues all his life and he wrote frequently on them.[16] In part this interest came from both religious and ethnic Jewish influence,[17] but much of it came out of his complex hostility and attraction to Christianity.[18]

There is even a very important way in which Freudian theory

---

[14]S. Freud, "Postscript to the Question of Lay Analysis," *Standard Edition* 20 (London: Hogarth, 1959), p. 256.

[15]E. Fromm, *Psychoanalysis and Religion* (New Haven, CT: Yale University Press, 1959); P. Roazen, *Freud and His Followers* (New York: Knopf, 1975).

[16]S. Freud, "Totem and Taboo," *Standard Edition* 13 (London: Hogarth, 1913); S. Freud, "The Future of an Illusion," *Standard Edition* 21 (London: Hogarth, 1927); S. Freud, *Moses and Monotheism* (New York: Knopf, 1939).

[17]For example, see D. Bakan, *Freud and the Jewish Mystical Tradition* (New York: Van Nostrand, 1958); J. M. Cuddihy, *The Ordeal of Civility* (New York: Basic Books, 1974); D. B. Klein, *Jewish Origins of the Psychoanalytic Movement* (New York: Praeger Publishers, 1981); M. Ostow, ed., *Judaism and Psychoanalysis* (New York: Ktva Publishing House Inc., 1982).

[18]See Zilboorg, *Psychoanalysis*; Freud and Pfister, *Psychoanalysis*; P. C. Vitz, *Sigmund Freud's Christian Unconscious* (New York: The Guilford Press, 1986); T. Pfrimmer, *Freud, lecteur de la Bible* (Paris: Presses Universitaires de France, 1982).

is an explicit anti-Christian theology. To exemplify this claim, consider the central concept in Freud's work—the now well-known Oedipus complex. In the case of male personality development, the essential features of this complex are the following: Roughly in the age period of three to six the boy develops a strong sexual desire for the mother. At the same time the boy develops an intense hatred and fear of the father, and a desire to supplant him, a "craving for power." This hatred is based on the boy's knowledge that the father, with his greater size and strength, stands in the way of his desire. The child's fear of the father may explicitly be a fear of castration by the father, but more typically it has a less specific character. The son does not really kill the father, of course, but patricide is assumed to be a common preoccupation of his fantasies and dreams. The "resolution" of the complex is supposed to occur through the boy's recognition that he cannot replace the father, and through fear of castration through remorse and guilt over wanting to kill the father, all of which eventually leads the boy to identify with the father, to identify with the aggressor, and to repress the original frightening components of the complex.

It is important to keep in mind that, according to Freud, the Oedipus complex is never truly resolved, and is capable of activation at later periods—almost always, for example, at puberty. Thus the powerful ingredients of rebellious, murderous hate and of incestuous sexual desire within a family context are never in fact removed. Instead, they are covered over and repressed. Freud expresses the neurotic potential of this situation:

> The Oedipus complex is the actual nucleus of neuroses. . . . What remains of the complex in the unconscious represents the disposition to the later development of neuroses in the adult.[19]

---

[19]S. Freud, "A Child is Being Beaten," *Standard Edition* 17 (London: Hogarth, 1919), p. 193; S. Freud, "Three Essays on the Theory of Sexuality," *Standard Edition* 7 (London: Hogarth, 1905), p. 226 ff; S. Freud, "Five Lectures on Psychoanalysis," *Standard Edition* 11 (London: Hogarth, 1909), p. 47.

Obviously, in most cases, this potential is not expressed in any seriously neurotic manner. Instead it shows up in attitudes toward authority, in dreams, slips of the tongue, transient irrationalities, etc.

The partial resolution of the Oedipal complex in the psyche of the individual has the boy, out of fear and remorse, choose to identify with his father rather than attempt to displace him. He ends up identifying with the father whom he can never truly escape. This identification involves the development, technically the introjection, of a representation of the father inside the self. This representation is the superego. Thus, the nature of the superego is determined by the character of the father as the child perceives him. Since the father is perceived as threatening and hostile, due to the Oedipal conflict, the superego is a hostile and punishing psychic system.

The formation of the superego "solves," that is, causes the dissolution of the Oedipal crisis by internalizing it. Unfortunately, the solution is profoundly unsatisfactory, for the conflict it contains is now permanently preserved. The child fears the father, and the adult fears the internalized father—the conscience. The child perceives the parent as furious at him for his incestuous and hostile desires; later as an adult the superego punishes the self, through moral condemnation, for these same desires. Perpetual fear and self-directed hostility are the scars of the Oedipus complex. According to Freud we all have these scars, to a greater or lesser degree, and psychoanalytic treatment devotes itself almost entirely to healing them. The best it can do is to remove much of the repression by bringing this pathology to consciousness and thus to some understanding. This alleviates the more severe neurotic component of the patient, but the Oedipus complex will still remain, though attenuated.

Jesus as the Anti-Oedipus.[20] Central to Christian theology is the doctrine of original sin, the essential nature of which is rebellion against God, the Father. This rebellion is an attempt to *replace* God in His role as ruler of our lives. Lucifer led an angelic army against God, hoping to take His place on the throne of Heaven. Adam and Eve disobeyed their Creator, being tempted by the promise "you shall be as gods" (Genesis 3:5). Freud's concept of the Oedipus complex is strong psychological evidence of the universal tendency to be as God, to sin by rebellion and disobedience; it is a specific representation of the struggle to become an autonomous ruler of our own and others' lives. Keep in mind that in Freudian theory the mental representation of God is assumed to be that of the person's father.

It is important to note again that for Christians there is no need to assume that the Oedipus complex is universal or that Freud's theory of the primal horde is historically or anthropologically true. But there is no barrier to Christian acceptance of the basic psychology of the Oedipus complex as a powerful though limited description of the psychological nature of original sin in the lives of many. In short, psychoanalysis has provided a widely influential interpretation of the traditional theology of our fallen nature.

Jesus, however, provides the perfect model for the negation, in fact for perfect love for God the Father. He also, by a life of chastity, renounces the sexual motive of the Oedipal brothers. The love of his father is expressed in what has been called "radical obedience," *i.e.*, total identification with his Father's will. Throughout the Gospels, Jesus consistently speaks of doing his Father's will and not his own, *e.g.*, "I seek the will of

---

[20]See P. C. Vitz and J. Gartner, "Christianity and Psychoanalysis, Part 1: Jesus as the Anti-Oedipus," *Journal of Psychology and Theology* 12 (1984), 4–14; P. C. Vitz and J. Gartner, "Christianity and Psychoanalysis, Part 2: Jesus the Transformer of the Super-Ego," *Journal of Psychology and Theology* 12 (1984), 82–90; and Vitz, *Sigmund Freud's Christian Unconscious*, for a more detailed rationale for this concept.

my Father" (John 5:30), "Not my will but thy will be done" (Luke 22:47).

The result of this radical obedience is the death of the Son. He is not killed by the Father, but by a group (horde) of conflict-filled, frightened and hateful men. It is the Son's death that occurs, nevertheless — and not the Father's. The result of this death is not guilt and remorse, but resurrection and joy. It is a "rebirth" in which the Father and Son are now together. The followers of Jesus, the new group of brothers (brothers in Christ) are called to become the sons of God by modeling their lives on that of Jesus. One important way in which this is done is through communion, when they eat the body and blood of the Son as represented in the bread and wine. In short, the life of Jesus is the life of anti-Oedipus.

It is in a radical love of Jesus, which is also an obedience to God's will, that this can take place. The price is radical forgiveness of one's enemies (including forgiving the self which hates itself) plus accepting of the cross. The latter is most difficult, for it involves a crucifixion or renunciation of self-will. All of these involve actions against the fundamental pride of Oedipal man. In view of the centrality and presumed permanence of the Oedipus complex, it should not be surprising that the cancellation of a structure psychoanalysis seen as the very source of all neurosis should result in a thorough transformation — in being born again.

Freud returned to this Oedipus and religion many years later in *Moses and Monotheism*. At the end of this, his last significant work, written when he was dying of cancer and surrounded by an increasingly virulent anti-Semitism, Freud nevertheless reiterated the same interpretation of Christianity as an example of religious "progress" in comparison to Judaism.[21] Although he considered the "glad tidings" to be "delusional," he could still appreciate the psychological power of the Christian message in

---

[21] Freud, *Moses*, p. 216.

Table I
Jesus as the Anti-Oedipus:
A Summary of the Ways in which the Life of Jesus is the Negation of the Life of Freud's Oedipal Man

Oedipal Man: The Old Man (from Freud)	Vs.	Jesus: The New Man (from Gospels)
1. Son who hates the father.		1. Son who loves the Father.
2. Son who shows radical disobedience to father.		2. Son who shows radical obedience to Father.
3. Son who wants sexual possession of mother (or all women of group).		3. Son renounces sexual possession of all women.
4. Radical disobedience results in death of father in fantasy or supposedly in fact in the ancient past.		4. Radical obedience results in death of Son.
5. Death of father caused by son or by band of brothers (sons) who hate the father.		5. Death of Son caused by band of brothers who hate the Son.
6. Death of father followed by failed resurrection in form of created father-totem and by emotions of guilt and remorse; permanent separation and estrangement of father and son.		6. Death of Son followed by resurrection of Son and by the emotions of joy and happiness; the complete reunion and identity of Father and Son.
7. Death of father leads to son's identification with the father now incorporated as superego; or to the band of brothers identification with totem-father.		7. Resurrection leads to the Son's identification with Son who is the center of morality and of ideals—a new superego; the new band of brothers identifies with the totem-Son.
8. The old sons identify with the father in a totemic meal in which the father is eaten.		8. The new sons (or band of Christians) identify with Son in a totemic meal in which the Son is eaten.
9. New band feeling guilt partly from their sexual motives renounce the women and create the rule of out-marriage (exogamy). Thus, the women take the name of some other group's father.		9. New band of sons *and daughters* takes the name of the Son (Christians); the women are not excluded from the "tribe" but take the same name.
10. In short: Hatred, disobedience leading to death of the father brings original sin.		10. In short: Love, obedience leading to death of Son brings redemption.

which "Original sin and salvation through sacrificial death became the basis of the new religion . . ."[22]

A summary of the logic of Jesus as the anti-Oedipus is shown in Table I.[23]

It should be clearly kept in mind that Freudian psychoanalysis never developed a positive synthesis to provide a clear meaning or answer to life. Instead, Freud always remained an analyst focused on the exploration of the unconscious. His attitude and that of psychoanalysis is pessimistic, stoical, and skeptical. He refused to provide a secular form of salvation since he saw religion in any form as an illusion to be rejected. Thus, Freudian theory, which is in important respects an anti-religion, was never made into a positive alternative to religion.[24] In fact, Freud was very critical of Jung, Adler, and others who did make psychology into such an alternative.

Analytic Psychology: Jung

Jung also was quite aware of the religious nature of psychotherapy, and the theological cast of much of his writing is apparent, for example, in a work like *Answer to Job*,[25] an extensive exercise in Scripture interpretation. Jung's explicit awareness of the religious issue is stated when he wrote:

> . . . patients force the psychotherapist into the role of priest, and expect and demand that he shall free them from distress. That is why we psychotherapists must occupy ourselves with problems which strictly speaking belong to the theologian.[26]

---

[22]*Ibid.*, p. 214.
[23]Vitz and Gartner, "Christianity and Psychoanalysis, Part 1."
[24]See P. Rieff, *Freud: The Mind of the Moralist*, 3rd edition (Chicago: University of Chicago Press, 1979; first published in 1959); Rieff, *Triumph*.
[25]C. Jung, *Answer to Job*, trans. by R. F. C. Hull (London: Routledge and Kegan Paul, 1954).
[26]C. Jung, *Modern Man in Search of a Soul* (New York: Harcourt, Brace, 1933), p. 278.

Unlike Freud's, Jung's psychology provided positive, synthetic concepts which could serve as a conscious goal not only for therapy but for life as a whole. Jung responded far more to the patient's demand for a general relief from distress than did Freud. As was noted earlier, Jung's answer to the search for salvation was the self-salvation of self-actualization.

Much Jungian psychology, of course, is not explicitly focused on individuation and self-realization, but is concerned with interpreting the patient's dream symbolism. Here Jung's analysis is focused on the collective and personal unconscious of the patient and on archetypes, the anima (or animus), shadow, and other concepts. This kind of Jungian psychology suggests a different way in which psychology can function as religion. Jung acknowledges the patient's basic religious concerns, and Jungian psychology is directly applied to the "archetypal" expression of the patient's religious motives, *e.g.*, in dreams about the wise old man (God archetype); dreams about rebirth, etc. Jung's discovery of the psychology of religious symbols is important, but there is with this a danger of substituting the psychological experience of one's religious nature for the religious salvation that comes through the transcendent God who acts in history.[27]

Those who make this mistake have truly treated psychology as religion.

Self- or Humanistic Psychology: Rogers, Maslow, and Others

The self-psychologies are those that place the self at the center of personality and make the growth or actualization of the self the primary goal both of life in general and of psychotherapy and counseling in particular. More specifically, self-psychologies share all or most of the following characteristics.

1. An emphasis on the conscious self as an integrated, or at least potentially integrated system.

---

[27]R. Hostie, *Religion and the Psychology of Jung*, trans. by G. R. Lamb (New York: Sheed and Ward, 1957); Rieff, *Triumph*.

2. An emphasis on the true self as entirely good and not characterized by any natural tendency to aggress against or exploit others; nor to make self-indulgent or narcissistic choices to its detriment or to that of others. Such undesirable phenomena are attributed to the false self created by external factors such as family, traditional religion, society, or the economic system.

3. An emphasis on the true self as having almost unlimited capacity for change through freely made decisions. This process of choosing brings about self-actualization, the ideal way of being; self-actualization is an ongoing process of change, not a finished state.

4. An emphasis on personality prior to self-actualization as primarily the result of learned social roles. That is, the false self is the product of social learning of an essentially arbitrary kind.

5. An emphasis on breaking with the past, especially with commitments to others, with tradition, with fixed moral codes. Morality is interpreted as personal, subjective, and relative.

6. An emphasis on getting in touch with and expressing emotions and feelings. This promotes a presumed greater awareness of the true self and greater self-acceptance and trust in one's instincts.

7. An emphasis on short-term counseling of relatively normal adults in contrast to theory focused on disturbed children or such problems as schizophrenia, manic-depressive symptoms, alcoholism, etc.

Examples of self-psychology theories are those proposed by Carl Rogers, Abraham Maslow, and Erich Fromm.[28] Rollo

---

[28]C. Rogers, *Client-Centered Therapy* (Boston: Houghton-Mifflin, 1951); C. Rogers, "A Theory of Therapy, Personality and Interpersonal Relationships, as Developed in the Client-Centered Framework," *Psychology: A Study of a Science*, Vol. 3, S. Koch, ed. (New York: McGraw-Hill, 1959); C. Rogers, *On Becoming a Person* (Boston: Houghton-Mifflin, 1961); Maslow, *Toward a Psychology*; A. Maslow, *Motivation and Personality*, 2nd edition (New York: Harper & Row, 1970; first published in 1954); E. Fromm, *Man for Himself* (New York: Rinehart, 1947); E. Fromm, *The Sane Society* (New York: Rinehart, 1955).

May's writings[29] and the Gestalt psychology of Fritz Perls[30] are also closely related. Such self-psychology had much of its origin in Adler,[31] in Jung's notion of self-realization, in Goldstein[32] and others. Most of the psychology that was immensely popular in the United States during the 1960s and 1970s was a form of self-psychology. For example, Transactional Analysis[33] and many others fit into this category. Movements such as Erhard Seminar Training (est) combine much of self-psychology with various other elements, usually from Eastern religions. (Indeed, much of recent humanistic, self- and transpersonal psychology is indistinguishable from Eastern religion.)[34]

Religious Aspects of Self-Psychology

The general framework noted above served as an interpretation of the meaning of life which undermined or replaced Christianity in many cases. Some of the more specific claims of the self-psychologists will make this clear. Carl Rogers[35] states that the goal of psychotherapy is to help the client become self-directing, self-confident, self-expressive, creative, and autonomous to such a degree that the client experiences unconditional positive self-regard. The client is increasingly to experience himself as the only locus or source of values.

Erich Fromm spends many pages in his books interpreting and reinterpreting parts of both the Old and New Testament.

---

[29]R. May, *Man's Search for Himself* (New York: Norton, 1953).
[30]F. S. Perls, *Gestalt Therapy Verbatim* (Lafayette, CA: Real People Press, 1969).
[31]A. Adler, *The Practice and Theory of Individual Psychology* (New York: Harcourt, 1927); A. Adler, *What Life Should Mean to You* (Boston: Little, 1931).
[32]K. Goldstein, *The Organism* (New York: American Book, 1939).
[33]E. Berne, *Games People Play* (New York: Grove Press, Inc., 1964); T. A. Harris, *I'm Ok – You're Ok* (New York: Avon Books, 1969).
[34]C. Tart, *Altered States of Consciousness* (New York: John Wiley & Sons Inc., 1969).
[35]Rogers, *Psychology: A Study of Science, and On Becoming a Person.*

The titles of some of his books give his religious agenda away, for example, *The Dogma of Christ* and *You Shall be as Gods*.[36] Fromm explicitly states that his psychology would be untenable if the doctrine of original sin were true. He believes that evil is in no way intrinsic to man's nature, and self-theory follows from this fundamental assumption, for obviously the self is to be perfectly trusted only if it is perfectly free of intrinsic evil.[37] The Pelagian assumption of "I'm OK and You're OK" found throughout Transactional Analysis is a recent popular expression of this position.[38]

Some of the popular American expressions of self-theory have gone so far as to claim that the self is God, *e.g.*, "You are the Supreme Being . . . Reality is a reflection of your notions. Totally, Perfectly."[39] Rogers's position, noted above, in which the self is the sole locus of values comes close to the same thing. The influence, often indirect, of Sartre and other existential thinkers on the American self-theorists has been substantial: Sartre states that once we've rejected God, "the Father," then

> . . . life has no meaning *a priori*. Before you come alive life is nothing; it's up to you to give it a meaning, and value is nothing else but the meaning that you choose.[40]

---

[36] E. Fromm, *The Dogma of Christ* (New York: Holt, Rinehart, and Winston, 1963); E. Fromm, *You Shall be as Gods* (New York: Holt, Rinehart, and Winston, 1966).

[37] Fromm, *Man for Himself*.

[38] Berne, *Games*; Harris, *I'm Ok*.

[39] C. Frederick, *est: Playing the Game the New Way* (New York: Dell Publishing Co. Inc., 1974; Delta Paperback, 1976), pp. 171, 177; also W. Schultz, *Profound Simplicity* (San Diego, CA: Learning Concepts, 1982), reaches the same conclusion.

[40] J.-P. Sartre, *Existentialism*, trans. by B. Frechtman (New York: Philosophical Library, 1947).

Since Sartre also argues that man's goal is to become God,[41] self-psychology often can be interpreted as a commercialized American packaging of much of European existentialism.[42]

The widespread acceptance of this self-psychology (called "selfism" by Vitz)[43] has been due in large part to works—*e.g.*, Transactional Analysis, Dyer[44]—which popularized the original theories. The strong public response has stemmed from various cultural and economic factors, and has had little to do with scientific knowledge. Contemporary upper-middle-class Americans—wealthy, increasingly secular, and with time on their hands—have been only too happy to find a rationale which encourages them to develop an extremely self-centered way of living ("life style"). Economic support for this kind of psychology came from the needs (and pleasures) of the consumer economy of the 1960s and '70s. Indeed, these self-psychologies can be viewed as justifications and descriptions of the ideal consumer.[45] It was not surprising that many expressions and catchwords of self-theory began showing up as advertising copy: Do it now! You're the boss! Honor thyself! Break tradition!

The problems posed by humanistic selfism are not new to Christianity. Indeed, they can be traced back to early conflicts with Stoicism, Epicureanism, and other sophisticated Graeco-Roman philosophical and ethical systems—especially Gnosticism. To worship oneself in the form of self-realization is in Jewish and Christian terms idolatry operating from the usual motive of unacknowledged egoism.

Indeed there is often a very specifically theological character to much self-theory. For example, consider much of the theoretical vocabulary of Carl Rogers. His psychology strongly emphasizes developing trust in the self, and developing uncon-

---

[41] J.-P. Sartre, *Existentialism and Human Emotions*, trans by H. Barnes (New York: Philosophical Library, 1957).
[42] For example, Schultz, *Profound Simplicity*.
[43] Vitz, *Psychology as Religion*.
[44] W. Dyer, *Your Erroneous Zones* (New York: Avon Books, 1976).
[45] Vitz, *Psychology as Religion*.

ditional positive regard for the self. Such statements can be made into standard Christian theology by replacing such words as "trust" with "faith" and "self" with "God." The familiar Christian emphasis on developing unconditional faith in God and His love has been reconceptualized in terms of unconditional trust in and love of the self. That is, often personality theory is nothing but Christian theology mapped from the spiritual domain into the realm of this world.

In developing his ideas Rogers took a particular brand of Protestantism with an extreme emphasis on personal experience of God and dropped out God. He ends up out with psychological experience and the self that has the experience.

Carl Rogers, who left the seminary to become a psychologist, apparently never consciously understood this although his antireligious motivation is clear when he wrote: "Neither the Bible nor the prophets . . . neither the revelation of God nor man . . . can take precedence over my own direct experience."[46]

One of the first psychologists to identify the way in which modern psychology with its emphasis on self-acceptance tended to undermine both the idea of sin and of personal responsibility was Mower.[47] The problem remained neglected, however, until its analysis by Adams and by Menninger in *Whatever Happened to Sin?*[48] Menninger notes the social and psychological benefits that follow from taking responsibility for one's actions, especially those that have hurt others, *i.e.*, one's sinful behavior. The same point was made by Adams in his early specific Christian critique of secular counseling theory and practice.

Some psychologists have justified self-theory by pointing out the large number of people that suffer from low self-esteem and associated depression. However, these are often caused by biological factors — something which self-theorists, because of

---

[46] Rogers, *On Becoming a Person*, p. 24.

[47] O. H. Mower, *The Crisis in Psychiatry and Religion* (Princeton, NJ: Van Nostrand, 1961).

[48] J. Adams, *Competent to Counsel* (Nutley, NJ: Presbyterian and Reformed Publishing Co., 1970); K. Menninger, *Whatever Happened to Sin?* (New York: Hawthorn, 1973).

their theoretical emphasis on social learning, usually fail to observe in patients. When biological factors are not involved, low self-esteem is itself often an inverted example of self-worship. At first this proposal might appear surprising, but the rationale is simple. Depression and low self-esteem are often the result of self-hatred or aggression against the self that occur when one fails to meet one's own high standards of value and worth. An enormous amount of pride lurks behind our attachment to the standards we fail to live up to. That is, optimistic self-confidence and pessimistic depression both result from the self taking on the prerogative of creating the standards of our self-worth and then judging how well one meets those standards.[49] In Christian terms, however, one's worth comes from God, not from one's self. Furthermore, a person is not to judge himself or herself as a success or failure—such judgments belong to God and so to judge is to set oneself in God's place. Psychologically, creating your own self-worth is like printing your own money—it leads to false prosperity: inflation followed by depression. It is not uncommon for self-psychology sessions to give short-term elation, only to be followed by depression. Kilpatrick accurately describes this creation of self-worth as wishful thinking.[50]

David Myers has collected much evidence from social and cognitive psychology which demonstrates that the self is intrinsically biased in its own favor—thus documenting the natural human tendency to pride.[51] Myers cites studies which show the following. (1) People are much more likely to accept responsibility for success than for failure. If I win, I accept credit, but if I lose, then it was bad luck, someone else's fault, etc. (2) Most people judge themselves as above average on most self-ratings. For example, 70 percent of the high school seniors taking the college board exams rated themselves as above average leaders,

---

[49]S. Strong, ed., "Christian Counseling," in *Counseling and Values* 21 (1977), 75–128.

[50]Kilpatrick, *Psychological Seduction*.

[51]D. Myers, *The Inflated Self: Human Illusions and the Biblical Call to Hope* (New York: Seabury Press, 1981).

only 2 percent as below average. In most marriages each person usually sees his or her positive contributions as greater than those of the spouse; in one survey 94 percent of college faculty reported themselves as better than their average colleague. (3) People have a natural but unrealistic tendency to think their own judgment and beliefs are especially accurate. (4) Most people are very optimistic about their own future, as compared to that of others. For example, most college students think things will work out much better for them than for the average student. (5) People tend to overestimate how morally they would act as compared with how they actually do act. For example, many more people say that they would help a stranger in need than actually do help when a real opportunity arises.

These and other studies led Myers to conclude that low self-esteem is not the great problem it is often claimed to be. Like other Christian critics, Myers notes that Christianity is not essentially concerned with building high self-esteem, but with admitting one's pride, and then, with God's grace, forgetting or letting go of the self.

Yet another analysis of how self-psychology functions as religion has been presented by Kilpatrick, who focuses on the way in which the psychological categories of humanistic or self-psychology function to replace religious categories.[52] Slowly, and often quite subtly, God disappears from our thoughts and concerns, and preoccupation with the self comes to dominate. This self-preoccupation has several pathological consequences, an especially destructive one being the growth of subjectivism[53] and the loss of contact with reality. A person begins quickly to perceive others only, or primarily, in terms of his or her own self-needs. This leads to serious misperceptions of others, as well as to an inability to view oneself objectively. Our desire for self-esteem gets in the way of objective self-awareness. Kilpatrick also points out how close self-psychology is to such Ameri-

---

[52]Kilpatrick, *Psychological Seduction*.

[53]Viktor Frankl, *Psychotherapy and Existentialism* (New York: Touchstone Books, 1968).

can traditions as the "self-made man" and the frontier man who is constantly changing, moving on, and always rejecting the notion of true commitment. Thus, self-psychology, in spite of its opposition to tradition, is an example of one of America's oldest social attitudes.

In summary, the overriding religious character of so much psychology is its tendency to replace God with the self. Intrinsic human pride and narcissism seem to have found one of their more effective expressions in modern psychology—a discipline that substitutes for the ancient, no longer appealing worship of the Golden Calf what might perhaps be called today's psychological worship of the Golden Self.

The Mystery of Human Nature

Charles Ransford

Charles Ransford is associate professor of psychology at Hillsdale College. He received his B.S. degree from Calvin College and his Ph.D. in experimental psychology from Wayne State University. While in graduate school, he specialized in the study of animal learning and the biological basis of behavior. Since coming to Hillsdale College thirteen years ago, he has published articles in both of these fields. Dr. Ransford is currently interested in synthesizing Christianity with major psychological theories of personality.

I hope this paper will lead to a better appreciation for both psychology and Christianity. It is interesting to consider how these two endeavors can be integrated. Some psychological findings are profound and can enhance Christian faith. In addition, Biblical revelation can steer psychological investigation.

There are several different investigative techniques that can be used to explore human nature. They include rational, scientific, intuitive, or authoritative approaches. In other words, we could depend on logic, observation, direct comprehension, or the assertions of someone else to improve our understanding of human nature.

The main strategy employed by most psychologists today is the scientific method. Science is a very powerful tool which has helped us understand chemical structure, plant life, disease, and brain function. However, science is not a perfect tool, nor the only one. In studying human nature, science has an additional burden. Science only works, or at least works best, when the subject matter is observable and measurable. The mind, however, is not directly observable. Psychologists must infer properties of mind from a subject's behavior. Usually these inferences require that we depend upon nonscientific assumptions about what people are really like.

One trick that psychologists use to deal with the unobservable is the operational definition, that is, defining the unobservable in measurable terms. Consequently, aggression is defined as the number of fistfights per day and love as the number of handshakes per hour. Notice that in the process of being objective, we have reduced or lost the essence of what we are studying. Another problem with empirical techniques is that subjects often change their behavior or their minds when they know that they are being observed. Is the subject trying to please the experimenter; is the subject trying to sabotage the proceedings; or is the subject trying to play a role that he thinks is demanded of him? The story is told of one participant who was asked to report to room 224 for an experiment. After waiting for hours in a very small, dark room, he finally realized that he had taken a wrong turn into a closet. The point is that subjects in experiments often behave artificially, so it is difficult to generalize from the unique experimental setting to the real world. A final handicap is that subjects' answers to questions are often clouded by their inclination for self-deception.

Psychology's continued infatuation with empirical methods has led to a narrow-minded investigation devoid of creativity and imagination. Some psychologists (*e.g.*, Calvin College professor Mary Stewart Van Leeuwen and Hillsdale College professor Jim Herbsleb) have more completely documented the shortcomings of this scientific approach.[1]

As mentioned before, there are other techniques that can be used to explore human nature. One such technique is intuition. Many of the so-called great scientific discoveries have really

---

[1] Mary Stewart Van Leeuwen, *The Sorcerer's Apprentice: A Christian Looks at the Changing Face of Psychology* (Downers Grove, IL: InterVarsity Press, 1982); and James Herbsleb, "Experimental Validity: The Problem of Relying on Common Sense" (unpublished manuscript, 1986).

been the result of at least some intuition. For example, scientists had been trying to determine the chemical configuration of benzene for years. The possibility that this configuration was in the form of a ring came to Kekule in a daydream when he had visions of snakes twining and twisting around and then grabbing onto their own tails. In another famous episode, Archimedes was asked to determine if the king's crown had been made out of the pure gold supplied to the goldsmiths. As Archimedes entered the bathtub one day, he noticed the water overflow as his body displaced it. Archimedes suddenly realized that he could determine the density of the king's crown using a similar technique.

There are many more examples of intuition. On more than one occasion, my wife's intuition has proven to be more accurate than my scientific approach. Some psychologists have made use of this intuitive or phenomenological approach to improve our understanding of human nature. Unfortunately, this intuition is subjective; the fact that we cannot all clearly measure or agree on the events makes us uneasy. Hope College social psychologist David Myers sarcastically refers to intuition as the "Luke Skywalker approach to psychology,"[2]: Put the controls aside and trust the Force. Myers argues that psychology is best conceptualized as a controlled science.

Another investigative approach is logic or reason; however, this approach is also limited. After centuries of debate, the most philosophers can say is that the philosophical case for the existence of God is just as strong as the philosophical case for no God.

It is my contention that logic, intuition, and science are all powerful yet limited techniques. Many theorists now agree that all theories of human nature are ultimately based on assumptions, beliefs or presuppositions rather than experimentally testable or rationally deducible ideas. In other words, assumptions

---

[2]David G. Myers, "Current Trends in Psychology Myths and Realities" (address to the annual convention of the Christian Association for Psychological Studies, Grand Rapids, MI, April 20, 1985), p. 10.

or world views guide our science, logic, and intuition. These assumptions cannot themselves be proven, but they can be modified by our investigations.

A different way to investigate human nature, then, is to study the great psychologists or theories of psychology and try to appreciate the different assumptions they make and the different perspectives of the world they offer. The collective wisdom of different psychologists using different investigative techniques should improve our understanding of human beings. Of course, these various perspectives are not equally appealing. Each of us has a perspective which we feel is correct. However, we may have made a few incorrect assumptions. By the same token, even though we may think that Freudian theory in general is distorted, Freud made some correct assumptions which led to some new insights.

This "perspectives approach" is now used in the Hillsdale College psychology department but is not to be confused with the perspectivalist position discussed and rejected by Mary Stewart Van Leeuwen. Perspectivalists "acknowledge that science cannot give a complete account of personhood but must be supplemented by literary, artistic, and other perspectives as well."[3] Unfortunately however, "to the perspectivalist the perspective of psychology must stay firmly within the paradigm of natural science, leaving to the humanities any consideration of ways to explore the accountable, transcendent aspects of persons."[4] In contrast to this, our psychology department does not revere nor discard the scientific method but rather uses it along with other investigative techniques. Psychology majors are asked to put on the glasses of Skinner, Freud, and Rogers and view the world as they did.

As we now explore what major psychological theorists have discovered, remember that my perspective is Christian and also

---

[3] Mary Stewart Van Leeuwen, *The Person in Psychology* (Downers Grove, IL: Inter-Varsity Press, 1985), p. 68.
[4] *Ibid.*

that I have limited space to discuss theories which are typically the topics for semester-long courses.

The major psychological theories we shall discuss are behaviorism, psychoanalysis, cognitive psychology, biological psychology, and humanistic psychology. Unfortunately, Christian psychology is not one of the current major psychological theories. In fact, it is rare to find mention of Christian psychology in a psychology textbook. Hillsdale College is somewhat unique in that we are willing to explore the merits of a Christian view of man. One of the core courses for psychology majors presents the Judeo-Christian perspective.

Behaviorism is a theory made popular by B. F. Skinner. Skinner spent a good deal of his life training pigeons and rats to perform elaborate behaviors for rewards. Skinner has concluded from his observations that animals and people are totally controlled by a punishing or rewarding environment. Man is very much like a rat in a maze that behaves in a certain way in order to obtain rewards. We need not allude to a mind or free will to explain the rat's behavior, nor should we, Skinner argues, to explain the human's. Man is not to be blamed for wrongdoing, because it is the poor environment which caused the inappropriate behavior. By the same token, man deserves no credit for achievements; these appropriate behaviors are simply the result of an enriched environment. Man needs to move beyond the illusion of freedom and dignity to the realization that we are nothing more than a set of behaviors totally controlled by the environment.[5] Man's major task is to design the best system of rewards and punishments so that correct behavior will emerge.

Skinner has claimed to be completely objective and scientific with his theorizing. To conclude that the behavior of an animal is influenced by reward is empirically demonstrable, but his assertions that there is no God, no soul, no mind, no freedom, and no dignity are not. This is another indication

---

[5]B. F. Skinner, *Beyond Freedom and Dignity* (New York: Bantam Books, 1972).

that theorizing even among "objective scientists" is guided by presuppositions.

Before we dismiss this narrow-minded or no-minded perspective, let's acknowledge that the behaviorists have documented the extent to which our behavior is influenced by rewards or punishments in our environment. Our children learn Bible verses for candy; businessmen who detest behaviorism work like slaves for their next free trip to Bermuda; and I will do just about anything for a hot fudge sundae.

The techniques of behavior modification have been found to be extremely effective, and the dilemma is how to affirm our autonomy and at the same time admit that we are at least partially influenced by our environment. Apparently our autonomy is limited. Most of us here, however, would argue that we have more of a mind and more free will than Skinner acknowledges. Let's see if cognitive psychology offers more of these desired characteristics.

There is yet no single coherent cognitive psychology, but all cognitive theories share an interest in cognitions or thoughts, *i.e.*, an interest in the mind. In contrast to asserting that the individual is totally at the mercy of external factors, the cognitive psychologist sees the role that internal factors have in exerting some influence on the environment. Here's an example of how a cognitive perspective would be employed in a treatment setting. Johnny is hyperactive and could be given rewards to calm down, or he could be given a shot of ritalin to control his hyperactivity biologically. Instead, he is asked to imagine that he is taking ritalin and challenged to fool the attending physician. Notice that this role-playing depends on cognition which originates internally.

Much of cognitive psychology is built on the computer metaphor; that is, the mind is an information-processing machine. Cognitive psychologists like to draw schematic models of the mind which suggest interactions between sensory input, short- and long-term memory, retrieval and response. Theorizing like this helps us understand the cocktail-party effect. At a party there might be several different conversations going on around us. Suddenly we hear our name mentioned in one of them. This recognition implies that we must have been monitoring all the conversations at some level even though all of these conversations were not stored in either short- or long-term memory.

Some cognitive psychologists are hopeful that this new computer model of the mind will enable us to assess reality accurately. Unfortunately, studies have shown that there is a filter in the system that determines what we will attend to. Notice how we can selectively attend to one conversation or another at the party. Sometimes this selective attention mechanism is under our conscious control, but sometimes it is steered by unconscious motivation. This unconscious motivation is in turn based on our lifetime experiences which are input to the filter from the long-term memory store. The bottom line is this: we see what we want to see, not necessarily what is there. The human information-processing filter becomes the 1980s' replacement for the ancient foggy glasses.

A major psychological perspective which focuses more heavily on unconscious motivation is that of Sigmund Freud. He saw man as basically driven by biological desires (id) which are usually opposed by civilization (superego). This creates a conflict which must be resolved by the individual (ego). Freud is not optimistic that man will successfully resolve this conflict between urge and restraint. Man, according to Freud, unconsciously denies his impulses in order to resolve his conflicts.

Although most of us like to emphasize our accountability and our responsibility to serve others, we can acknowledge with Freud that man has the potential for selfishness and self-deception. It is interesting to speculate on how our tendency to deny our shortcomings interacts with our ability to be aware and responsible. Christian psychologist H. Newton Malony suggests that we allow self-realization only after self-preservation is assured. In other words, we play little tricks on ourselves to survive, and once we think we are going to make it, we can allow more understanding of our true selves.

Let's look back on our own lives and see this principle in action. When the child was four she wanted all the doors in the bedroom closed in order to keep the ghosts and monsters away. Now even at four, she knew that there could not really be a monster in the house, but at the time she was not prepared to admit that she was really afraid of herself—alone, in the dark, with no parents around. Later on at age eight, she was certain that a stomachache was the only reason she didn't want to go to school. At fifteen, she becomes overweight in order to avoid an intimate relationship that she fears she cannot control. Later on in life with self-preservation somewhat assured, she allows herself realization of her original motivation to overeat. So how did we fool ourselves at eighteen, and what blind spots do we have now?

Freud poses a dilemma for modern psychologists who value science. Freud did not use traditional scientific techniques to arrive at his theory. Psychologists want to accept his ideas because they are profound, yet they are reluctant to do so because they are not empirically based. If only psychologists would be willing to accept the credibility of nonempirical techniques.

Another perspective which sets limits on man's autonomy is biological psychology. Whereas cognitive psychologists like to diagram the mind, biological psychologists like to map the brain. Present-day maps of the brain are like ancient maps of the world. The major landmarks are known, but many of the details are disputed. Here are some general ways in which brain structures influence behavior. The occipital lobe has something to do with vision. We know that because patients with lesions (*i.e.*, damage) to this area report visual deficits. Other areas of the brain are responsible for hearing, speech, reading, input of touch, and output of movement. One area of the brain is responsible for sensory memories; a person with a lesion here could copy a picture of a cup but could not draw one from memory. Another area of the brain is responsible for motor memories; a person with brain damage here could not show you how to row a boat or unlock a door.

The front portion of the brain, the cortex, is responsible for executive control; it enables a person to plan ahead, to execute a complex series of actions, and to restrain himself when necessary. This is the site of the notorious prefrontal lobotomies that were an attempt to alleviate the symptoms of schizophrenia, but rather just produced a number of undesirable side effects. The patients could no longer plan ahead; they lost their ability to reason abstractly; they no longer had the initiative to dress themselves. Further, they tended to perseverate, *i.e.* they could not switch their plan of action. One patient wrote to his doctor, "Dear Dr. Luria: I want to tell you, that I want to tell you that I want to tell you . . ." These people also lose their self-restraint; they become very rude, crude, lewd, frivolous, and obscene.

There are other structures in the brain which influence the emotions of pleasure, rage, fear, motivation for food, sex and aggression. Students in my biological psychology course are introduced to Mark Larebis on a videotape. Mark has just admitted to assaulting and almost killing his girlfriend's 2½-year-old daughter. Before being sentenced by the judge, a hospital examination reveals that Mark has a tumor involving a part of the brain which influences aggression. The tumor is removed, Mark is declared cured, and the judge sets Mark free with no punishment. Most students in my class argue that the judge made the correct decision because the tumor rendered Mark not responsible for his actions.

Students next see a woman charged with child beating who claims that premenstrual syndrome (PMS) has diminished her responsibility. She is also found not guilty; however, most students object to this, arguing that she should somehow have been able to restrain herself. It is interesting to speculate on what sort of interaction exists between the ability to control ourselves and the biological, environmental, and unconscious factors that control us. On the one hand, we become irritable when we are tired or hungry; on the other hand, some of the greatest acts of heroism, achievement, creativity, and unselfishness have occurred during times of tremendous physical pain and deprivation.

Man's belief in goodness, free will, autonomy and responsibility, and his dissatisfaction with the pessimism of Freud and the mechanism of Skinner and biological psychology have led to the appeal of humanistic psychology. Both Carl Rogers and Abraham Maslow proclaim man's potential for growth and goodness. According to them, man strives for self-actualization, *i.e.*, a full development of his talents and a full appreciation of nature. According to Rogers, man is like a potato plant which naturally grows from darkness toward the light. According to Maslow, there is a hierarchy of needs. Only after satisfying basic physiological, security, and esteem needs can we cultivate higher needs for beauty, trust, and creativity. The observation that there are people who are tremendously creative and yet physically or mentally ill serves as negative evidence for Maslow's hierarchy. Van Gogh and Handel are some of the names that come to mind.

Many critics have argued that humanistic psychology is narcissistic; however a more careful reading of Rogers and others reveals that concern for others is supposed to be a characteristic of the actualized individual. On the other hand, there is an important way in which humanistic psychology is self-centered. Since most humanistic psychologists do not believe in God, man becomes the supreme being. There may be absolute truth, but it is best discerned by man rather than revealed by God. Indeed, Rogers at one time asserted that the directions of fully functioning persons "would be wiser than the commandments of gods or the directives of governments."[6]

All these theories offer us only a partial portrait of man. For example, humanistic psychology accurately points out man's potential for good but neglects man's potential for evil. I doubt that many of us would agree with pop singer Madonna who, after a recent episode, proclaimed, "I have never done anything that I am ashamed of." Freud knows better. His theory focuses on man's self-deception and selfishness but unfortunately does not do justice to our potential for knowledge, kindness, and greatness.

One of the strengths of Christian psychology is that it accu-

---

[6]Carl Rogers, *Carl Rogers on Personal Power* (New York: Dell, 1977), p. 251.

rately depicts man's dual nature, *i.e.*, his potential for good and evil. In this vein, Christian psychology is in line with the literature from Shakespeare to *Star Trek* which has described the battle within.

Of course, the most distinguishing characteristic of Christian psychology, in contrast to the other major schools, is that it is the one which explicitly argues that we do not only live in a natural world but also in a supernatural one. Christian psychology argues that, yes, we are influenced by our biology, our environment, and the conflict between urge and restraint, and we do have a mind and some self-will to deal with life's challenges and opportunities. In fact, it is important that Christian theorists not totally reject natural explanations of man. Christ was after all a man who was thirsty and hungry. He enjoyed the company of friends. He was not only offered great things in the desert by Satan, but he was truly tempted by them. There is, however, a supernatural component to man which somehow changes us.

Some biblical counselors, for example Jay Adams, have suggested that God's power can be used to cure mental illness. Man's anxiety, confusion, failing, and depression are the result of his sin; therefore, a confession of sin and the presence of the Holy Spirit will cure neuroses. Natural theories of man such as Freud's are seen as incompatible with this Christian viewpoint.

The major issue here is whether there are separate or unified spiritual, mental, and physical realms. There are some who would attempt to use only prayer to treat a patient's broken arm, but most of us would *also* go to a physician. It is the doctor's God-given understanding of the natural laws of healing which will prove most helpful. By the same token, C. S. Lewis argues that Freudian techniques can be very helpful in treating the neurotic. It is after the person is cured, he holds, that Christian ethics makes a crucial difference in that person's life.

The following case study illustrates the separate roles of natural psychotherapeutic techniques and Christian ethics. A woman has four children and has no desire for a fifth. She enjoys her children but would like to return to some of the activities which she has given up; she does not want another financial or time-consuming burden. To her surprise and disappointment she finds out that she is pregnant again. A healthy response to this situation might be an initial expression of anger, frustration, and disappointment (id) followed by an adjustment to the responsibilities of life (ego). Notice, however, that civilization tends to frown on prospective mothers who appear to be selfish and unloving (superego). If the mother does not have a strong ego, she might deny her hostility and indeed mask it by trying to take better care of this child than she did of the other four (this is an example of the defense mechanism of reaction formation). For this anxious and confused mother to submit to biblical counseling and a confession of sin would probably be a mistake. She is already being too hard on herself in some ways. A knowledgeable and caring therapist can help her cut through her self-deception to see her buried hostility. It is at this point that therapy ends and Christian ethics begin. Is she going to have an abortion so that she can do the things she wants to do, or is she going to make a sacrifice for the benefit of another?

The sad fact is that many therapists are not only ill-equipped to get patients in touch with their hidden feelings, but they also lack the strong moral values to influence patients to make ethical decisions once they have better self-understanding. It is also important to note that there are many other therapists who are quite competent.

What is being suggested here is that in some ways the spiritual, mental, and physical realms are separate. If one acknowledges this, it is easier to understand an individual like Abraham Lincoln who was apparently a very God-fearing yet at the same time despondent man. Some historians have claimed that friends kept knives away from "honest Abe" for fear he would "do himself in." This illustrates that the power of belief does not always lead to mental health, but it does allow for a meaningful life of commitment, purpose, and value.

Many of us suffer from pride and falsely believe that we are the masters of our fate and the captains of our souls. At the same time, there are many people, especially neurotics, who often fail to take responsibility for their own actions. It would, therefore, be dangerous for these people to ask *only* for the healing power of the Holy Spirit. As a patient with a broken arm was advised to also seek a physician, these neurotics should *also* work hard to develop their character.

The following story illustrates the point I am trying to make. A church service is interrupted by news of an approaching tornado. One of the elders stands up and says, "Pastor, please continue, God will take care of us." However, another elder responds by saying, "No, God has given us a warning to take responsible action."

If the main purpose of the spiritual is not to cure physical and mental disabilities, magically and automatically, then what is it? One of the most outstanding characteristics of a Christian psychology is that it sees man as both capable of loving others in spite of human imperfection and required to do so. This is not just a love for friends but also a love for enemies.

Corrie Ten Boom offers us a glimpse of this love in the midst of human hate. During World War II, she hid Jews from the Germans in Holland. On one occasion a neighbor asked her for help for his imprisoned wife. A Nazi policeman would accept a 600-guilder bribe and release the wife. Corrie gave the man 200 guilders of her own money and raised the rest in an hour. Five minutes after she gave her neighbor the 600 guilders, the Nazis were at her door to arrest her. This neighbor did not need help; he was a quisling, that is, a betrayer, who not only informed on his countrymen but made money in the process. As a result of this betrayal, Corrie and her family suffered greatly. Her father and sister died in a concentration camp, and her brother died after being released from one. Corrie herself barely survived living in three different camps.

This betrayer's behavior is an example of extreme selfishness and unkindness. At the same time, we all have a tendency to look out for ourselves first; consequently, there is potential for hurt in any human relationship. If relationships are to survive, there must be instances of kindness in the midst of pain. We must be able to supplant our quite natural reaction of hate with an unnatural reaction of concern for the person who has disappointed us. That is, we must at least sometimes be able to love someone in spite of his weaknesses rather than because of his attractiveness.

Corrie Ten Boom's initial reaction was one of hatred; however, she asked forgiveness for her hostility and then wrote to her betrayer offering to forgive him. One may argue that unselfish love and forgiveness do not necessitate the existence of the supernatural. Indeed, the kindness of "nonbelievers" often surpasses the unkindness of Christians. But Christians argue that allegiance to someone other than ourselves, *i.e.*, God, lays the groundwork for performing acts of kindness that are not simply self-serving. In addition, Christ's sacrificial death serves as an example of pure, unselfish love. This example, plus Christ's supernatural power, makes unselfish motivation possible. Indeed, Corrie Ten Boom's betrayer said to her, "That you could forgive me is a great miracle."[7] What is being suggested here is that Christianity offers the greatest amount of intimacy between man and others, between man and God, and between man and his world. This is possible because a Christian psychology both accurately sees the dual nature of man and also supplies the supernatural influence to assist him.

Humanistic psychologists like Carl Rogers and Leo Buscaglia have an appeal because they also emphasize love. Leo Buscaglia argues that the Golden Rule is a fundamental principle in almost all human cultures, and Carl Rogers suggests that therapy proceeds best when we have unconditional positive regard for others. Remember, however, that humanistic psychology is based on a delusion that deemphasizes man's dark side. It is easy for a therapist to accept just about any client unconditionally when he is paid for it, but how does that same therapist fare when in the midst of an intimate relationship he is stung by human unkindness?

---

[7]Corrie Ten Boom, "The Greatest of These is Love" (audiotaped lecture for "Focus on the Family," 1982).

Freud, on the other hand, is more fully aware of man's selfishness but offers no real hope for man. Even the individual who has a strong ego and is in touch with his urges and restraints is destined for a life of relative unhappiness.

In summary, there is a natural part of man which psychologists can help us understand. We are all influenced by rewards, by hunger and thirst, and by unresolved unconscious conflicts. We also have cognitive abilities and a self-will which enable us to determine our destiny in part. There is, in addition, a supernatural aspect to each of us. The primary function of that supernatural aspect is not to alter physical or mental health, but rather to transform the human heart miraculously.

D. Ivan Dykstra, professor emeritus of philosophy at Hope College, once preached a sermon on the addition of the supernatural. He said,

> Spirituality can never be a substitute for nor an excuse for ignoring the requirements of living in a natural order, nor the provider of novel kinds of skills. But as a superaddition, spirituality is never merely tacked on; by adding the superstructure, everything we do undergoes a transformation. The spiritual man still looks at nature's things and processes, but he sees them as never either merely things or processes; now nature has an extra dimension, an extra meaning: it is related to its Creator, who gave it to man not with rights of exploitation but with the responsibility of stewardship. The spiritual man works hard, like everyone earning his daily bread in the sweat of his brow, but at mealtimes he prays—in gratitude for what he has, knowing that what he has comes more from what he has no control over than from what he can control. The spiritual man still produces his art, but his art is never in and for itself, for the titillation of the senses; its measure remains its capacity to ennoble the soul. The spiritual person still buys and sells in the marketplace, but beyond the prudential considerations of profit and loss or the satisfaction of his wants, he knows that the things he possesses he holds in trust and is responsible both in his act of extracting from nature the things that are there and in his act of consuming them and sharing them. Spiritual persons still marry, and mar-

riage is a relationship between two people, but whatever the social meaning of the relationship there is for them always that capitalized "Other" who adds a vertical relation to marriage and thus seals it in a bond which even loose convention still calls "holy" matrimony.

The dictionary defines mystery as "something that is secret or impossible to understand." Rock Hudson recently was reported to have said, "I spent so much time trying to figure out what life was all about; I still don't know. But now I don't give a damn."[8] We can sympathize with him, but most of us do not like to participate in a mystery and come away without an answer. At the same time, we do not like to go to a lecture on the mystery of human nature and have one person tell us "the truth." There is another dictionary definition for mystery: "unknowable except by divine revelation." I do not think that science or logic or intuition will ever enable us to understand human nature completely, nor will behaviorism, psychoanalysis, or phenomenology. These are all techniques that originate with man. It is as if these techniques have become man's modern Tower of Babel. In his delusion of self-sufficiency, man attempts to use powerful yet very limited tools to reach toward what might be a heaven. One of the distinguishing characteristics of Christianity is that it depends on a revelation of knowledge from God to man rather than a search for knowledge originating with man. We do see through a glass darkly, not because we have not yet perfected our scientific process of investigation, but rather because our sinful nature prevents a clear view. I suggest that biblical revelation combined with rational, scientific, and intuitive exploration will give us the best understanding of human nature possible in this life.

---

[8]"Rock: A Courageous Disclosure," *Time* (August 5, 1985), 51.

Philosophy, Faith, and Personality Theory

Merold Westphal

Merold Westphal is chairman of the philosophy department at Hope College in Holland, Michigan. He received his M.A. and Ph.D. from Yale University and since then has been awarded a host of fellowships and honors in his field. He has taught at Wheaton College, Yale, SUNY-Purchase, and Juniata College. He is an editor for *Clio, The Owl of Minerva*, and *Perspectives: A Journal of Reformed Thought* and is the former chairman of the Hegel Society of America. Dr. Westphal is the author of *History and Truth in Hegel's Phenomenology* (1979, 1982) and *God, Guilt and Death: An Existential Phenomenology of Religion* (1984) as well as the co-author of *Inflation, Poortalk, and the Gospel* (1981). He has published nearly 100 essays and book reviews in professional journals.

The difference between a behaviorist and a magician is well known. The behaviorist is the one who can pull a habit out of a rat. This old saw is not without its serious point, for behaviorism involves the claim that human behavior can be understood by treating it as if it were but a special form of prehuman or subhuman behavior. It is sometimes useful to distinguish between humble and pretentious behaviorism. Humble behaviorism is a research program which claims that we can learn important facts about ourselves if we treat ourselves as organisms and carefully study the observable and quantifiable functional relationships between the organism and its environment. Medical science for the most part also reduces the human self to its organic dimensions. It sometimes pays a price for leaving out the psycho side of the psychosomatic totality, but it also has made enormous strides in the conquest of disease and the sustaining of human life. And it seldom turns speculative by making the claim that what it studies is the whole story about human life, saying, in effect, whatever my net doesn't catch isn't a fish.

It is just this sort of claim which pretentious behaviorism makes. It turns a research program into a philosophy of human nature, or, in the language of the psychologist, a personality theory. The heart of this theory is the claim that human behavior is simply a function of the rewards and punishments offered to us by our environment.

The finest response to this version of behaviorism with which I am acquainted comes from Hannah Arendt, the German-American philosopher. She writes, "The trouble with modern theories of behaviorism is not that they are wrong but that they could become true, that they actually are the best possible conceptualization of certain obvious trends in modern society."[1] I like to paraphrase that slightly by putting it in the present tense. The trouble with behaviorism is not that it is false but that so much of the time we allow it to be true.

In this latter form Arendt's response to Skinner and company becomes a summary of the reply which philosophical existentialism makes to all naturalistic, objectivistic, and reductionistic theories of the human self. Kierkegaard and Nietzsche, Heidegger and Jaspers, Marcel and Sartre unite to tell us that unlike the animals, we have the capacity to distance ourselves from the immediacy of our life sufficiently to take up an attitude toward it and significantly to preside over it.

We get, for example, a conversation between Freud and Sartre which parallels quite exactly the one between Skinner and Arendt. Freud quotes Groddeck when he says, "We are

---

[1]Hannah Arendt, *The Human Condition* (Chicago: University of Chicago Press, 1958), p. 322.

'lived' by unknown and uncontrollable forces."[2] These forces, which make of human life an event in the passive voice, are not environmental, as with behaviorism, but instinctive. It is nature and not nurture which is the agent of human life.

It would be a mistake to think here exclusively of the id, the libido, the sex drive. It is no accident that Freud speaks here of forces in the plural. For when he wrote this in 1923 he had not forgotten the discoveries of *The Interpretation of Dreams* nearly a quarter of a century earlier. He needed to illustrate his theory from actual dreams and the largest supply at hand was his own. But propriety forbad him from getting too specific about the sexual dimension of his own dreams and there emerged again and again the repressed demands, not of his id, but of his ego. The "absurd megalomania" which he confesses turns up constantly as a will to power every bit as powerful as any sexual will to pleasure. And eventually, the superego is introduced as a social force which takes up residence within us and lives our lives according to its agenda. The only problem with Freud's picture of the poor ego as harassed and overpowered by the id, the superego, and the external environment is that we must add to this list the ego's own drive to self-assertion as a power before which we are essentially inert and by which we are lived.

To all of this Sartre responds that when we view ourselves in this way we are in bad faith, which is to say that we are deceiving ourselves. We flee from our freedom in order to flee from the responsibility which comes with it, and we posit ourselves, ironically a free act, as pure facticity, as purely passive, to avoid the tasks of becoming a person which are otherwise as unavoidable as they are strenuous. (Of course at other times, when we think it humiliating to be mere things, we flee from our facticity to our freedom and, in an equal but opposite bad faith, deny the giveness which makes us inescapably situated and finite. But Sartre's critique of the resultant romantic idealism is not part of

---

[2]Sigmund Freud, "The Ego and the Id," *Standard Edition* 19 (London: The Hogarth Press, 1923), p. 23.

his reply to Freud, which is what concerns us at present.) Whereas Arendt would say that the trouble with Freud's claim (that we are lived, essentially passive beings) is not that it is false but that so often we allow it to be true, Sartre would locate the problem in the frequency with which we think and talk as if it were true, even when it is not and when the very act of thinking and talking as if it were is itself an act and thus an evidence of freedom—freedom misused, to be sure, but freedom nevertheless.

These conversations between Skinner and Freud on the one hand and Arendt and Sartre on the other call for several comments. First, the point is not that psychologists have reductionistic, "low" views of human personality, while philosophers have truly humanistic, "high" views. It would be just as easy to juxtapose a humanistic psychologist to a reductionistic philosopher. On both sides of the disciplinary fence we find theoretical interpretations of human selfhood which we can usefully if not too precisely distinguish as low and high.

Second, if we look at these theories from the perspective of biblical faith, we will notice quickly that both of them remind us of theological themes. The low views remind us not merely of the fallenness of human life, but of the bondage to sinful self-centeredness which this involves. The high views, by contrast, remind us of the created dignity and destiny of human personhood. In our creativity and freedom we are indeed "little less than God" (Psalms 8:5, RSV). So we find among these theorists what might be called secular theologies of original sin and of human dignity, calling these theories theological because they address genuine theological themes, and secular because they do so not without reference to God but with God conspicuously absent.

Third, these theories represent plurality which cannot find unity. On the low side of the fence there is the unresolved dichotomy between nature and nurture. On the high side of the fence there is the unresolved tension between a social and an individualist perspective on the self. Most importantly, between the low and the high side there is such an isolation of the negative themes from the positive that we end up with accounts which have a high degree of phenomenological support, since we can see their truth in our own lived experience, but which ultimately leave us unsatisfied, not just because they do not please us, but because they do not ring true to the whole of our experience. Thus, for example, Skinner ends up having to deny freedom and dignity quite thoroughly, while Sartre sees our efforts to affirm our freedom and dignity as the impossible task of becoming God, from which he concludes that human life is a useless passion, a futile and self-contradictory project.

Perhaps the reason for the unresolved dissonance of these secular theories is that they are theoretically immature and have not pursued conceptual wholeness far enough. Perhaps, as I suspect, the problem is rather that they are secular, that the wholeness and integrity they seem to lack, for all of their disturbing truth, cannot be found in the absence of the theological affirmations they so assiduously avoid. While it would surely be the task of developing a Christian personality theory to address this issue, it is not my task here. The question that I shall address is rather this one: in seeking to develop a personality theory within the perspective of the Christian faith, what resources are available from philosophical sources? For I hope that if nothing else the discussion to this point has indicated the relevance of philosophy to personality theory. Questions about the nature and destiny of the human self, its structure, and development are inseparable from philosophical reflection. In any case, these issues are too important to be left to the psychologists alone, especially to those who define their discipline exclusively in terms of experimental procedures and sometimes end up saying in their own way, whatever my net of quantifications does not catch is not a fish.

In order for philosophy to provide useful input to the development of personality theory, it is not necessary that its theories have the wholeness and balance of which I just spoke. We are looking for raw materials, or perhaps those which are but partially cooked. So the insights we are looking for must have the ring of truth about them, but they need not have the form of the whole truth. An immediate and important implication of this is obvious: even if secular theories should turn out to be deficient in comprehensiveness by virtue of their secularity, they will not thereby be rendered useless for present purposes. They may contain indispensable insights which any satisfactory theory will have to incorporate.

I want to propose two broad areas in which I believe modern philosophy provides just such indispensable insights for a personality theory developed in the context of the Christian faith. For purposes of identification they will be called self-knowledge and intersubjectivity. What I shall say about each falls under the general heading of the movement away from Descartes. The seventeenth-century French philosopher René Descartes is indisputably the father of modern philosophy. But it is frequently said that since World War II the Western tradition in philosophy has been moving steadily against his most basic assumptions. It is true that in spite of important differences, the one thing that seems to unite the Anglo-American tradition, often termed "analytic," with the continental European tradition during the postwar period is the anti-Cartesianism they share.

If, however, one looks at the latter tradition by itself, it becomes clear that the break with Descartes comes much earlier. Though Descartes is still a hero for Hegel, the latter makes a significant break with Descartes on the issue of self-knowledge and a total break on the question of intersubjectivity. And by the time we get to Marx and Kierkegaard in the 1840s, the break with Descartes is complete. (This is not to say that someone like Husserl won't try to go back to Cartesian ways of thought. It's just that his immediate followers revert immediately to the anti-Cartesian paths.)

Underlying the Cartesian position on self-knowledge is a radical dualism of mind and body. Each of us is not one substance or entity but two, a thinking substance (a mind) and an extended substance (a body). How far this picture is from biblical thinking is perhaps best indicated by the fact that Descartes thinks this sharp distinction of mind and body is essential to the belief in immortality, whereas the biblical idea of life after death is that of the resurrection of the body, implying that the human self is essentially and not accidentally embodied. The human self is an incarnate self, and human incarnation is scarcely less a mystery than The Incarnation. The union of the human and divine natures in Christ was declared by the Council of Chalcedon to be "without confusion, without change, without division, without separation." This is a good formula for the union of mind and body in the human self, both in the holistic, Hebrew-based thinking of the Bible and in contemporary philosophical discussion of the embodied self and the lived body. Since there is not time now to develop this into a third major theme under the heading of philosophical contributions to a biblically oriented personality theory, I shall have to be content simply to point to it and to move on to its relation to the theme of self-knowledge.

Having sharply distinguished mind from body, Descartes went on to claim that the mind is more easily known than the body. The physical world of extended substances is, on his view, opaque. Descartes was present at the birth of modern physical science, both as an observer of people like Copernicus, Kepler, Galileo, and Harvey, and as a participant whose own research taught him firsthand that it is no small task to tease nature's secrets from her. But he was misled by the fact that it is easy to know whether I am in pain or not, or whether that seems to be a book in front of me or a koala bear, or whether it seems to be orange or blue. The conclusion he drew was that while nature is opaque, the mind is transparent to itself. There is a kind of infallibility to self-consciousness which makes it a candidate to replace the Catholic infallible church and the Protestant infallible Bible as the guide for the self's journey. A modern rationalism demanding clarity, certainty, and freedom from all authority and tradition was born. The human self was redefined as independent of a lot more than its body.

This tradition prevailed (did you notice the irony involved in the fact that the repudiation of tradition becomes itself a tradition?) through Kant and Fichte into the early nineteenth century. But in his great masterpiece of 1807, *The Phenomenology of Spirit*, Hegel points out that a great deal goes on in the life of consciousness unnoticed and, so to speak, behind its back.

This is for two reasons. First, consciousness is like a visual field; it has access to but part of a larger whole. But the larger whole of assumptions and implications is at work in all the parts, and we do not fully grasp the parts until we have grasped the whole. Second, consciousness objectifies itself and lives outside itself. It gives birth to social and cultural systems and institutions which in turn reshape the self which was their source but now becomes their product. The self is both parent and child of its society and culture. It can fully understand itself only through the task of deciphering and interpreting its social world, and this task, while different from research in the natural sciences, is by no means an immediate and introspective task. Because of the dialectic of whole and part in consciousness itself, and because of the dialectic of inner self and outer social world, the self is also opaque and not transparent. It is precisely because the soul is not more easily known than the body that we have the social sciences.

A second and much sharper rejection of the Cartesian assumption about self-knowledge is to be found in Freud. In a typically modest passage, he links himself with Copernicus and Darwin. "In the course of centuries," he writes,

> the *naive* self-love of men has had to submit to two major blows at the hands of science. The first was when they learnt that our earth was not the centre of the universe but only a tiny fragment of a cosmic system of scarcely imaginable vastness. This is associated in our minds with the name of Copernicus. . . . The second blow fell when biological research destroyed man's supposedly privileged place in creation and proved his descent from the animal kingdom and his ineradicable animal nature. This revaluation has been accomplished in our own days by Darwin. . . . But human megalomania will have suffered its third and most wounding blow from the psychological research of the present time which seeks to prove to the ego that it is not even master in its own house, but must content itself with scanty

information of what is going on unconsciously in its mind. We psychoanalysts were not the first and not the only ones to utter this call to introspection. . . .[3]

If we ask why this is the "most wounding blow," we will be reminded that the omniscience and infallibility of self-consciousness on Cartesian assumptions make of the self something of a godlike ground for itself, a ground which requires neither trust nor obedience, both of which are galling to the "megalomania" which is at the heart of this secular theology of original sin. If this blow cannot be fended off, the self will either have to humble itself before a ground outside and above itself in power and authority, or it will have to pursue its course ungrounded, which means both unjustified and undirected. Unable to be its own god, and either unable or unwilling to find God beyond itself, the self fits the Pauline description of alienation, "having no hope and without God in the world" (Ephesians 2:12, RSV).

If we ask who has preceded psychoanalysis in wielding this "most wounding blow," the first people who come to mind are post-Hegelian philosophers, including Feuerbach and Marx, Schopenhauer and Nietzsche, atheists all, and Kierkegaard, as passionate and articulate a believer as the others are unbelievers. In the face of the self-assurance of self-consciousness they unite to practice the art of suspicion. They are suspicious that what appears on the surface of consciousness is a mask designed to hide both from the public and from the self who wears it what is really going on inside. The interpretation of human persons as systematically self-deceived about the real meaning of their beliefs and practices has come to be called the hermeneutics of suspicion. Freud and the philosophers I've mentioned are the masters of unmasking our truths and our values. To be more precise, they unmask the way we use our truths and our values to hide from others and especially from

---

[3]Sigmund Freud, "Introductory Lectures on Psychoanalysis," *Standard Edition* 16 (London: The Hogarth Press, 1916-17), pp. 284-285.

ourselves the forms of self-interest we cannot acknowledge without shame.

I believe that any personality theory in a Christian context will have to take the school of suspicion seriously, in spite of the temptation to dismiss their unwelcome insights on the ground that they are, for the most part, atheists. For if we listen to them carefully and with any degree of objectivity, we will have to admit that what they say is all too true all too much of the time. And it should hardly be the task of Christian reflection to refute or ignore the truth. We would do better, I think, to take them seriously as theologians of original sin, and to listen to the hermeneutics of suspicion as a long sermon on Jeremiah 17:9, "The heart is deceitful above all things, and desperately corrupt; who can understand it?"

Each of these thinkers has a distinctive contribution to make to the hermeneutics of suspicion. But I shall have to be satisfied with a composite portrait for the present. I will give you an example of the kind of self-deception it seeks to expose, and then a brief sketch of the theoretical picture which emerges.

Several years ago I was on a study tour in Jamaica. With others in my group I went one evening to what appeared to be a public forum on international relations. It turned out to be a propaganda event sponsored by the very tiny Communist Party in Jamaica, and it featured a speaker from the Soviet embassy. Apparently we were not the only ones there expecting something quite different from what was offered, and the crowd was not entirely friendly. In response to one very hostile question about the violation of human rights in the Soviet Union, the embassy official assured us that this could not be the case. In evidence of this claim he read from the Soviet constitution, in which the kinds of abuses alleged are forbidden.

Apologists for communism often employ essentially the same tactic in a slightly different form. They point to the very real suffering which has always accompanied capitalism, from unemployment to slave labor or its near analogue to the brutality of the repression often required to sustain a favorable climate for investment. To this they compare, not the equally concrete, real communism with its gulags, its Berlin Walls, etc., but the ideal communism of theory. This communism fulfills the promise of liberty and justice for all, but, unfortunately, it exists only on paper.

Apologists for capitalism are naturally irate at this tactic, which they see through right away. But since their task is to be apologists, their response is to play exactly the same game. They compare real communism with ideal and theoretical capitalism, which fulfills the promise of liberty and justice for all, but, unfortunately, exists only on paper.

Sometimes the apologists for both sides are careful to stick closely to concrete historical actuality while playing what remains essentially the same game. They compare the lot of the beneficiaries of their system with that of the victims of the other.

The masters of suspicion are not fooled by all of this. As theologians of original sin they are not surprised to find that "all have sinned" and are more or less equally adept at this style of patently propagandistic polemic. The question they ask is this: how is it those who do this often seem to be entirely sincere, not noticing what they are doing? And how is it that their numerous followers, for whom they are heroes, allow themselves to be persuaded by arguments whose entirely fallacious form they recognize instantly when presented by apologists for the other side?

Freud presents us with a model which is helpful in understanding this phenomenon. Suppose I am told under hypnosis that when I awake I will go to the corner of the room, pick up a large umbrella, and open it, though it is not even raining outside; and I am also told that I will not remember having been given this command under hypnosis. What happens when I awake from hypnosis? I open the umbrella, and, either in response to the question why I did so, or just in response to the peculiarity of the situation, I make up out of whole cloth a reason to account for what I have done. The school of suspicion has as its first basic principle that human reason is not pure and disinterested but readily in the service of the need for self-justification. Freud, thinking of individual self-justification calls this rationalization. Marx, thinking of corporate attempts at legitimation, calls it ideology.

A second principle of suspicion is that the fundamental motivations for human action are forms of self-interest. Like the theological traditions which see the essence of sin as pride, the masters of suspicion detect a ubiquitous self-centeredness at the heart of individual and social behavior.

By itself this would not lead to rationalizing self-deception. We have to be ashamed of our selfishness in order to need to mask it. So the third principle of suspicion is that we are not immoral and shameless but just moral enough to be dishonest with ourselves and others. In other words, we are not moral enough to act consistently on the principles of equality, justice, neighbor love, and general benevolence which we profess. We continue to act largely out of self-interest. But our (professed) morality serves to blind us to this fact. It would be unpleasant to recognize the degree to which our practice violates our profession, and so we simply manage not to notice. We give false but flattering accounts of what motivates our beliefs and our practices, sometimes deceiving others, more frequently deceiving ourselves.

To the degree that this picture is correct the human self emerges as systematically estranged from genuine self-knowledge. Far more serious than the whole/part and inner/outer problems posed by Hegel is the self's very tenuous commitment to truth in self-knowledge. It develops habits of thinking more highly of itself than it ought to think, of thinking quite unfairly about its competitors and enemies, and even of creating its gods in its own image.

The masters of suspicion are especially sensitive to self-deception in the religious realm, whether they be atheists or believers. Noticing the tendency to believe what would be nice, they note the tendency to domesticate God. It would be nice if all that power were unconditionally on our side, individually and collectively, and if it were quite permissive, making very minor demands on us. It would, for example, be very nice if

God would be satisfied with metaphysical compliments or ritual observances and leave us to live our daily lives on our own terms. Or, if He were to insist on butting into our daily lives, it would be nice if He required nothing more of us than our society asks, rendering it unnecessary for us ever to question the sacred bond between Him and our social order which all but equates the national interest with the divine will. Suspicion predicts, in other words, that two of the most popular forms of piety will be the religion of self-esteem without repentance and the religion of God and country. Both are, of course, patently unbiblical. What the masters of suspicion help us to see is how those who profess the Bible as their authority can nevertheless be the purveyors and purchasers of these pieties.

In summary, it seems to me that any comprehensive personality theory needs to address the question of self-knowledge, and that any attempt to do this in a Christian context will require taking the hermeneutics of suspicion very seriously in its understanding of the human self. For this tradition has a view of sin which is "biblical" in several important ways. First, it recognizes the pervasiveness of sin in human experience. Second, it recognizes that it permeates our cognitive life as well as our affective and volitional life. Third, it recognizes that we are surrounded by sin insofar as the temptation to self-deception both arises from within the individual and comes to the individual from the social environment where its corporate practice has all but coercive power.

I want to turn now to a second area where I believe modern philosophy provides valuable insights for anyone trying to think in a Christian way about personality theory. It is what I referred to earlier as intersubjectivity. Descartes's model can be described as atomistic or individualistic. Here individualism signifies not so much the primacy of private self-interest, but the essential completeness and self-sufficiency of the individual prior to relations with any other. In the context of mind–body dualism it is nature to whom the self is only accidentally related. But here I want to focus attention on relations with other selves. The question here is not whether they exist or can be known (though these become problematic on Cartesian assumptions) but whether my identity is essentially mediated by my relations to other selves.

The modern anti-Cartesian tradition on this point can be summarized in three claims. First, it is affirmed by thinkers as divergent as Rousseau, Hegel, Marx, Kierkegaard, and Sartre that both who I am and who I think I am are grounded in my relations to others. The category of substance, signifying that individual entity which needs only itself in order to be itself, is declared to be inadequate for understanding human personality. I may be a biological individual from the moment of conception, but even at birth and on into adult life, I am far from being an individual self. To become one is the task of a lifetime, carried out only in interaction with others who become significant precisely by playing important roles in this process, the roles of parent, playmate, sibling, teacher, teammate, friend, lover, rival, competitor, boss, etc.

What is true of personal identity at the ontological level is just as true of self-consciousness at the epistemic level. Here it is possible to prescind from the question whether self-consciousness is veridical self-knowledge or some form of self-deceptive mystification. The point is simply that I do not see myself as myself until I notice you looking at me, that I do not learn to say "I" except in the presence of a Thou.

The second claim is a negative one in which modern philosophy again speaks as if original sin were its point of departure. The other selves, who are seen to be utterly essential to my own selfhood, are now seen to be threats which I encounter in fear, hostility, and defensiveness. Others are threats to me in several ways. For example, if I am not careful, they will take advantage of me, use me for their purposes, and eventually dominate me simply in the attempt to establish their own importance. Or, they may evoke my love, respect, and trust, only to disappoint me by proving unworthy of my esteem. Or again, taking the point of departure from friendship rather than hostility, others may have the loving courage to tell me what "even your best friend won't tell you," just as parents sometimes impose punishment on children which, even when it is recognized as an expression of loving care, is anything but welcome. Finally, others can be threats to me simply by being there. Their mere presence represents a claim to be ends in themselves and not merely means to my ends. The "megalomania" which constantly wants to put myself at the center of the universe and make everything and everyone else subordinate to my wishes (or even whims) is challenged by the simple being of other selves, prior to any gestures of friendship or hostility they may make.

It is this last feature which leads to perhaps the gloomiest philosophical expression of this depressing picture, Sartre's claim that love is nothing but the demand to be loved. By this he means that when I say, I love you, I really mean nothing more than, You must love me. We might call this cheese omelet love. Consider this question: I love cheese omelet; would you like me to love you too? In spite of the fact that this is a perfectly legitimate use of the word love, your answer would surely be no. For to love cheese omelet is to have a need which can be satisfied only by possessing and devouring, using and using up the omelet for my own purposes without any concern for its purposes. While that may be quite all right in relation to eggs, which presumably have no purposes of their own, there is nothing to keep me from relating to other selves in just that way, although they do have purposes of their own. And when Sartre says that love is just the demand to be loved, we hear the secular theology of original sin claiming that all of us do just that.

If we ask what leads us to treat others in this way, Sartre's answer is in terms of the "megalomania" in each of us which makes us want to be absolute, our own ground, our own justification, dependent upon and answerable to no one. His blunt way of putting it is hopelessly theological. Each of us is, he claims, the desire to be God. For this reason every other self, just to the degree that we cannot reduce him or her to an it, just to the degree that we must continue to encounter another subject and not just an object, is a threat to our fundamental project, our deepest identity.

Sartre applies this picture to sexual life, and it is easy to extend the application to other domains, including international politics, for the selves that want to be God are collective as well as individual selves. But at any level the results are the same: hostility, mistrust, and the kind of defensiveness which is itself a form of aggression.

However depressing this picture may be (and I always hope it isn't raining on the days we read Sartre), we cannot simply dismiss it as morbid cynicism. For it corresponds all too well both with the biblical picture of sin and with our experience of ourselves and others all too much of the time, if we are really honest about it. But it does not correspond to the whole of either the biblical account or our daily experience. There is another side, and its expression represents the third claim of modern philosophy on intersubjectivity, namely that in spite of the obstacles and the barriers, genuine dialogue, presence, and fidelity do occur between selves.

Among the most eloquent defenders of the human race on this point are Martin Buber and Gabriel Marcel. While presenting his vision of that true dialogue in which I and Thou really meet one another in mutual subjectivity, Buber anticipates an objector who will challenge him to show by what authority he is going around telling other people what to do. His reply is that he is telling no one what they must do but simply what they can do. Presence is possible. Masks and moats and mail are not the only tools of the soul.

Marcel expounds the same concept of genuine presence in terms of the categories of vulnerability, permeability, disposability (not as in disposable diapers, but in terms of being at someone's disposal), and receptivity. Using the notion of receiving guests, he insists that receptivity is an activity and not a passivity, and that making room for the others in our life is the act by which in receiving others we give ourselves to them. Marcel is aware of the Sartrean picture, and he reminds us of it when he talks about the meaning of saying to another, You belong to me. But he insists that we are also able to say, I belong to you, and that the meaning of belonging is as different in these two situations as the word love is in the statements, I love cheese omelet, and, God so loved the world . . .

The philosophers in the modern anti-Cartesian tradition insist that our relations with others are fundamental to whom we are; and they present the alternatively depressing and hopeful picture of defensive aggressiveness and vulnerable openness as modes in which we live out our relatedness. Hell is other people. Yes indeed. But so is heaven. What neither Marcel nor Buber nor Sartre nor any of the other philosophers in this tradition do is give a cogent account of how it is that both accounts ring so true to our experience. To help us see that they do, let us consider two events from ordinary daily life.

When I teach a unit on the criminal justice system, I ask my students to develop their own incipient theory of punishment by reflecting on their own experience of being punished as children. Where do they give their parents or guardians high marks, where do they give low marks, and why? What generalizations might we tentatively formulate about what distinguishes good punishment from bad? The two accounts which follow won't take us very far with that question, which is not our present concern in any case, but they may help us gain a deeper understanding of the issue which is before us — the essential intersubjectivity of human personality.

One student described being the oldest child in a large family. She was at the age where she liked to think herself a big kid in distinction from the little kids. She liked to think, for example, You are still little kids. You get spanked when you are naughty. But I'm grown up. I'm past all that. Unfortunately her behavior did not live up to this image, and on the occasion in question she acknowledged that she had left her father no alternative consistent with established family practice but to spank her.

But instead of taking her to her room as she expected, he told her to bend over the railing by the stairs and grab hold of her ankles. She realized that for the first time (had her father been able to read her mind?) she was going to get spanked in front of a small congregation of younger siblings. Realizing that her options were few, she quickly decided that at least she would not give them the satisfaction of seeing and hearing her cry. To her great surprise, she succeeded in not crying. To her even greater surprise, her victory left a bad taste in her mouth that lasted long after the physical pain had disappeared. Without having read Marcel, she put it this way: "I wasn't able to receive what he was giving."

It is important to notice that it was her dignity and not her backside that she sought to defend. The gift her father offered in anger but also in love was painful both physically and spiritually. At the former level she was quite able to receive it. She made no attempt to protect herself physically. But at the spiritual level her pride made it impossible to receive what he was giving. As Joseph fled from Potiphar's wife, leaving only his coat behind, so she fled from her father's discipline, leaving her backside fully vulnerable to his whacks while barricading her soul behind the impregnable defenses of her spiritual act of refusal.

Quite different was the response of another student. In her family, spankings always occurred on the spot of the offense, and thus in front of whatever other family members happened to be present. To make matters worse, they were always administered to the offender's bare bottom. It was hard to say whether the physical pain outweighed the embarrassment or vice versa. But this student was able to write in her journal, "The spankings I received as a child were good for me. No, I take that back. They were very good for me." No doubt much of the credit for this belongs to her parents for establishing patterns of fairness and consistency in a larger context of loving care. But some of the credit surely derives from her own ability to receive what they had to give, at least if we take at face value something else she wrote. "In baring my bottom to my father's hand I bared my soul to his rebuke."

The point of these stories is not, of course, that we encounter the other primarily as punisher. But, as we have already noted, the other poses a threat to us in a variety of ways whether encountered in friendship or hostility, love or anger, or both. And our experience tells us that each of us is both of these children. Much of our life is shaped by the pain that comes, not so much from what others do to us, as from our inability to be genuinely open and present to them, to receive them and what they have to give into our lives. Thus we barricade ourselves behind a variety of masks and conventions, or we make matters even worse by elevating a good football strategy, the best defense is a good offense, into the principle of our relations with others. We ourselves become the aggressor self, and in so doing guarantee that we will not achieve the loving mutuality for which we long.

But sometimes, somehow we find the strength to bare our souls to the unfiltered presence of the other. We do what is required of us in the situation by convention or self-interest, but we do something more at the same time. We render ourselves present without protection to the subjectivity of another. We risk receiving what the other has to give, knowing it may involve pain.

Powerful descriptions of both these moments can be found in modern philosophy and in modern literature as well. What is needed is a theoretical account which will illuminate how a single self can be both of these moments so essentially that failure to include either makes any account of the self as false as it may otherwise be illuminating. The raw materials are there in abundance. The synthetic and integrative task remains as a major challenge for a personality theory with a Christian perspective. That task will require more than reciting as shibboleths the terms "creation" and "fall." It will be necessary to cash these slogans in for genuine insight.

Finally, a word about the unity of the two issues I have discussed, self-knowledge and intersubjectivity. Their point of intersection, it seems to me, is the question of courage. The task of becoming a self, a real person, includes the challenge to that honesty which makes self-knowledge possible and to that receptivity which makes intersubjectivity something other than hell. The question which arises from the preceding analysis is very direct: Do I have the courage for that honesty and that receptivity?

This question leads to another. Once I become clear what sort of courage is at issue and how central its practice is to real selfhood, I will want to know where this courage comes from and how I get it. In a Christian context this will immediately involve the theology of sanctification and the role of the Word and the Spirit in the process by which the self becomes itself.

All this leads to still a further question. If this courage comes from the work of the Spirit in my life, is there anything I can do to be open, vulnerable, and receptive to God's working in my life? Clearly there is a circle here. My contribution to the Spirit's work in building me up in the courage I need to be myself is itself a form of courage. The traditional answer to this dilemma, which purports to keep the circle from becoming a vicious catch-22, is the practice of the spiritual disciplines in which I deliberately place myself at the disposal of the Word and Spirit, so far as I am able, so that they may enable me to be more fully at the disposal of God and neighbor and more fully honest about what is going on in my life.

It now looks as if the personality theory I have in mind is quite peculiar. In itself it will be visibly incomplete. It calls for and opens out into an ethics (of the tasks of selfhood and the virtue of courage), a theology (of the work of the Word and the Spirit in sanctification), and a practice (of the spiritual disciplines). Typically, personality theories do not do this. Either they omit reference to the goals and ideals which distinguish genuine from pseudopersonality, and they confine themselves to the kind of explanation which serves the prediction and control of behavior; or they address the normative issues in a secular, humanistic framework. We see here the ambiguity of the concept of humanism from a Christian perspective. It affirms the ideal beyond the facts, but seeks to do so in a purely "rational" way. Thus "reason" becomes the attempt to establish human values without God.

Because of its understanding of human bondage to sin, Christian thinking about personality theory will have powerful affinities with the theories of Skinner and Freud. Because of its concern for the task of becoming a self, it will have noticeable kinship with the thought of Rogers and Maslow. But it will have its own distinctive contributions to make, both in unifying the realistic and idealistic motifs and, perhaps most importantly, in its analysis of the courage without which personality is an empty name with which we flatter ourselves.

Why Secular Psychology Is Not Enough

William Kirk Kilpatrick

William Kirk Kilpatrick is professor of educational psychology at Boston College. He holds a B.S. from Holy Cross College, an M.A. from Harvard University, and a Ph.D. from Purdue University. His fields of special interest are the social effect of psychology, Christianity and psychology, and the Christian imagination. Dr. Kilpatrick has published three books: *Identity and Intimacy*, *Psychological Seduction: The Failure of Modern Psychology* (translated into French and also awarded *Cornerstone Magazine's* Book of the Year Award in 1983), and *The Emperor's New Clothes: The Naked Truth about the New Psychology*. He has also written numerous articles and reviews for journals such as *Policy Review*, *The Human Life Review*, *America*, *Communio*, and *Newsday*. Professor Kilpatrick is currently working on a study of the relationship between stories and moral growth.

"Would you like to hear a story?"

It's a question to which adults as well as children respond with anticipation. In this case, however, I'm afraid it's only a hypothetical question because I'm not going to tell you a story, I'm going to give you a paper. But I suspect you'd rather hear the story. I hope you'll forgive me, but I only ask the question to make a point. We love stories. We respond to them in a way we do not to papers or lectures. Stories speak to our hearts. You might even say we have an appetite for stories just as we do for food and drink. Certainly, a meal is much more enjoyable when there are good stories going round the table. And certainly we can all remember times when we were so engrossed in hearing and telling stories that we forgot about food altogether.

When we were younger we made up stories in our heads—daydreams. Needless to say, the heroes and heroines of these stories were always ourselves. The other day I was re-reading one of Flannery O'Connor's short stories in which the main character, a girl, daydreams about being a Christian thrown to the lions in the Coliseum. Quite to the surprise of the Romans, all of the lions lie down at her feet and lick her hand. Reading this triggered something in my mind, and I remembered that I used to have similar daydreams. But, of course, mine were the daydreams of a boy. My preference was to strangle the lions or rip their jaws apart. That would teach them to fool with Christians! The daydream didn't always end there. Sometimes the emperor would be foolish enough to send a dozen armed gladiators after me to do what the lions couldn't do. As a Christian I could not, of course, kill the gladiators. I merely disarmed them and knocked them out. After that, the emperor decided it was best to let all the Christians go free. Once, as I recall, one of these daydreams ended in the conversion of the entire Coliseum.

As we grow older, we tend to daydream less, but I'm not sure we ever get over wishing that our lives were more like stories and we more like heroes and heroines. Even grown ups still love stories of adventure and romance. And, surprisingly, even in this highly sophisticated and technological world, old-fashioned stories are still the popular favorites—stories in which there are elements of love and hate, good and evil, heroes and villains, and even the suggestion that there is some great force at work in the universe. That is why people flock to see *Star Wars* and *Close Encounters*, *E. T.* and *The Emerald Forest*, *Return of the Jedi*, and *Raiders of the Lost Ark*. People have a need for stories. Without stories they become less human.

In this paper I am going to argue not only that we need stories in our lives, but also that our wishful instincts do not mislead us. A life *is* a story. That is the proper way to look at it. The best way to interpret and explain a life is in a narrative way. No other way will do.

But, of course, this is not the prevalent way of interpreting lives. The prevailing mindset is what Phillip Rieff calls the therapeutic mentality. Within the therapeutic framework, lives are explained in terms of theories or studies or observations. At best, a life amounts to a case history; at worst, we have, as Stanley Hauerwas would put it, the story that there is no story.

In what follows I want to make a case for a narrative interpretation of lives rather than a therapeutic interpretation. I want to suggest that secular psychology doesn't understand the storied nature of our lives and that Christian psychology had better not forget it.

Let me begin by addressing the question of meaning. The Old Testament prophet says "Without a vision the people perish." I do not think secular psychology offers a meaningful vision. I am not sure that it offers any vision. Whatever it offers, it is not enough. People are not flourishing. They still swallow bottles of pills and hold revolvers to their heads just as people did in the Depression when they didn't know a tenth of the facts and theories we know today.

Why isn't secular psychology enough? It offers plausible explanations, good insights, good techniques. It offers very good pills. But it doesn't offer the one thing that people require most: a sense of meaning. Quite the contrary, we can even say that the psychological sciences tend to reduce meaning. One comes away from the psychology textbooks with the feeling that though life now seems more explainable, it somehow seems less meaningful. Everything we thought was of value gets explained away. Symphonies and paintings turn out to be sublimations of the sex drive or productions of the right brain hemisphere. Love turns out to be a matter of stimulus and response or a series of transactions conditioned by family patterns.

In thinking about love, for example, we are subtly encouraged to forget about Romeo and Juliet, and to think rather in terms of some new study of the sexual behavior of 2,000 couples in the Midwest, or some observations on the mating patterns of chimpanzees or to reorder our understanding along the lines of some such formula as "She is the mother that he always wished to possess."

And not only is the noble side of our nature reduced, so is the ignoble side. We are allowed to be neither saints nor sinners because, as it turns out, there is no sin; only synapses. I'm sure the day is not far off when some psychologically minded committee of theologians will get together to rework the Lord's Prayer along more scientific lines. The new version will no doubt read "Give us this day our daily bread and forgive us our synapses as we forgive those who synapse against us. . . ."

What I am suggesting here is that though the social sciences are long on analysis they are very short on meaning. Tom Howard handles this matter nicely in his book *Chance or the Dance?* "The myth sovereign in the old age," he writes, "was that everything means everything." That is, everything pointed to something of vast significance standing behind it. But, he observes, "The myth sovereign in the new is that nothing *means* anything." Howard continues: "the old myth said, 'I have a father, and this is to be expected since there is, in fact, a Father who has set things up so that I will have some way of grasping this notion of fatherness which is the stuff of things. . . .' The new myth says, 'You have projected your experience of your father onto the cosmos, so that the Father exists strictly as the extension of your own situation.'"

The upshot of our continual exposure to the new myth is the complete frustration of the human imagination, since the imagination is forever asking for significance, and it is forever being told by the keepers of the new myth not to ask that question. Let me quote once more from *Chance or the Dance?* This time it's the imagination that is speaking: "Well, if *this* doesn't mean anything then (the imagination replies), does *this*? No? Well then, let's look over here. What about this? No? Well, here then? No again? Alas, the world is weary, stale, flat, and unprofitable."

I think we may be close here to the reason why the rise of psychology has not ushered in the reign of happiness. Try as it might to give us skills for living, psychology has never been able to give a reason for living. It offers no vision. And, as I have suggested, the reductionist nature of so much psychology often has the unintended effect of making life seem less important, less significant, less worth the struggle. Let me give an example. In one of his books, Victor Frankl quotes a psychoanalyst to the effect that values "are nothing but defense mechanisms, reaction formations, or rationalizations of instinctual drives." Maybe so, replies Frankl, but in that case one would have to be a damn fool to care much about values. He writes, "I would not be willing to live for the sake of my 'defense mechanisms' much less to die for the sake of my 'reaction formations.' "

Frankl's point is that psychology can assign no significant meaning to human values or, for that matter, to any human activities. Everything is explained in terms of the lowest common denominator; everything that first appeared to carry meaning is explained away. Consequently, within its own terms, psychology has little to offer in the way of motivation. Why should we work on improving our lives? When you boil it down, the only answer that mechanistic and physiological models of psychology can offer is something in the order of "Do it for the sake of your synapses" or "You have a duty to your neurotransmitters." Well maybe, but to paraphrase Frankl, I'm not sure I want to live for the sake of my neurotransmitters. Even the much-touted motivation of self-actualization won't do the trick. It may work for a while, but in the long run people yearn for a meaning outside themselves. Sooner or later (and it may be sooner for highly perceptive and sensitive adolescents) people ask, "What's the point of becoming a self-actualized person in a meaningless world?"

Now admittedly, some secular therapists do employ higher aspirations and more noble considerations in trying to motivate their clients. They say things like: "You have so much to contribute" or "Have you thought about the effect this will have on your parents?" or "I know you don't care about your own life anymore, Mrs. Jones, but can't you see how much your family needs you?" and so on.

I would only point out that when they say these things they

138   The Christian Vision: Man and Mind

are usually stepping outside of the limits of the psychological sciences and are making use of other traditions and belief systems. Where do these ideas come from? Where do we get the idea that individuals ought to put their families first, or that they ought to contribute to society, or that they ought to care how other people feel? Why should people love one another, or go out of their way, or act in any but purely utilitarian ways? These ideas did not originate in psychology.

Christopher Dawson once wrote "As liberalism did not create moral ideas, so too it cannot preserve them. It lives off the spiritual capital that it inherited from Christian civilization. . . ." I think secular psychology is in an analogous position. It assumes in its clientele a fund of good will, love, and caring that it is incapable of creating. We can go further and say that it assumes the existence of meaning systems which give order and purpose to people's lives but does nothing to sustain or preserve those meaning systems. It depends on those meaning systems at the same time that it is doing much to undermine and weaken those systems. In short, it is like a man sawing off the branch on which he sits.

Now, so far, my contention has been that secular psychology can assign no particular meaning to emotional distress and traumatic situations. It has no ultimate answer to the question that plagues us when we are distressed and broken by the circumstances of life. That question is: "Why me?" "Why is this happening to me?"

Secular psychology can only answer that question in one of two ways. It can answer that your suffering is pure chance, randomness, the result of a bad concatenation of genes or chemicals, family patterns, or environment. Or it can answer like the friends of Job and tell you in very subtle ways that perhaps you really brought this on your own head. If you had only done this or if you hadn't done that; if you had only had a better understanding of family dynamics; if you had only given your children more freedom, or if you had only given them less. And so on. But such explanations, though they may be plausible, and though they may actually fit the facts of our lives, seem insufficient. They are explanations, but they are not meaningful explanations. They don't answer the question, "Why me?" For we may be well aware of others—friends, neighbors, relatives—who have made just as many mistakes in life as we, who are perhaps less caring and more self-absorbed and who, nevertheless, go sailing through life. Why not them? Why me?

Moreover, the kind of explanations we get very often serve to trivialize our lives. Our struggles, sufferings, and triumphs when placed in the cool light of therapeutic analysis are made to seem much less significant than we feel them to be. And there's the rub. We are forever searching for significance in our life and we are restless till we find it. To be told by a well-meaning therapist that the particular problem we suffer from is a typical reaction of mid-life or that this particular family situation is "something we see quite often in the people we work with"—that kind of response just doesn't seem to do justice to the story of our lives.

The fact is we do look upon our lives as stories. However difficult to elucidate, we feel there is something like a point or purpose or plot to life. We are even audacious enough to want the story to have a nice *sensible* plot, preferably like a nineteenth-century novel. We decidedly do not want to think of our life as "a tale told by an idiot . . . signifying nothing"—although that seems to be the interpretation favored by the social sciences. This concept of life as story helps to explain why we like to tell stories, listen to stories, and read stories. As G. K. Chesterton put it, all life is an allegory and we can understand it only in parable.

I, for one, take that very seriously. I believe that if you are not looking at life poetically and dramatically then you are not looking at it properly. And this, it seems to me, is also the way Christianity instructs us to look at life. After all, Christianity has come to us as a story, not as a theory or a philosophy or a science. Or perhaps we might say that it is many stories that are part of one vast tale. There is the story of Creation, the story of Abraham, the story of Joseph and his brothers, the story of King David, the story of the Good Samaritan, the Christmas story, the Gospel stories. Moreover, we speak of God as the author of Creation and the author of our Salvation, and sometimes we refer to the drama of Salvation and the part we are meant to play in it.

It is a story of God's goodness but, since it is a true story, it is not an idyllic fable. The Dark Lord plays his part as does the Good Lord. A good story will not exclude the unpleasant side of life. The characters will encounter humiliations, accidents, misfortunes, and sorrows, but these calamities serve a purpose and are never without meaning. Indeed the calamity is very often the occasion for the growth or transformation of the story's protagonist. For example, in one of Tolstoy's short stories, a mortal sickness causes Ivan Illych to see his life as he has never seen it before. In Jane Austin's *Persuasion*, Louisa Musgrove is transformed into a better person by an accident and her subsequent convalescence. In *Great Expectations*, Pip is transformed by his illness. In *Captains Courageous*, a fall overboard transforms a spoiled child into a loyal friend. And, of course, in the Gospel story, we find that it is through suffering that we are redeemed and the world is saved.

In stories, and particularly in the Gospel story, hardships, setbacks, persecutions, rejection, sickness, and abandonment are not mere random events. They can be occasions of *revelation*, of seeing something for the first time or remembering something that had been forgotten. And they can be an occasion of *transformation*, of turning lives around or turning them back to the right path. And the interesting thing is that the events in a story may serve not only as occasions of revelation and transformation for the actors in a story but also for readers and hearers of the story as well. Augustine takes and reads and the pattern of his life is revealed to him, and perhaps a thousand years later another man picks up the *Confessions* and the miracle is repeated. And it still happens. Despite the spirit of the age, we feel there must be a point to our lives. One of the great services which a story may render then is to help us see what that point may be. Stories may help us to recognize a moral or spiritual meaning in a personal situation that might otherwise seem chaotic or pointless.

Now I'm not saying that the significance of events is always crystal clear either to the characters in the story or to the hearers or readers of a story. There is always much that cannot be articulated, much that remains mysterious. There is indeed a sense in which all good stories are mystery stories. And that's because good stories are true to life and life *is* mysterious. You get the sense in reading Dickens or Tolstoy or Dostoyevsky that they are not only propounding the great and solid facts of life but also the marvelous and uncanny nature of those facts, and the mysterious bonds that connect facts and events and people together. But to say that the events in a story or in a life are mysterious is not to say they are random or senseless. Mystery and meaning are not opposites. Rather, a mystery is something that has more meaning than we can comprehend.

The problems we encounter in life, however, do not usually follow from a sense that there is too much mystery or too much meaning in our lives but a complete absence of both. We can sometimes reach a point where we feel not only that life is meaningless but also that there seems nothing mysterious about the fact. We look at life clearly and unsentimentally (so we tell ourselves) and it seems quite obvious that it is meant to be meaningless; and as soon as we can get up the courage we will exit stage left and put up with it no more. With David Copperfield, we all set out to see whether we will turn out to be the hero of our own story. Along the way, however, some of us come to the conclusion that not only are we not the hero, but that there is no story. I have suggested that secular psychology unwittingly encourages that bleak view. Let me suggest now that one of the tasks of Christian psychology is to challenge the notion that there is no story.

But first, lest you think I've been reading too many stories and not paying enough attention to nonliterary views of human nature, let me add that this view of life as story corresponds to some of the very best thought in contemporary psychology and philosophy. For example, the developmental scheme worked out by Erik Erikson is quite compatible with this view. For Erikson, the major element in ego identity is a sense of *continuity* over time. A healthy self, like a novel, requires a theme or narrative thread. And though this narrative thread may not tie up all the loose ends of one's life, it still ought to give us a conviction that our life ties together.

In the field of philosophy one of the most important books in recent years is Alasdair MacIntyre's *After Virtue*. Much of this book is devoted to the problem of defining personal identity. Although I can't do justice here to MacIntyre's full argument, I can give a rough summary. The best way to understand a person's life, says MacIntyre, is to think of it as a story. Not as being *like* a story but *as* a story. He writes: "All attempts to elucidate the notion of personal identity independently of and in isolation from the notions of narrative intelligibility, and accountability are bound to fail." Elsewhere he writes, "The unity of a human life is the unity of a narrative quest." And again, "I can only answer the question 'What am I to do?' if I can answer the prior question 'Of what story or stories do I find myself a part?' "

MacIntyre also notes that "When someone complains—as do some of those who attempt or commit suicide—that his or her life is meaningless, he or she is often and perhaps characteristically complaining that the narrative of their life has become unintelligible to them, that it lacks any point, any movement toward a climax or *telos*. Hence the point of doing any one thing rather than another at crucial junctures in their lives seems to such a person to have been lost."

When a man comes to the point in his life when he begins to ask "What's the use?" or "What's the point?" or "What does it matter?" it's a sign that he has lost the narrative thread of his life. One of the major tasks of Christian psychology is to help him find it again. Christian psychologists are in a much better position to do this than their secular counterparts because they are in touch with a tradition in which every individual life, no matter how desperate and seemingly pointless, can find a place. Christian psychology can encourage people to see their lives as stories within a larger story, to locate themselves within a tradition of people who have been similarly tested. Many life experiences which appear meaningless or accidental from secular perspectives are more properly viewed as points of testing or revelation or transformation from the perspective of the Christian drama. Christian psychology has the task of helping us go beyond the level of merely "working on our problems" or seeing our lives as clinical studies, and on to the level of discerning the distinctive part we are meant to play and the importance of playing it well.

In all of this the role of faith is crucial. So too is the role of imagination. The distressed person needs the power to imagine an interpretation other than the bleak one he has assigned to his life. In the words of the old hymn, he must be able to say, "I was blind, but now I see." "I looked at life that way, but I was wrong. Now I see it this way." The imagination needs to be fed, of course. And it feeds, naturally enough, on images. What kind of images? Well, it will try to nourish itself with whatever images are available. But I would suggest the kind of images the dispirited man needs are not clinical images or psychological images or sociological images but images that will give him back his spirit. Inspirational images, if you will.

Now, I'm afraid the word "inspirational" has fallen on bad times, and has come to mean a sort of spiritual pep talk, as though the Holy Spirit were some variation on college spirit or team spirit. That view is a bit superficial. We'd do better perhaps to think of a commander rallying his soldiers at the darkest hour of battle, or of a family facing hard times, or natural disasters, or a serious illness with the attitude, "We've seen this before, we'll come through it again, we'll sustain each other with our love." Better yet is to look at the actual images of our faith: images which say "God is with us, He will see us through."

What are some of these images, and how might they relate to the lives of those who seek help in counseling? Well, to someone who feels abandoned, desolate, without friends, it is no little thing to call forth the image of Christ in the Garden or on the cross. He, too, felt abandoned. To someone who is ashamed of his life but feels it is too late to start over, it makes a difference to know that Peter was a coward, Paul an accomplice to murder, and Augustine a libertine. When family life seems to have lost its point, when children seem only an occasion for heartbreak, it makes a difference to know that God, too, experienced the disobedience of his first children; and it helps to know that prodigal sons and daughters do come back. When someone's life seems to have been reduced to simply waiting and hoping year after year, it makes a difference to recall that the Israelites wandered for forty years, or that Monica, Augustine's mother, waited thirty years for an answer to her prayers. And finally, when someone can find no earthly explanation for his tribulations, it is no little thing to recall that we battle with principalities and powers, that we have an enemy who goes about seeking our destruction, and that in our sufferings we may help to destroy the power of the Dark Lord.

Does a narrative approach to understanding human lives explain everything? No. After all, mysteries are at the heart of our faith. And ordinary people are also mysteries. Christians are not called upon to understand everything but to believe and act. The power of narrative, however, is not limited to the power to explain. It also has the power to sustain. It can sustain us even when it does not explain everything. It sustains us by assuring us that we are part of something important even though the connections are not always visible. God does have a plan for each of us. Our gestures and struggles which may appear to lead nowhere or to bear no fruit may yet have great significance. As Christians we really do believe that there are other lines of connection than those the world sees, lines which may run in completely different directions. The logic of stories and of lives, then, is not the same as the logic of the logicians.

Nor is it the same as the logic of the social scientists. The logic of the social sciences can be characterized as a cause-and-effect logic: this happened, therefore this happened next. It's a kind of rough mathematics of the psyche. Multiply three psychological factors by three environmental factors, and it works out to a psycho-social total of nine. For example, one prominent psychologist, in explaining the behavior of would-be assassin John Hinckley, points out that John's older brother and sister had preempted all the positive identities held out as valuable by his parents. "Consequently," the psychologists reasoned, "John adopted a negative identity—one of extremism, aloneness and social disruption—the negative of what his parents valued."

Now this is a plausible application of the concept of "negative identity" and it happens to fit the facts of "the case" very nicely. It is a logical explanation, although I can't imagine that for the Hinckley family it is a comforting explanation or a sustaining one. Somehow, it doesn't answer the question, "Why me?" And I'm not even sure it's good mathematics. It seems to be one of those cases where three times three equals nine hundred ninety-nine instead of nine. To let the prominent psychologist off the hook, let me confess that in my own courses on psychology I have used the Hinckley example to illustrate the formation of a negative identity. I also offer neat and plausible psycho-social explanations of the reasons why some young people join cults, and some motorcycle gangs, and why some take drugs, and some take their lives. But I'm always conscious in doing so that these explanations are not nearly sufficient. And I know in my own case, when trouble strikes my life, such formulations seem beside the point.

I'm not saying that there is not an order to our lives or that there is not a coherence by which *that* connects with *this*. I would only suggest that this order is in a different order from what the social scientist supposes. It is better understood as a narrative order than a cause-and-effect order. The parts of our life story are not connected in a logical way but in a narrative way. In his book, *Vision and Character*, Craig Dykstra, in trying to characterize the progress of both lives and stories puts it this way: "What happens next cannot be deduced from what happened first, though what happens next must follow narratively from what happened first." To illustrate what he means, pick up a literary classic with which you're unfamiliar, read a few chapters, and try to figure out what will happen next. Reading *War and Peace* who could guess that Natasha would suddenly break off her engagement with Prince Andrew and attempt to run off with the playboy Anatole Kuragin? Reading *Anna Karenina* who could guess that Alexey Karenin, the classic case of a mechanical man, would suddenly undergo an emotional conversion? Or that Vronsky would attempt to kill himself? Yet these things do happen. And when they do happen they seem like an inevitable part of the story. But these events proceed by a pattern which simply transcends the logic of cause-and-effect.

In this connection, it is worth noting that when social scientists get hold of great literature, or when literary critics employ a narrow social science analysis, the results are far from happy. Before we too readily adopt the social science explanation of lives we might consider what a failure the social science interpretation of literature has been. Even a naïve reader realizes there is more at work in *David Copperfield* than sociology, more at work in *The Brothers Karamazov* than psychology, more at work in *War and Peace* than Tolstoy's sex life, and more at work in *Pride and Prejudice* than proto-feminism. Such attempts at narrow analysis always end up as petty endeavors next to the thing they pretend to analyze. The characters and events in Tolstoy, Dickens, Homer, and Shakespeare cannot be reduced to social science categories. They transcend such categories. And just as psychological criticism misses much of the significance of literature, psychological analysis can miss much of the significance of individual lives.

Again, it is a question of imagination. A human life can be imagined in strikingly different ways from different perspectives. Imagine, if you will, a game of connect-the-dots, the kind of game children play. Only this time, imagine that the dots are arranged in such a way that more than one picture can be formed from them. One person will connect them this way, another person that way depending perhaps on how they have been trained to look at things. Secular psychology will tend to connect the dots of our lives along certain lines and not others.

They can make a picture, it is true, but you have to wonder if it's the right picture. Now take it a step further and imagine a three-dimensional game of connect-the-dots—a game where some of the most important dots to be connected may be completely missed by players who are conditioned to think only in terms of two dimensions.

Or think of that other children's game in which you look for a hidden picture, perhaps a face in a tree. If you look at it one way all you see is the tree, but if you change your perspective in the right way it becomes apparent that the face was there all along.

Most introductory texts in psychology contain illustrations of such perceptual reversals. The idea seems to hold a certain fascination for secular psychologists. But they stop short of making the logical application to their own field. For it implies, of course, that there are other ways of looking at life than those employed by secular psychology. Christian psychologists, on the other hand, are in the fortunate position of looking at life's vagaries in a dual perspective. They can see both the tree *and* the face. The Face was there all along, of course. The picture has never made sense without it.

Telling The Truth:
A Biblical View of Personality

John S. Reist, Jr.

The Reverend John S. Reist, Jr. is professor of Christian studies and literature at Hillsdale College. He earned his M.A. and Ph.D. in theology and literature at the University of Chicago. He has taught at a number of colleges, including Kansas City's Central Baptist Theological Seminary and North Central College in Illinois where he received the Sang Award for excellence in teaching. His articles, essays, and reviews have appeared in *Cross Currents*, *The Journal of the American Academy of Religion*, *The Anglican Theological Review*, *The Journal of Religion*, *Christianity and Literature*, *Christian Century*, *Religious Education*, *Foundations*, *Perspectives in Religious Studies*, and *The Journal of Religious Thought*.

I. Introduction: Chaos or Canon?

It is wise that I assert at the beginning that it seems to me there *is* no theory of personality, as such, in the Bible. In his still definitive study of 1952, *The Body: A Study In Pauline Theology*, the late Bishop J. A. T. Robinson declared:

> From the standpoint of analytic psychology and physiology the usage of the Old Testament is *chaotic*; it is the nightmare of the anatomist when any part can stand at any moment for the whole and similar functions be predicated of such various organs as the heart, the kidneys and the bowels — not to mention the soul. But such usage is admirably adapted to expressing the unity of the personality under the various aspects of its funda-

mental relation to God. The Hebrew had little or no interest or competence in psychology or physiology.¹ (Italics mine)

But he then goes on to say: "But that must not blind us to the fact that there is in the Old Testament a profound anthropology or doctrine of man."²

The New Testament, also, has overlapping uses of and references for such words as sarx, soma, psyche, and pneuma (flesh, body, soul, spirit), and Paul and the gospel writers never organize references into a composite whole to be studied scientifically, as modern psychiatrists wish to do. It is *man* who is created in God's image, not just a *part* of man. The biblical understanding of humanity is rooted in revelation of knowable truths and also in inexplicable mystery—the mystery of God's creation, judgment, preservation, and salvation of His people, all of whom live in relation to each other and, more basically, to God. It is possible to extrapolate a doctrine of humanity from the testimony of Scripture; but just as the Bible is not a metaphysical argument for the existence of God or a philosophy text, neither is it a psychology textbook.

The mystery of human personality is preserved for us in the etymology of the word "person"; it derives from the Latin *per*, which means "through," and *"sonare,"* which means "to sound." Thus, the mysterious core of each individual is shared through, or sounds through, his or her personality; and just as the word *persona* was used to describe the mask through which an actor spoke in ancient drama, so the human personality seeks expression of its unique being. However, the mystery of human existence should not prevent us from grasping and sharing what it is that Scripture tells us about ourselves, for the witness of Scripture provides knowledge and truth about whom we are. The Psalmist declares of God, "for with Thee is the fountain of life; in thy light do we see light" (36:9); and "Oh send out thy light and thy truth, let them lead me, let them bring

---

¹John A. T. Robinson, *The Body: A Study in Pauline Theology* (London: SCM Press Ltd., 1961), p. 16.
²*Ibid.*

me to thy holy hill and to thy dwelling" (43:3). Instead of a theory of personality, what we have in Scripture, as an inspired account *by* human beings *about* human beings, are actual men and women encountering God in relationship to His world—including other persons. For theoretical definitions of personality, we need to go to psychology texts; for example:

> For us, personality will mean the dynamic organization of interlocking behavior systems that each of us develops through learning processes, as he grows from a biological newborn to a biosocial adult in an environment of other individuals and cultural products.[3]

I need hardly point out the great difference between this kind of language and the powerful, personal truths of the Bible—"Oh Lord, what is man that Thou dost regard him, or the son of man that thou dost think of him?" (Psalms 144:3)

"What is a human being?" Ten years ago, when I was chaplain to a small, private, independent, liberal arts college where "scoping" is practiced, I once spent a week participating in interviews of candidates for a student counseling position. Each candidate came to my office at the end of the day, around 4:30—tired, and hopeful; and when I began each conversation with the question, "What is a human being?" each candidate reacted with shock, puzzlement, fear, and wonder. Not a single one of the interviewees, who were going to provide vocational, emotional, academic, sexual, and abortion counseling, could, or would answer the question, except for one 30ish woman who finally confessed that she was Episcopalian and that her faith "meant a lot" to her. Each evening I went home, as Wordsworth once did, "in grave and serious mood,"[4] for the student services staff had spent each day asking such questions as "What filing

---

[3]Norman Cameron, *The Psychology of Behaviour Disorders* (n.c.: Houghton-Mifflin, 1947), p. 16.

[4]William Wordsworth, "The Prelude," 1,389-390, in *English Romantic Poetry and Prose*, Russell Noyes, ed. (New York: Oxford University Press, 1976), p. 156.

system do you use?" and "How do you plan and manage your time?"—surely important questions, but not nearly as important as the fundamental question, "What is a human being?"

To appeal to the Bible for our understanding of human personality is not merely an option; it is essential, for if we are indeed *homo creatus*, *homo peccator*, and *homo sapiens*, we are probably not going to discover that truth from modern secular society, which is built on the confidence syndrome. Advertisers sow seeds of self-doubt in all of us, for we are not driving the right cars, not using the right perfume, not socially mobile, not fragrant enough, not slender enough, not macho enough, not chic or cool or laid back enough—then they ruthlessly seize that doubt to sell us luxuries as if they were essentials. One must paint one's house with Glidden's or one's face with Oil of Olay. This obsession with "image," with confidence, belies the emptiness at the heart of our life together, for certainly a confident society would want to continue its culture, its life, its values. Ironically, however, this confident, blasé society has become bankrupt, for we have actually asked, for the first time in our history, whether or not we should reproduce ourselves. At the same time in which test tube babies, created in the image of God, become a reality, the pill and the bomb have reduced our confidence to a mad pursuit of fleeting happiness; and the future stands by as a time bomb ready to explode on our Three Mile Islands.

However, it is not only the slick commercial syndrome that misinforms and seduces us; Robert Coles, Professor of Psychiatry and Medical Humanities at Harvard University, has written:

> Especially sad and disedifying is the preoccupation of all too many clergy with the dubious blandishments of contemporary psychology and psychiatry. I do not mean to say there is no value in understanding what psychoanalytic studies, and others done in this century by medical and psychological investigators, have to offer any of us who spend time with our fellow human beings—in the home, at school, at work, and, certainly, in the

various places visited by ministers and priests. The issue is the further step not a few of today's clergy have taken—whereby "pastoral counseling," for instance, becomes their major source of self-satisfaction. Surely we are in danger of losing our religious faith when the chief satisfaction of our lives consists of an endless attribution of psychological nomenclature to all who happen to come our way.[5]

To substitute "passages" and "stages" and "complexes" and "crises" and "empathy" and "analysis" for the truth of the biblical witness is alarming. In a letter he wrote in prison, Dietrich Bonhoeffer declared, "In short I know less than ever about myself, and I'm no longer attaching any importance to it. I've had more than enough psychology, and I'm less and less inclined to analyze the state of my soul. . . . There is something more at stake than self-knowledge."[6] However, this is not to say that the insights, knowledge, and strategies that modern psychiatrists have discovered are to be ignored; for example, Freud's conception of the id has reinforced the biblical truth about the demonic powers in mankind, and C. Roger's notion of "empathy" and "client-centered therapy" exemplifies, at its best, the Christian doctrine of incarnation and the Christian virtue of compassion. Indeed, the same D. Bonhoeffer, six months closer to being hanged by the neck until dead by the Nazis, also wrote to Eberhard Bethge, his biographer: "Now, having, I think, got over the dangers of psychology, I'm very interested in it again, and I should like to discuss it with you."[7]

Which is to say that all truth in the world—theological, biblical, psychological—originates with God and belongs to God, for it is made possible and plausible by the Divine Logos, the Second Person of The Trinity, through whom the world was created, and who for us all became like us that we might

---

[5] Robert Coles, "Critic's Corner: Psychology as Faith," *Theology Today* (April, 1985), 70.
[6] Dietrich Bonhoeffer, *Letters and Papers from Prison*, Eberhard Bethge, ed. (New York: MacMillan Publishing Co., 1971), p. 162.
[7] *Ibid.*, p. 245.

become like Him, so that we might know what human personality is. We are not then constructing a *theory* of personality, or examining a universal *conception* called humanity; but we are endeavoring to discern *actual* humanity—Jacob wrestling with his angel, King Saul struggling with his melancholy, Paul enduring his thorn in the flesh, Mary trembling with her adolescent awe and wonder. Richard Eberhart, a gunnery instructor during World War II, wrote this moving poem about the individual young men he had trained:

The Fury of Aerial Bombardment

You would think the fury of aerial bombardment
Would rouse God to relent; the infinite spaces
Are still silent. He looks on shock-pried faces.
History, even, does not know what is meant.

You would feel that after so many centuries
God would give man to repent; yet he can kill
As Cain could, but with multitudinous will,
No farther advanced than in his ancient furies.

Was man made stupid to see his own stupidity?
Is God, by definition, indifferent, beyond us all?
Is the eternal truth man's fighting soul
Wherein the Beast ravens in its own avidity?

Of Van Wettering I speak, and Averill.
Names on a list, whose faces I do not recall
But they are gone to early death, who late in school
Distinguished the belt feed lever from the belt holding pawl.

They are actual, concrete men and women of whom the biblical canon speaks also; never of human persons merely alone, or alienated, or schizoid; but always in dependence of God (whose covenant they broke), in relationship to each other (Am I my brother's keeper?), and in internal organic wholeness (Thou shalt keep him in perfect peace, whose mind is stayed on thee).

Our attempt to discover a biblical view of personality raises the question of whether there is such a thing as "Christian" psychology. Graham Greene, the contemporary Roman Catholic novelist, once complained of his being labeled a "Catholic novelist," to which he responded, "I would not claim to be a writer of Catholic novels, but a writer who in four or five books took characters with Catholic ideas for his material."[8] Greene wanted to preserve the distinction between the novelist and his novel, lest he rig the plot according to his Catholic faith. As we determine a biblical view of personality, we do so, not to deny or denigrate the germinal truth in such contemporary concepts as "client-centered empathy," "reality therapy," "approach-avoidance complex," and the like, but to forthrightly declare that these conceptions, whatever objective truth or therapeutic efficacy they contain or connote, are fundamentally and fatally flawed without the biblical revelation of the image of God (Genesis 1 and 2); the "glorious liberty of the children of God" (Romans 8:21); and the image of Christ, for as Paul declares, "Do not lie to one another, seeing that you have put off the old nature with its practices, and have put on the new nature, which is being renewed in knowledge after the image of its creator" (Colossians 3:9-10). No theory of personality which examines *only* human personality can account for or explain personality; and it is human beings who know that they are sons and daughters of the canonical biblical Creator, Judge, and Redeemer who are aware of this. Our contemporary TV society provides meretricious material to look *at*; contemporary depth psychology looks deeply *into*; all of us look *around* for the truth; the biblical canon looks at, into, around, and also *up*. Without this transcendent keystone, which is revealed in Jesus Christ, the Word made human, every theory of personality—rational, existential, Rogerian, Freudian, Buscaglian—can offer only partial knowledge; and those who know of the personal God of the biblical canon are motivated thereby to examine all theories of personality—whether they come from B. F. Skinner or Hills-

---

[8]Graham Greene, *In Search of a Character: Two African Journals* (New York: The Viking Press, 1961), p. 13, n. 3.

dale hallway scopers. The biblical *canon* orders for us the *chaos that is always threatening us.*

In Part II, I will briefly expound one of many encounters persons have had with Jesus Christ—the meeting of Christ with the woman who had an issue of blood—in order to suggest what it is to "Tell The Truth" about human personality.

II. Telling The Truth: Mark 5:25-34

And a great crowd followed him and thronged about him. (25) And there was a woman who had a flow of blood for twelve years, (26) and who had suffered much under many physicians, and had spent all that she had, and was no better, but rather grew worse. (27) She had heard the reports about Jesus, and came up behind him in the crowd and *touched* his garment. (28) For she said, "If I *touch* even his garments, I shall be made well." (29) And immediately the hemorrhage ceased; and she felt in her body that she was healed of her disease. (30) And Jesus, perceiving in himself that power had gone forth from him, immediately *turned* about in the crowd, and said, "Who touched my garments?" (31) And his disciples said unto him, "You see the crowd pressing around you, and yet you say, "who *touched* me?" (32) And he looked around to see who had done it. (33) But the woman, knowing what had been done to her, came in fear and *trembling* and fell down before him, and told him the whole *truth.* (34) And he said to her, "Daughter, your faith has made you well; go in peace, and be healed of your disease." (Mark 5:24b-34 RSV) (Italics added)

What is the truth about us? Or, more fully, *who* is the truth about us? "But the woman, knowing what had been done to her, came in fear and trembling and fell down before him, and told him the whole truth" (v. 33). The Greek word for truth— *aletheia*—means "that which has certainty and force," "trustworthy," and "the state of affairs as disclosed." The root meaning is "unconcealed" or "unveiled." Here, then, the personal power of Christ has revealed what has been hidden beneath the woman's expressed personality and also beneath the facade of the society in which this fearful reject lived. The truth is that, although many persons crowd and throng about Jesus, it is those who personally experience the Christ who desire and divine the truth.

Notice that this woman's condition is psychosomatic, caused in part by her body; and psychosocial, caused by her social exile. Notice too that her personality is phobic in two ways: she fears people and she (therefore?) fears God. Ironically, her fear of people was a fear of the ostensibly religious people, the crowds around Jesus.

"And there was a woman who had had a flow of blood for twelve years, and who had suffered much under many physicians, and had spent all that she had, and was no better but rather grew worse" (v. 25-26). It is important to know the background of this woman's situation. Leviticus 15:25 required that a woman during her menstrual period be rejected. She could not come to the temple; she could not be touched while she was in her period. But, *this* woman was ostracized, not just every 28 days, but daily for twelve years! And she had spent all her money and was herself spent. Thus, the woman's alienation and loneliness, since she was perpetually menstruating, stretched into years.

Her fear of God is in part a consequence of the way she has been treated. When she touched Jesus, she fell down, thinking once again that she has been judged and rejected—the same old thing experienced this time, ironically, in the midst of the crowds around Jesus.

Mark then gives us a poignant fourfold movement by which she is dramatically renewed—Touching, Turning, Trembling, and Truth.

1. *Touching*—"She had heard the reports about Jesus, and came up behind him in the crowd and touched his garment. For she said, 'If I touch even his garments, I shall be made well' " (v. 27-28). She reached out in hope against hope, in *fear* but also in *faith*. She had only heard reports about Jesus, for she could not throng with the throngs; she was a social outcast. So she sneaked up behind him, amongst those who were whole, or who

thought they were whole, or who at least could appear confidently in public. Alienated from God and from fellow humanity, nonetheless she is still aware of her need, which indicates that humanity, even in the estrangement of the Adamic condition, is never completely separate from her Creator, God.

2. *Turning* — Christ immediately turns to her. "And Jesus, perceiving in himself that power had gone forth from him, immediately turned about in the crowd, and said, 'Who touched my garments?' " (v. 30). Who touched me? Who *are* you? Who are *you*? God, who created us, also sustains us; and Jesus, the personal Word incarnate, is available to those who seek their personal identity. God first turned to us in creation; He turns to us again in redemption.

3. *Trembling* — "But the woman, knowing what had been done to her, came in fear and trembling and fell down before him, and told him the whole truth" (v. 33). Having been recognized by Jesus but rejected by the crowd, she would hear them again say, "Woman, go home; you are ill; you are unclean; you are unworthy; you are a woman." And this new leader in town, this man who had attracted others in great numbers, would be just another person who looks through her, who notices her only to judge her and to reject her.

I do not wish to turn this essay into a feminist tract, but I cannot help remarking how often women have been ridiculed, or ignored, or hindered, simply because they are women. Jokes about women — "Generally speaking, they are generally speaking," or "A woman is only a woman but a good cigar is a fine smoke;" *epithets*, such as "gals," or "honey," or "the girls"; and aphorisms, such as the Jewish prayer, "I thank God I was not born a woman," or Oscar Wilde's, "Wicked women bother one; good women bore one. That is the only difference between them" — all of these transmit powerful and rejective messages to women.

4. *Truth* — But this woman will not be denied. She told Jesus the whole truth. What *is* her truth? That she has an alienating physical ailment; that she is unacceptable on a daily basis; that she is searching and hoping, but finally that she knows what

had been done to her—both by townspeople, like her created in God's image, and by Jesus, the image to which she is to be transformed.

Telling the truth about human personality means to see persons as created in God's image, as open to God's call and command; the truth about us is that we are whole persons—the woman's diseased body is healed, but it is her volitional, searching, thoughtful, courageous act that precipitated Jesus' redemptive gesture. As the Psalmist declares (139:1-6):

> O Lord, thou hast searched me and known me!
> Thou knowest when I sit down and when I rise up;
> thou discernest my thoughts from afar.
> Thou searchest out my path and my lying down,
> And art acquainted with all my ways.
> Even before a word is on my tongue,
> lo, O Lord, thou knowest it altogether.
> Thou dost beset me behind and before,
> And layest thy hand upon me.
> Such knowledge is too wonderful for me;
> it is high, I cannot attain it.

III. The Human Personality: The Image of God—Mirror or Mirage?

Who is this humanity that is embodied and ensouled in this woman's encounter with Jesus? Who is the God who defines us in creation and redemption? The prophet Isaiah asks, "To whom then will you liken God, or what likeness compare with him?" (40:18). There are three modern commonplaces among dilettante students in psychology, theology, and religion: (1) the Freudian dictum that religion is an infantile neurosis which must be overcome, although Freud himself was pessimistic that this could happen; (2) the Feuerbachian claim that man created God in man's image, instead of God creating man in the divine image; and (3) the Comtean positivist assertion that this universe is simply there; that phenomena are cold, bald facts; that what many of us would call the soul or spirit of each person is merely the epiphenomenal vapor that is momentarily created by the physiological motion of the blood, by synapses in the brain, and by the bright spark in the eye, in much the same way that a locomotive puffs out elusive and transitory clouds of steam. Once the trip is over, the vapor disappears. Hamlet's "immortal longings" are mortal, indeed!

The biblical claim challenges the view; and if that claim is true, as I believe it to be, then it follows that any claims that do not take into account the biblical revelation of the prior personhood of God in which humanity's personality is grounded are basically mistaken. For example, whatever truths or information most secular introductory psychology textbooks contain, the biblical view declares that such information can never comprehensively describe a human being without references to God, the image of God and their implications. It is the secular wisdom that is a *mirage*; the biblical view of created humanity is that the image of God is the *mirror*, or reflection of God's creative power and sustaining presence in us. It is the fool who claims that there is no God (Psalms 14:1, 53:1), for even those who ignore or reject Him or seek to define Him outside the biblical revelation could not do so did He not exist. They are living on borrowed capital.

Professor Elder Olson, a wise and brilliant poet-critic (now retired) under whom I studied literary criticism at the University of Chicago, has written these poetic lines:

> Not in God's image was man
> First created, but in
> Likeness of a beast;
> Until that beast became man,
> All travailled in death and pain
> And shall travail still
> Til man be the image of God
> And nothing shall transform
> Man to that image, but love;
> And this I believe is God's will.

> And all shall work that will:
> Planet and planet shall spin,
> Atom and atom, until
> The scriptures of heaven and earth,
> Mountain and ocean, spell
> The one unnameable Name
> Of One we know nothing of,
> Save what we learn from love.[9]

These lines are a curious combination of evolutionary truisms and religious hope; a truncated view of the image of God, the poem nonetheless bears secular witness to the universality of the image, for both Paul Tillich and F. D. E. Schleiermacher have claimed that the human quest for elusive meaning and straying significance, the very consciousness that I *am*, but need not ever have been, and one day, indeed, will *not be*, are prevailing and prevenient clues to our relationship with God.

Schleiermacher writes:

> I want to show you from what disposition of humanity religion proceeds and how religion interlocks with what you yourselves most highly value. I want to take you up to the heights of the temple, so that you may survey the whole sanctuary of religion and discover its innermost secrets.[10]

> The sum total of religion, then, is to feel all that moves us in our feeling, in the supreme unity of it all, as one and the same, to feel all that is individual and particular as mediated only through that unity—that is, to feel our being and life as a being and life in and through God.[11]

Thus, he rightly enjoins us: "As you look at each individual, for once seek religion alone; view the existence of each person as a

---
[9] Quoted in James Dickey, *Babel to Byzantium: Poets & Poetry Now* (New York: Farrar, Straus and Giroux, 1968), p. 115.
[10] F. D. E. Schleiermacher, *On Religion: Addresses in Response to Its Cultured Critics*, trans. by Terrence N. Tice (Richmond, VA: John Knox Press, 1969), p. 51.
[11] *Ibid.*, p. 94.

revelation of religion to you."¹² . . . in some sense every other person is also to be regarded as a special representation of humanity.¹³ Paul Tillich calls this same common human situation and experience, "ultimate concern about the ground and meaning of our being."¹⁴ It is this human consciousness of possibility, of dependence, of search, to which the biblical account of personality addresses itself. In Paul's address to the cultured Athenians on Mars Hill, we hear him reminding his listeners that they, too, are conscious of God's presence, even in their unbelief and ignorance.

> So Paul, standing in the middle of the Areopagus, said: "Men of Athens," I perceive that in every way you are very religious. For as I passed along, and observed the objects of your worship, I found also an altar with this inscription, "To an unknown god." What therefore you worship as unknown, this I proclaim to you (Acts 17:22-23) . . . he is not far from each one of us, for "In him we live and move and have our being"; as even some of your poets have said, "For we are indeed his offspring." Being then God's offspring, we ought not to think that the Deity is like gold, or silver, or stone, a representation by the art and imagination of man (28-29 RSV).

In this section, I will seek to adumbrate and extrapolate a biblical view of personality, keeping in mind that the Bible is not a psychology text, nor does it theorize about human nature or action.

First of all, we should observe that some thinkers have sought to identify the image of God with a certain, or single aspect of the human being. Many times, but not always, this meant that the human faculty or aspect so singled out was also considered to have avoided the ravishes of Adam's fall, so that man's reason, or his imagination, for instance, was thought to be that

---

¹²*Ibid.*, p. 122.
¹³*Ibid.*, p. 126.
¹⁴Paul Tillich, *Systematic Theology: Vol. I* (Chicago: University of Chicago Press, 1951), p. 42.

human natural grace by which man might naturally know God and do His will.

1. Some have argued that the *will* of man by which he chooses his path, or his destiny, shows the divine image. It was, then, the body which hindered man from true self-knowledge.

2. Others have thought that our *freedom*, by which persons are open to the future, to God, to possibility, radically distinguishes us from animals and therefore is the voice of God in us.

3. Certain thinkers have regarded our *consciousness* of our *finitude*, our sense of "being-toward-death," our awareness that we are conscious, that we can reflect on our selves, stand outside our selves, so to speak, and interpret our selves; all this reflects the image of God.

4. Others have identified *reason* as the image of God in man, pointing out that Jesus is the logos by whom all was created, and through whom all things consist. Our ability to engage in inductive research and deductive proof reflects the order and wisdom of the divine.

5. Still others have contended that *imagination* is the way we boldly and vividly construct our universe and our selves; maid and man, man and maid reflect the creative power of God.

6. It has also been asserted that the essence of the image of God is *relational*; humanity can be understood only as we understand and undertake God's covenant with us, and only as we do this mutually — male and female, old and young, Jew and Greek — in relationship, can we discover our true being.

7. Some, but few, would argue that our *bodies* are necessary to the image of God; although God has no hands or ears, these biblical bodily analogies indicate that our bodies are not to be considered secondary, or inferior parts of God's image in us. It is impossible to be a human being without a body, for the body is an integral means by which the self is individuated and expresses its self. And the incarnation of Jesus Christ indicates the bodily character of God, for the incarnation was crowned with the bodily resurrection.

8. Finally, some have declared that the image of God, the

human personality, is to be found in the *composite unity* of human being; the person is to be identified with no particular aspect of the individual, but is reflected in the body-soul unity and wholeness of human existence. One does not *have* a body; one *is* a body-soul entity; there is no more authentic *you* inside your body. Nor is the body an encumbrance, or a hindrance, or a prison, by nature; it is inherently good, and suffers under the sway of sin and death only in tandem with the mind, soul, and heart of man.

This unity is the human reality of personality—not an idea or theory—which one finds in the Bible. Whether or not one should first turn to the Old Testament or New Testament—to Adam or Christ, the Second Adam—in order to understand personality is a debated question. Karl Barth has stated:

> . . . Christ who seems to come second really comes first, and Adam who seems to come first really comes second. In Christ the relationship between the one and the many is original, in Adam it is only a copy of that original. Our relationship to Adam depends for its reality on our relationship to Christ. And that means, in practice, that to find the true and essential nature of man we have to look not to Adam the fallen man, but to Christ in whom what is fallen has been cancelled and what was original has been restored. We have to correct and interpret what we know of Adam by what we know of Christ, because Adam is only true man insofar as he reflects and points to the original humanity of Christ.[15]

Barth's extreme view of man's radical sinfulness by which the image of God is totally smashed requires him to say this; yet it seems that man separated from God is still man, who is conscious of God's power, for after Adam and Eve have eaten the forbidden fruit, . . . "the Lord God called to the man, and said to him, 'Where are you?' And he said, 'I heard the sound of thee in the garden, and I was afraid, because I was naked; and I hid

---

[15]*Christ and Adam: Man and Humanity in Romans 5*, trans. by T. A. Smail (New York: Collier Books, 1962), pp. 74-75.

myself.' He said, 'Who told you that you were naked? Have you eaten of the tree of which I commanded you not to eat?' " (Genesis 3:9-11). Humanity, estranged from God, our Creator, with God's image obscured, recognizes God's call, but also requires to be renewed in Christ, for "He is the image of the invisible God, the first born of all creation" (Colossians 1:15).

Who is this person who reflects God's person, rebels against His command, remembers his divine origin, and must be renewed? Although many would state that it is anthropocentric arrogance and human *hubris*, the Genesis creation account indicates in Chapter One that we are the pinnacle of divine creation which ascends chronologically from the creation of the firmament and the waters, through the dry land, vegetables, birds, sea monsters, and every living creature, to the crowning creation of humanity on the sixth day; and in Chapter Two, the account *begins* with our creation, indicating that humankind enjoys thematic priority in the order of creation.

Genesis 1:26-28, 2:7, and 2:21-22 are key passages. Notice first in v. 26 that man (Adam) is created in God's image (tzelem) and likeness (demuth). Since they are immediately given dominion over the world, humanity is to be distinguished from lower animal life. This dominion is not to become tyranny, for which some contemporary ecological critics of the Jewish-Christian tradition have blamed us, for in Genesis 2:15 where God commands Adam to till and keep the garden, the work translated "till" is (abhad), which comes from the same root as the word translated "servant" in the Isaiah suffering servant passages. Thus, man is to till (serve) the land in his lordship.

In Genesis 1:27 gender is distinguished; thus humanity includes male and female in mutual relationship. This relational aspect is reinforced through the body and sexuality, for (*zakhar* = male) possibly means "sharp or pointed" indicating phallic presence, and (*neqabhah* = female) in its root meaning signifies "to bore, to pierce." Humanity in its genderification, then, shares a mutual dependence on the transcendent God, as well as on each other. Since man also in 2:20 "gave names to all cattle, to the birds of the air, and to every beast of the field," the image of God is intellectual and cerebral; and the imperative in 1:28 to "be fruitful and multiply" accentuates the complementary genderic bodiliness.

In 1:27 we are told that we are formed from dust; but here the breath (ruach) of God invigorates the body, and humanity becomes (hayah = the verb "to be") a living soul (nephesh). The Hebrew psychology lacks precise terminology, for (nephesh) includes mind, feeling, inclination and reason. Even animals have nephesh, the vital life principle that is not always clearly distinguished from ruach, God's life-giving breath or spirit. Suffice it to say that our nephesh or life vitality originates in and depends upon God's ruach (spirit); we are open to God's presence, but we do not create Him out of our imagination or infant neurosis. Further, our relation to the sovereign God who placed us in the world gives the lie to Skinnerian determinism, for it is the source of the fertile brilliance of Skinner himself, by which he thought it possible and necessary to move "beyond freedom and dignity!"

In 2:21-25 the relational, mutual and sexual partnership is strengthened in the following ways: (1) Woman is taken from man's rib, indicating the intrinsic goodness of the body; (2) Adam is asleep, indicating that the source of woman is God, also, for Adam wakes up and accepts and confirms what God had created; he does not create it himself; (3) Adam, the male, does not know himself as such, until he sees a woman, at which time he declares, "she shall be called woman (ishah) because she was taken out of man (ish)." In v. 24, when we are told that a man and his wife should become one flesh (basar), the whole person is meant, for in biblical thought, and body are indeed distinguished, but both comprise a single unity, as when the Psalmist declares, "My flesh (basar) also shall see God" (16:9), meaning the whole person.

In the New Testament, this wholistic psychology is confirmed by Paul in Romans 12:1, for he uses the word "body" (ta somata = plural) when he exhorts us to "present our bodies, our full selves, or whole selves, body, soul, mind, and spirit, as a living sacrifice to God which is our reasonable (logiken) service or worship." And Jesus, the logos, in Matthew 22 and Mark 12 requires that the whole person—body, soul, mind, and spirit or "heart, soul, mind, and strength"—must be united in love toward God, self, and neighbor. The New Testament further heightens the soul-body unity of the person by listing the works of the flesh as both sensual and rational; in Galatians 5:19-20 Paul states: "Now the works of the flesh are plain: immorality, impurity, licentiousness, idolatry, sorcery, enmity, strife, jealousy, anger, selfishness, dissension, party spirit, envy, drunkenness, carousing, and the like." In addition, in Romans 13:14, the lusts of the flesh are much more than sensuality: "let us conduct ourselves becomingly in the day, not in reveling and drunkenness, not in debauchery and licentiousness, not in quarreling and jealousy. But put on the Lord Jesus Christ, and make no provision for the flesh, to gratify its desires." In these two passages, the word for flesh is *sarx*, which means the whole person hostile or indifferent to God's image, judgement, and command; the fleshly person in the New Testament is the whole human personality—body, soul, and spirit—wrongly motivated and totally seduced.

The New Testament also uses (psyche) and (pneuma) to refer to the intellectual, psychic, and transcendent nature of persons. Pneuma denotes the whole human personality; for example, in II Corinthians 7:1 and I Corinthians 5:3a, where Paul writes "for though absent in body I am present in spirit (pneumati)." But pneuma may also refer to that aspect of man that survives death with his transformed body: Matthew 27:50, "And Jesus cried again with a loud voice and yielded up his spirit." Compare also, Acts 7:59, "And as they were stoning Stephen he prayed, 'Lord Jesus, receive my spirit.' " The use of psyche is various; at times it means a higher level of psychic life: I Corinthians 15:45, "Thus it is written, 'The first man Adam became a living being; the last Adam became a live-giving spirit' "; psyche is used for "living being," pneuma for "spirit." But psyche can also refer to the higher human powers (intelligence, will) as opposed to the lower (feelings and appetites).

It would be impossible and irresponsible to discuss human

personality in the Bible without noting that all of us—every one of us and every aspect of each of us, of the individual human being—is flawed and wounded by sin; thus Cain slew Abel, David slept with Bathsheba and murdered Uriah, and Peter denied our Lord. "All we like sheep have gone astray; we have turned every one to his own way" (Isaiah 53:6a-b). In solidarity with Adam, we all sin; that is, we do not become sinners by sinning, but we sin because we are sinners. The Adamic nature that we all share means that a person may be guilty, even though he does not feel that he is; and a woman may feel guilty, even though she may not be; and vice versa. Although psychology and faith are required to help all of us, psychology largely helps the person who feels unnecessarily guilty, while biblical truth corrects and renews the proud man or woman who arrogantly imagines that he or she is not accountable to God, who judges and loves and calls us all. Paul in Romans 1:20 and 2:1 informs us that we are all without excuse, and that whatever the nature of human personality psychologically considered, man needs radical renewal through the Second Adam, in whose image we are to be renewed and by which we are to be clothed.

IV. Conclusion: *Who* Is A Person

The question, finally, is not *what* is a person, which thingifies the deeply and uniquely personal qualities of God's created image within us, but "*Who* is a person?" God is the suprapersonal one who creates personal creatures; each person is a composite unity of body, soul, mind, and spirit. Further, such a creature is *liable*, in that he is responsible to and respondable to God and his neighbor; she is *loving* in that she needs to be loved and is loved by God's gratuitous agape, and she loves by the power of God's image in her. In addition, we are *longing*, for we *long* for the kingdom from which we are separated; and we *look* through a glass darkly, seeing in the neighbor penultimately and in Christ ultimately the glorious reflection of the personal God.

Professor Robert Coles has rather stridently called for a careful preservation of the Christian distinctives concerning personality; weary of the condescending attitude toward and the astonishing ignorance about religion of many secular psychologists who, at most, merely tolerate a patient's religious faith as the grid by which he screens out the painful events and realities of his life, and who grant such faith no truth claims; and wary of pastors who substitute "another gospel" for the Christian faith, he writes:

> I am tired, for instance, of the unwarranted, undeserved acquiescence some ministers (and alas, recently, priests as well) show to various "experts" who tell them about important "relationships" (talking about psychological jargon) and about "mental health" (whatever *that* is) and about the supposed "value" of religion (the height of condescension) in a person's "psychic economy." I am tired of watching ministers or priests mouth psychiatric pieties, when "hard praying" (as I used to hear it put in the rural South) is what the particular human being may want, and, yes, urgently require. I am tired of all the "value-free" declarations in the name of what is called "social science"; tired, too, of the complexities, ambiguities, and paradoxes of our moral life being swept into yet another "development scheme," with "stages" geared to ages.[16]

Victor Frankl has more calmly stated:

> As soon as we have interpreted religion as being merely a product of psychodynamics, in the sense of unconscious motivating forces, we have missed the point and lost sight of the authentic phenomenon. Through such a misconception, the psychology *of* religion, often becomes psychology *as* religion[17] in that psychology is sometimes worshiped and made an explanation for everything.[18]

---

[16]Coles, p. 70.

[17]Persons interested in this distinction should read Paul Vitz's *Psychology as Religion: The Cult of Self-Worship* (Grand Rapids: Wm. B. Eerdmans Publishing Co., 1977).

[18]Victor Frankl, *Man's Search for Meaning* (New York: Washington Square Press, 1968), p. 210.

The preacher has stated in Ecclesiastes 3:19-22:

> For the fate of the sons of men and the fate of beasts is the same; as one dies, so dies the other. They all have the same breath, and man has no advantage over the beasts; for all is vanity. All go to one place; all are from the dust, and all turn to dust again. Who knows whether the spirit of man goes upward, and the spirit of the beast goes down to the earth? So I saw that there is nothing better than that a man should enjoy his work, for that is his lot; who can bring him to see what will be after him?

That quest for such personal wisdom is asked again at the last supper—"Is it I?" A biblical view of personality declares, "yes, it is you—created, placed, judged, loved, called, and inspired by Him who works *order* out of *chaos*, creates mirrors instead of *mirages*, and who enables us to *tell the truth* about ourselves. Writing poetry in prison less than a year before his death, Dietrich Bonhoeffer asked and affirmed:

> Who am I? They mock me, these lonely questions of mine.
> Whoever I am, thou knowest, O God, I am thine.[19]

---

[19]Bonhoeffer, *Letters*, p. 222.

Personality Theorizing Within a Christian World View

Mary Stewart Van Leeuwen

Mary Stewart Van Leeuwen is professor of interdisciplinary studies at Calvin College in Grand Rapids, Michigan. Born in Ontario, Canada, she received her M.A. and Ph.D. from Northwestern University. She has conducted research in Africa as well as in Canada and the United States. She is the author of two books, *The Sorcerer's Apprentice: A Christian Looks at the Changing Face of Psychology* and *The Person in Psychology: A Contemporary Christian Appraisal*, and co-author of two others, *Knowing Ourselves: Reflexivity in Social Science* (in progress) and *Intergroup Relations*. Dr. Van Leeuwen's articles appear frequently in professional journals, and she lectures on a variety of Christian and psychological topics.

Although not a central concern of the present conference, in laying the groundwork for the construction of a Christian theory of personality, it has been necessary to document the indifference, if not the outright hostility, of contemporary personality theorizing towards a Christian world view. But the more positive agenda of the conference is the attempt to answer not merely the question, "Can there be a Christian theory of personality?", but also the more basic question, "Can there be Christian theories of personality?"

This is the more basic question because even among those who confess every clause of the Apostles' Creed, there are

---

Much of this paper is a revision of Chapters 5 and 10 of Mary S. Van Leeuwen, *The Person in Psychology: A Contemporary Christian Appraisal* (Grand Rapids, MI: Wm. B. Eerdmans Publishing Co., 1985).

bound to be individual and group differences in the way such a task is approached. We deceive ourselves if we believe that our social, cultural, and theological backgrounds will make no difference in the way, and the degree to which, we use Scripture as a source of control beliefs for personality theorizing.[1] Admittedly, such self-deception is still common among Anglo–American psychologists, many of whom exempt themselves from the laws of selective perception that they have so carefully shown to be at work in others. It has been observed that "the average psychologist seldom applies his [*sic*.] technical knowledge to himself. Ostensibly, his is the only immaculate perception!"[2] This, however, only underscores our obligation to articulate not only the assumptions which divide Christian from non-Christian personality theorists, but also those in-house differences which may divide us from each other.

We also deceive ourselves if we forget that, for many Christians, Scripture is *not* the sole, authoritative source from which to derive control beliefs for personality theorizing, but rather that Scripture is coequal with certain received traditions and present-day pronouncements by church authorities. This too is bound to make a difference in the process and the results of doing personality theorizing from a Christian perspective. Above all, we do ourselves no favor if we forget that at all times and in all places, we see through a glass darkly; consequently, our best efforts to apply a Christian world view to our personality theorizing are bound to yield results which are at best partial, and at worst larded over with sin, self-deception, and self-interest.

I begin with the above caveats not to promote skepticism or faintheartedness, but only to suggest that we must be ready to make haste slowly, and to avoid premature dogmatism, in the task of doing personality theorizing and research as Christians.

---

[1] See Nicholas Wolterstorff, *Reason Within the Bounds of Religion*, 2nd edition (Grand Rapids, MI: Wm. B. Eerdmans Publishing Co., 1984).

[2] Anthony C. Thiselton, *The Two Horizons* (Exeter, UK: Paternoster Press, 1980).

I mention them also in the hope of promoting an irenic spirit among those who feel called to such a task. I have suggested that differences in background, temperament, conviction, and specialization are bound to result in different emphases as we do our personality theorizing. From one point of view, this can be regarded as unfortunate — just as denominationalism can be regarded as evidence of the tragic and sinful fragmentation of the church, which Christ specifically prayed would remain united (John 17:20-23). From another point of view, however, such pluralism can be seen as at least neutral, and perhaps even healthy. Even the Roman Catholic church, although united under a single hierarchy, retains a plurality of emphases in its various orders and lay movements. This suggests that, in our human finitude, none of us can cover all the bases adequately; consequently, in our task as personality theorists, we may as well be ready to accept help from fellow believers, and from nonbelievers in whom we discern that God's common grace is at work.[3]

Having made these preliminary remarks, let me now outline the three points around which the remainder of my presentation will be structured. First of all, it is true, as I have said, that we should make haste slowly in the task of filling in the details of a Christian personality theory, then perhaps a useful, *prior* task would be to look at the process of personality theorizing *as a whole* and to see what it is trying, at least implicitly, to accomplish. Salvatore Maddi of the University of Chicago is the one theorist who has been both bold and thorough enough to come up with such a "metatheory" — that is, a theory about the nature and scope of personality theorizing *per se*, and a resulting typology of current theories which he categorizes in terms of this metatheory.[4] Maddi's scheme has evidently been a helpful one to the Anglo-American psychology community, as the text in

---

[3] See Arthur Holmes, *The Idea of a Christian College* (Grand Rapids, MI: Wm. B. Eerdmans Publishing Co., 1975).

[4] Salvatore R. Maddi, *Personality Theories: A Comparative Analysis*, 4th edition (Chicago, IL: Dorsey Press, 1980).

which he lays it out is now in its fourth edition. A working knowledge of his scheme would be helpful to Christian students, critics, and architects of personality theory as well. So my first task will be to introduce you to the contours of Maddi's metatheory and typology of existing personality theories.

Having done that, my second task will be a preliminary application of Maddi's scheme to a Christian theory—or perhaps I should say "prototheory"—of personality. That is to say, I will try to show that it is possible to talk about a biblical model of personhood using the categories suggested by Maddi with the result that comparisons and contrasts of this model with other theories of personality can be made. In attempting such an exercise I am not suggesting that my conclusions are the only possible ones that a Christian could come to. Nor am I suggesting that all Christians should do their personality theorizing within Maddi's framework, although I believe it to be a theologically defensible one for reasons which will become apparent. I see this exercise merely as a preliminary effort to show how Christian control beliefs can interact with existing concepts in personality theory in a way that does justice to the latter without necessarily compromising the former. It is a tentative platform, open to revision and/or addition by others.

Maddi's Metatheory of Personality

Henry Murray, an early personality theorist at Harvard, once remarked that the entire enterprise of personality theorizing is centered around the affirmation that every person is in some respects (a) like *all* other persons; (b) like *some* other persons; and (c) like *no* other person.[5] When phrased in this manner, I think we can see a clear relationship between personality theory and that area of theology traditionally known as the doctrine of man. Personality theories, whatever else they do, make general statements about human nature: they postulate, explicitly and

---

[5]Henry A. Murray, in *Personality in Nature, Society and Culture*, Henry A. Murray and Clyde Kluckholn, eds. (New York: Knopf, 1948), p. 35.

sometimes implicitly, the irreducible motives, abilities, and liabilities that are assumed to be distinctively human. Many go on to theorize about group differences—between men and women, for example, or between broadly defined personality "types" such as Jung's intraverts and extraverts, or Freud's oral, anal, and phallic personality types.[6] Finally, at the most differentiated level, personality theories may suggest ways of mapping unique trait-constellations in individuals through the use of psychometric techniques.

For the theologian, the doctrine of man, or the doctrine of persons, is constructed on the same three levels. Systematizing from Scripture, it tries to say what it is that is uniquely and irreducibly human, partly by exegeting what is meant by that intriguing and elusive biblical phrase, "made in the image of God." The doctrine of persons has also distinguished between two large subgroups of human beings, the regenerate and the unregenerate, or those who have responded to the salvific call of God and those who have not. Finally, at least on the implicit level, the doctrine of persons has something to say about individual differences, inasmuch as it assumes without favor the importance of each individual life, and concedes that even within their common imaging of God, human beings exhibit varieties of gifts and talents which they are to exercise as diverse members of the church.[7]

In attempting to relate the task of the personality theorist to that of the theologian considering the doctrine of persons, Maddi's scheme offers us a framework which helps to show (whether he intended it to or not) that all personality theorizing is an anthropological and, indeed, a covertly religious endeavor. That is to say, it shows us that each personality theory is an attempt to erect an alternative doctrine of the person. This is

---

[6]Sigmund Freud, *New Introductory Lectures in Psychoanalysis*, trans. by J. H. Spratt (New York: Norton, 1933).

[7]As used in psychology, the phrase "individual difference" actually refers to *group* differences: men vs women, analytic vs intuitive thinkers, engineers vs artists, etc. But I am using the phrase in its literal sense, to designate personality differences between single individuals.

not to say that, in doing so, every such theory is totally antithetical to the Christian doctrine of the person, thereby rendering it completely useless to the Christian student of psychology: I will argue that non-Christian theories of personality may have their most basic categories improperly *ordered* from a Christian point of view, yet still contain valuable insights about personhood if these are relocated at lower levels. For either task—that of ferreting out what is at odds with a Christian analysis, *or* discerning what is redeemable in a given personality theory—Maddi's metatheoretical analysis is a useful tool.

Core, Peripheral, and Developmental Statements in Personality Theory

I have pointed out that personality theories are attempts to describe and explain both the commonalities and differences among human beings—to say something both about human nature in general and about the origin and nature of group and individual differences. When a theory refers to things that are claimed to be common to all people—to inherent attributes of humanness that exercise a pervasive and relatively stable influence throughout life—it is making, in Maddi's terms, a *core statement* about personality: "It is in core theorizing that the personologist makes a major statement about the overall directionality, purpose, and function of life."[8] (Refer to Figure 1 and Table I.) Thus, for example, Freud held that instinctual gratification and the avoidance of psychic pain and guilt were the core, organismic tendencies of all human beings. Alfred Adler theorized that the human core tendency was the striving toward superiority or perfection, while Abraham Maslow said that it was the urge to actualize all of one's inherent potential.

In essence, what Maddi identifies as the core tendencies of any personality theory are those uniquely human requirements, or overall *directionalities* which, in the mind of the theorist, are so basic as to be common to all people. A core tendency is not required to have conscious awareness in Maddi's scheme and,

---

[8]Maddi, *Personality Theories*, p. 14.

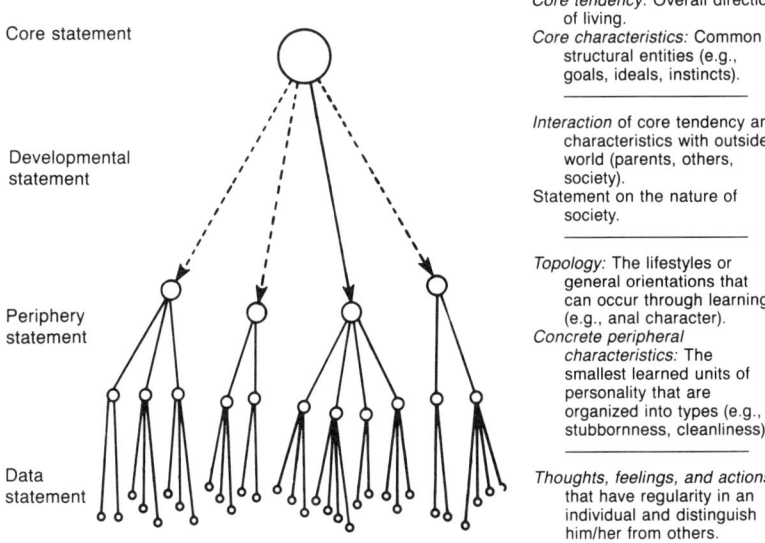

Figure 1. Maddi's schematic representation of the structure of personality theories. The single solid line between the core statement and the periphery statement indicates that each theorist postulates an ideal course of postnatal development resulting in an ideal type, or character. (From Maddi, *Personality Theories*, p. 16, reprinted with the permission of the publisher [see footnote 4].)

Table I
A Summary of Maddi's Typology of Personality Theories

Basic Type	Subtypes	Representative Theorists
I. Conflict Model	A) Psychosocial Version B) Intrapsychic Version	Sigmund Freud, Henry Murray, Otto Rank, Carl Jung, Andras Angyal
II. Fulfillment Model	A) Actualization Version B) Perfection Version	Carl Rogers, Abraham Maslow, Alfred Adler, Gordon Allport, Erich Fromm, various existential theorists
III. Consistency Model	A) Cognitive Dissonance Version	George Kelly, David McClelland
	B) Activation Version	Donald Fiske, Salvatore Maddi

indeed, being so general and all-encompassing, usually does not. Rather, it is a pervasive "tropism" (to borrow a biological term) which affects all behavior and thought in a general way. In its service will develop, throughout the life of the individual, more individually unique and specific *motives*—i.e., learned, conscious goals and proactive, intellectual strategies which, although usually consistent with core tendencies, do not express them directly.

Core theorizing also includes what Maddi calls the *core characteristics*—structural entities common to all persons and implied by the core tendency or tendencies. Thus, if one theory's core tendency is instinct gratification and avoidance of psychic pain, its core characteristics, assumed to be present in all persons, may comprise a list of the mechanisms through which these tendencies are optimized. Freud's id, ego, and superego give us an example of such a list. Or if another theory's core tendency is the actualization of human potential, a theoretical list of those potentials (such as Maslow's "need hierarchy," which includes emotional, social, and cognitive elements) comprise the core characteristics of the theory. Core characteristics can be conceived in terms of common human goals, ideals, or psychic structures, depending on the theorist. But the important things about them are, first, like core tendencies they are considered to be uniquely human and humanly universal and, second, unlike core tendencies they express *structure* rather than *direction*. That is, they are invoked to express presumed "what" of the generic human personality, rather than its "whither," or its overall orientation.

At this point I think it would be useful to return to the parallel task of the theologian attempting a theoretical elaboration of the doctrine of persons. Conservative theologians have distinguished between what they call the *broad* and the *narrow* image of God in persons.[9] In the broad image, they include

---

[9] See, for example, G. C. Berkhouwer, *Man: The Image of God*, trans. by Dirk W. Jellema (Grand Rapids, MI: Wm. B. Eerdmans Publishing Co., 1962).

those abilities and motives which distinguish human beings from other species—facets of humanness which have been conjectured over the centuries to include any or all of rationality, self-consciousness, dominion, sociality, sexual complementariness, and the quest for meaning.[10] The narrow image, by contrast, refers to the core tendency or directionality toward (or, by its absence, against) the worship and service of God.

This distinction between broad and narrow images was developed, in part, to deal with the question of the continuity of God's image in human beings after the fall. To this question traditional theology has given us a twofold response: yes, they write, the *broad* image persists in everyone despite the fall. Human beings are still unique imagers of God, whatever motives and capacities this may be said to include. But in the *narrow* sense, by which is meant the orientation of one's entire life God-ward, human beings did indeed lose an essential aspect of the *imago Dei*, restoration of which is only possible through Christ. I think you can see that there is a methodological parallel with Maddi's metatheory in all this: Maddi's idea of the *core tendency* parallels the theological concept of the *narrow* image or its absence, while his *core characteristics* parallel the theological concept of the *broad* image.[11] More on this a little later, when I will try to use Maddi's categories in a kind of "prototheory" of personality from a Christian perspective. For the moment, however, let us continue with our description of Maddi's scheme.

You should be able to see by now that it is in the core state-

---

[10]A good summary can be found in Cornelius Plantinga, Jr., "Images of God" (paper given at the Wheaton Conference on Christian Theology in a Post-Christian Age, Wheaton, IL, March 1985).

[11]The notion of "structure" versus "direction" to express the broad versus the narrow image of God has also been developed in a slightly different way by H. Evan Runner in his "Scriptural Religion and the Political Task," *Christian Perspectives* (Hamilton, Canada: Guardian Publishers, 1962). For a more accessible treatment, see also Malcolm Jeeves, R. J. Berry, and David Atkinson, *Free to Be Different: Varieties of Human Behavior* (Grand Rapids, MI: Wm. B. Eerdmans Publishing Co., 1984), especially the chapters by Atkinson.

ment of a theory (including statements about a core tendency plus some core characteristics) that a personality theorist tells us what he or she believes is most distinctively and universally human. But Maddi also suggests that every theory of personality makes (or should make, in the service of completeness) what might be called a *peripheral statement*. It is at this level that the theorist goes on to distinguish the personality styles that are believed to distinguish groups and individuals from one another, beyond the common human heritage represented by the core tendency and the core characteristics. It is at this level that the theorist describes the personality styles and traits he or she believes most clearly distinguish groups and individuals from each other. At the most individual level, there are *concrete peripheral characteristics* — more traditionally known as personality traits — which refer to individual aspects of a person's style, for example, timidness, generosity, affiliativeness, stubbornness, etc.; the relevant list and the terms used vary from theorist to theorist. In Maddi's scheme, these are the smallest, *learned* units of personality, although others (including myself) might argue that genetic predisposition interacts with learning to make some traits more likely than others to appear in specific individuals.

Regularly associated bundles of traits may be organized into specific personality *types* — that is, lifestyles or characteristic orientations acquired by virtue of exposure to certain common developmental patterns, especially in the course of early family life. For example, Freud distinguished among oral passive, oral aggressive, anal passive, anal aggressive, phallic, and genital character types; Jung distinguished intraverts from extraverts; and Otto Rank wrote about artistic versus neurotic personality types. Different theoretical orientations lead to different "cuts" in the typology concept.

Finally, linking the core to the periphery of personality is what Maddi calls the theorist's *developmental* statement, which outlines the way in which the undifferentiated core tendency and characteristics interact with the social and physical environment to produce adult personality types. I have already alluded to the importance ascribed by most theorists to the family: the personality type displayed by any adult is almost always seen as heavily, if not exclusively, influenced by the type of family in which he or she was raised. In addition, all personality theories imply or specify what Maddi calls an *ideal personality type*, one that most fully expresses what the theorist believes to be the core tendency and core characteristics of human nature, and the result of supposedly ideal developmental conditions. Thus, Carl Rogers writes about the "fully functioning person" as his ideal type, one who respects, values, and knows (virtually) all there is to know about herself, and who as a result, values and supports others and is flexible and open to new experience. In contrast to Rogers, Freud insisted that even his ideal "genital character type" could not be free from unconscious defense mechanisms whose function it is to mediate the conflict between instinctual desires and societal prohibition; the best that could be hoped for, he wrote, is that this conflict can be contained via the mature defense mechanism of sublimation of the instincts.

This brings us to the end of our summary of Maddi's metatheory, or metastructure, of personality theories. In concluding it, perhaps two additional points should be made. The first is that Maddi's scheme is, in effect, *his own* "ideal type" for a logically coherent and complete personality theory, regardless of the theoretical direction taken in it. Many theories are lopsided in their stress on one or another of the core, peripheral, or developmental statements. Nor does Maddi suggest that a theory must be complete on all levels before being offered for consideration. But he does suggest that the most useful theories, from both a theoretical and an applied standpoint, are those which, regardless of their original emphases, continue toward greater completeness along the lines described above.

The second point is that this theoretical elaboration normally takes place through a variety of channels, as psychologists do psychometric assessments of people, practice psychotherapy, or conduct empirical research aimed at demonstrating aspects or implications of a particular theory. All of these activities are grist for the theoretical mill. But Maddi readily appreciates (more than most Anglo-American psychologists) that the opposite is also the case: psychologists cannot help but conduct their research and applied activities according to their preferred world view and its implied theory of personality; this is clear from the examples just cited of Rogers's and Freud's ideal personality types. Maddi writes:

> When you assess a person's personality, you are working with a particular explicit or implicit sense of typology and its component, concrete peripheral characteristics. This is so because it is here that a personality theory permits pinpointing of differences among persons. . . . When you attempt to do psychotherapy, you must decide, on the basis of your view of human nature (core of personality) and the particular peripheral personality confronting you (is it ideal or not?) what is to be done. Looked at this way, psychotherapy is also a special case of development, so the therapist's view of development is also involved.[12]

Here is a rare personality theorist who recognizes the inevitable metaphysical underpinnings of his work. Maddi is in effect conceding that the theorist's prescientific convictions about human nature, its ideal unfolding and its ideal endpoint cannot help but influence his or her research and applied activities. Moreover, after reviewing a total of twenty-two major and minor personality theories, he concludes that their theoretical orientations are of only three basic types, although each type seems also to divide into two subtypes. Typologies of this sort, he concedes, are always risky, inasmuch as many of the elements one is dealing with defy neat classification in one or another single category. Nevertheless, Maddi's is a useful typology for Christian students who wish to compare personality theories with each other at the level of world view concerns, and also to compare them with theological elaborations of the doctrine of persons. So let us look briefly at Maddi's typology of personality theories in anticipation of using it as an alternative way to express the Christian doctrine of persons.

---

[12]Maddi, *Personality Theories*, pp. 16-17.

Maddi's Typology of Personality Theories

Broadly speaking, Maddi contends that one can classify any personality theory as being *conflict*-oriented, *fulfillment*-oriented, or *consistency*-oriented, depending on the theorist's basic view of human nature and of the social and physical milieu in which it unfolds and with which it must continue to reckon in adulthood. (Also see Table I, p. 177.)

In the first of these, the *conflict model*, human nature is seen in terms of a perpetual opposition between two great, unchanging forces, with life at best a compromising balance between the two, and at worst an unsuccessful attempt to deny one or the other. Sometimes, as with Freud and his later disciples, the conflict is seen as *psychosocial* in nature, with the biological instincts of the individual at war with the demands of organized society. Alternately, in the second subtype, the conflict may be seen as occurring completely within the individual—as being *intrapsychic* in character, and reflecting a profound ambivalence with which all persons are said to struggle. A classic example is Otto Rank's theory, according to which all human functioning is ultimately traceable to what is known as the "schizoid paradox": the tension between wanting to be unique (but at the risk of being alone), and wanting to be part of a group (but at the risk of losing one's identity).[13]

By contrast with the conflict model, the second major type of personality theory—the *fulfillment model*—assumes only one great force for human nature to respond to and locates it within each individual. Life then becomes, in its ideal unfolding, the progressively greater expression of this force. Conflict is *possible* within this model (the force can be thwarted in various ways), but is not *inevitable*. This model also divides into two subtypes. In the *actualization* version the "great force" is likened to a genetic blueprint that determines the individual's capabilities and additionally urges him on toward complete development. Abraham Maslow is probably the best-known

---

[13]Otto Rank, *The Trauma of Birth* (New York: Harcourt, Brace, 1929).

American theorist of this genre; indeed, his ideal personality type, the "self-actualizing person," has become something of a catchphrase among many readers of popular psychology.[14] Carl Rogers is another example of a fulfillment theorist of the actualization genre.[15]

Alternately, the *perfection* version of the fulfillment model places less stress on innate capabilities operating under their own momentum and more upon active striving toward ideals of what is noble and meaningful in life. The "great force" in this version is the *motivation* to strive toward such ideals, regardless of whether or not one's native endowments are perfectly in tune with that end. The theories of Alfred Adler and various existential psychologists (*e.g.*, Médard Boss, Victor Frankl, Ludwig Binswanger) are current examples of this approach; Gordon Allport and Erich Fromm seem to be primarily perfection theorists, but with something of an actualization orientation as well.[16]

The third and final kind of personality theory Maddi terms the *consistency model*, according to which the single universal and most formative influence on all persons is feedback from the external world. If such feedback is consistent with what one has known before or with what one expects, a state of quiescence reigns. But inconsistency produces tension which results in psychic pressure to decrease this uncomfortable state. Human life is thus viewed as an endless attempt to maintain consistency. In this model, the inevitable tension of the conflict orientation is rejected, as is the fulfillment model's presumption of either predetermined capacities or chosen ideals as blueprints for living. That is, the *content* of beliefs or capacities is not what is important in this model, but rather the *process* of balancing expectations against reality in the attempt to keep them consistent with one another.

---

[14]Abraham H. Maslow, "A Theory of Metamotivation," in *Nebraska Symposium on Motivation*, M. R. Jones, ed. (Lincoln, NE: University of Nebraska Press, 1955).

[15]Carl R. Rogers, *On Becoming a Person* (Boston: Houghton-Mifflin, 1961).

[16]See Maddi for the basic bibliographical references on these theorists.

Of the two subtypes in this model, the *cognitive dissonance* version holds that the inconsistency with which we all struggle is always cognitive in nature: two thoughts, perceptions, or values may be experienced as "dissonant," or more often it is an *expectation* that is in conflict with an actual *experience*. The resulting dissonance must then be reduced by reinterpreting one or another of the elements involved. The theories of George Kelly and David McClelland are in this tradition.[17] In the *activation* version of the consistency model, it is not cognitive elements that we strive to keep consistent, but rather a habitual and an actual level of bodily tension, or "activation." This is a homeostatic model which postulates that if events underexcite us relative to an accustomed level of activation, the resulting state of boredom will produce an impulse toward greater stimulation. Conversely, if events overexcite us in comparison with habitual levels of activation, the resulting stress will become the impulse to correct downward to the accustomed level. Maddi himself, working with psychologist Donald Fiske, has advanced this kind of personality theory[18] — but recall that it is Maddi's analysis of personality theories *in general*, and not his own preferred theory in particular, that is the primary focus of this discussion. What is most significant about consistency theories as a group is that the *content* of beliefs and activities is deemed less important than the *process* of reducing inconsistency *per se*, which is seen to be the core tendency of human nature.

Core Statements about Personality from a Biblical Perspective

You may have noted that in the preceding section I have concentrated on the core statements of each of the three broad

---

[17]George A. Kelly, *The Psychology of Personal Constructs*, Vol. 1 (New York: Norton, 1955); David C. McClelland, *Personality* (New York: Dryden, 1951).

[18]Donald W. Fiske and Salvatore R. Maddi, eds., *The Functions of Varied Experience* (Homewood, IL: Dorsey Press, 1961).

types of theory, because this is the level of discourse that first concerns most Christians—*i.e.*, the level at which statements are made concerning what all human personalities have in common. This leads us to an interesting question: is it possible to express the basic contours of the doctrine of persons using the categories Maddi has suggested? Furthermore, can we legitimately do so, not losing theological essentials in the process of translation? I suggest that the answer to both questions is yes, and that such an exercise can help us to clarify what Wolterstorff has called our Christian control beliefs—those basic assumptions about the world and human nature by which we are aided in understanding theories in psychology and evaluating them in order to accept, reject, or possibly adapt them.[19] The following is a very preliminary attempt to do this.

The narrow, process orientation of the consistency model would seem to render it immediately incompatible with a biblical anthropology, and this suggests that our first task is that of deciding whether a biblical perspective on the core of personality is best seen in terms of conflict or fulfillment. But even as we ask this question, there is a further complication to consider. For the Bible alludes not only to the inborn personality heritage common to all persons, but speaks also of the possibility of a "second birth," and a completely "new creation." So even as we speak of our common, human core, we must also (distinct from all other personality theories) hold open the possibility that, through the grace of God, this very core tendency can be changed and that moreover, this can happen during any phase of the individual's life span. However, I believe there is a way of conceptualizing this without ending up with a theory that is so awkward as to leave no room for dialogue with other theoretical traditions, or for acknowledgement of possible truths they may have uncovered.

Let us begin with a consideration of the common heritage of all human beings who, as the Bible puts it, have been born "in Adam." Saint Augustine wrote that God made us for himself,

---

[19]Wolterstorff, *Reason*.

and that all human hearts would be restless until they found their rest in him. This is as succinct an expression of the core tendency as a Christian could ask for—provided we understand by it that human hearts are not merely restless, but *rebellious* as well. From a biblical perspective, the core tendency that all persons share from birth is in the nature of a *conflict* between total fidelity to the God who created us and total concentration on oneself or any other of a variety of idols that we try to force into the God-shaped void of which Augustine wrote. But recalling that Maddi referred to two different types of conflict theory, we are further led to ask whether this basic conflict is a purely *internal* one, with two parts of ourselves (the God-oriented and the idol-oriented) at war with each other, or an *internal-external* conflict (analogous to Freud's postulated war of the instincts with societal limits)—that is, with our inborn tendency one of total rebellion against God until He intervenes with the grace that brings about conversion?

Already we can see how Maddi's categories may be too simple for us, since the Bible seems to imply that the conflict may be of *both* sorts. When Paul writes in Romans 1 of the wicked who "suppress the truth," he seems to be saying that the unconverted are in a state of total war with God, not wanting to respond to *any* of the hints about his nature and lordship that he supplied. Yet the same Paul preached to the Athenians about the "unknown god" whom they *already* worshipped in a confused way, and announced, "What you therefore worship as unknown, this I proclaim to you" (Acts 17:22-30).

So how might we conceptualize this ambivalent core tendency, which seems on the one hand to be between our own inclinations and God's call, and on the other hand to be within ourselves, or between two warring halves of ourselves? Perhaps a helpful analogy would be to think of the core tendency in terms of a balance scale. That is, human beings are born with the potential to recognize and even be vaguely attracted to the call of God (one side of the balance); yet for the most part they suppress it, and cannot do otherwise in the absence of divine intervention to change their core. In other words, the balance of this intrapsychic conflict is so decisively tipped toward rebellion that neither intuitive knowledge of God nor any intermittent interest in Him is enough to swing the balance the other way.

Yet I believe that we must still see this conflict as basically *intra*psychic; for if unregenerate human beings were *totally* against God and everything he stands for at every moment of life, it is hard to see how common grace could ever operate — that common grace which Calvin defined as "the merciful disposition or act of God that holds the spread of corruption in check"[20] and without which unregenerate persons would be devils, not human beings, since none of the core characteristics by which they continue to image God could ever be used in a creationally normative way.

What, then, *are* the "core characteristics" by which, in the systematic theologian's terms, human beings broadly "image God"? I think it should be pointed out to begin with that there has been a distinct tendency among modern theologians to avoid this question completely. G. C. Berkhouwer, summarizing the thrust of European theology in the twentieth century, concedes that the distinction between "broad" and "narrow" images (*i.e.*, what I have been labeling structure versus direction, or core characteristics versus core tendency) is important in that it reminds us that even unregenerate human beings are still uniquely human. But he resolutely refuses to systematize a *list* of essential, human core characteristics from Scripture, concluding rather that

> the word of God is concerned precisely [*i.e., only*] with the whole man in his relation to God. Thus the various terms and concepts it makes use of give us no exactly expressed or scientifically useful definitions, but rather are related always to [this] same basic reality of humanness.... It is indeed true that the various aspects of humanness are spoken of in extremely varied ways, but ... the biblical witness makes use of this composition

---

[20]John Calvin, *The Institutes of the Christian Religion*, trans. by Henry Beveridge (Grand Rapids, MI: Wm. B. Eerdmans Publishing Co., 1957), 2:3:3.

as an anthropological given only incidentally, in order to speak of man as a whole.²¹

What this position amounts to is a reduction of the image of God only to the narrow image—to what Berkhouwer elsewhere calls "concretely visible sanctification" in the believer²² and by implication its absence in the unbeliever. In other words, it is an attempt to avoid taking a stand about any biblically based core characteristics in humankind as a whole. This is a position which I, as a Christian psychologist, find both questionable and theoretically unhelpful. Philosopher Stephen Evans has referred to it as

> the contemporary swing towards relational and away from substantial categories . . . [the view that] the uniqueness of the human person is not to be found in the possession of a soul of a certain type, or in a particular set of qualities which constitute the *imago*. Rather [it is said] human beings are special because of the relationships which they are part of . . . including especially [their] roles in relation to God.²³

Evans goes on to suggest that this purely relational anthropology, initiated during the Reformation and developed further in succeeding centuries and especially our own, is indeed important as "a theological barrier to human pride and autonomy."²⁴ It began as a Reformation rejection of the Catholic scholastic tendency to equate the image of God with an independent human rationality which predates the Fall and remains unaffected by it. The Reformers, by contrast, were suspicious of *any* qualities or virtues attributed independently to human beings,

---

[21]Berkhouwer, *Man*, pp. 199–200.
[22]*Ibid.*, p. 112.
[23]Stephen C. Evans, "Healing Old Wounds and Recovering Old Insights: Towards a Christian View of the Person for Today" (paper given at the Wheaton Conference on Christian Theology in a Post-Christian Age, Wheaton, IL, March 1985).
[24]*Ibid.*, p. 6.

stressing instead the total dependence of all human life and activity on God's sovereign providence and grace.

But although the Reformation position was theologically sound and a needed corrective, it is too one-sided: Catholic theologians rightly pointed out that such a position stripped God's human creation of all its value, and did inadequate justice to the basic dignity and value that even unregenerate human beings possess. Moreover, it was a position which made it hard to show how it is that Christ's redemptive work *restores* Creation, inasmuch as it holds that nothing is left of that fallen, human creation to *be* transformed. On this account, anything good or positive about human beings is merely an "imputed righteousness" which is completely external even to the life of the believer and, by extension, totally absent in the unbeliever.

Evans concludes (and I agree) that this is a dispute which has outlived its usefulness and that, in the end, we need *both* substantial *and* relational categories—*both* a theology of core characteristics *and* a theology of core tendency—to do justice to the image of God in all human beings. (In fact, a closer reading of both Catholic and Reformation theologies shows that at root each side realized this and argued only, in effect, that the other was lopsided in its emphasis.) Nevertheless, even though Protestant himself, Evans concludes that the bad effects of this controversy are still especially noticeable in Protestant theologies such as those summarized and espoused by scholars like Berkhouwer—theologies which refuse to take any kind of stand regarding human core characteristics. Writes Evans:

> The heart of the matter seems to me to be this. Whatever else the *imago* is, it must be a resemblance between God and human beings. I do not see how a mere relationship [such as dependence, acceptance] could be this resemblance. Whatever resemblance there is between God and human beings may be—indeed must be—*derived* from a relationship to God. But the relationship cannot itself be the resemblance.[25]

---

[25]*Ibid.*, p. 8.

And so we return to the knotty question as to what these core human characteristics comprise from a biblical perspective. Let it be pointed out that although Scripture does contain material which, when systematized, helps us to answer this question, it does not do so in a way that renders psychological and other social-scientific theorizing redundant. What the Bible rather gives us, in its journey through salvation history, are some broad categories in terms of which we should think about humanness and in light of which we can judge the adequacy of more systematic personality theories, especially as regards their core statement. In attempting to harvest the scriptural yield concerning human imaging of, or resemblance to God, theologian Neal Plantinga (also drawing on current biblical scholarship) points first to the theme of *accountable dominion* in the Genesis creation account. In these, human beings are seen as divinely "equipped to keep, control, and care for the earth.... Though servants to God, they are landlords to the rest of creation. They are at once God's agents and patented images, and their dominical agency is a part of the image of God."[26]

Note that, by itself, this is not so specific as the conclusion that all human beings have rational capacities of a certain quality or degree, or that they have freedom of choice and action, at least to some degree. But in order to have the accountable dominion of which Genesis speaks, in a way that animals have not, both of these more specific attributes would seem to be necessary. Thus, any personality theory which rejects or renders illusory the existence of a reflexive, problem-solving, human mind, or asserts no freedom, and hence no accountability in human activity (as does radical behaviorism, for example) is rightly to be seen as suspect by the Christian. Moreover, Plantinga notes, Psalm 8 places the theme of dominion side by side with the theme of *glory and honor*. Thus,

> All human beings carry by design a weight of glory ... they have weightiness, value, *dignitas*. They deserve due respect.... This

---
[26]Plantinga, "Images," pp. 3-4.

weight of glory calls to account the various greasy human degradations that smear the image. All sad indignities, indelicacies, indecencies, and pornographies of the human spirit are called to account. Every frightening video image of humans as slaves, snakes, slobs, or sleazebags; all attempts to objectify humans as mere bedfellows, manufacturing devices, career stepladders, or disposable inconveniences—all these things are called to account. For humans are Godlike. Because of the acids of sin they are nobility in ruins, but they are nobility who will, one way or another, live forever. They must therefore be handled with care, for [in C. S. Lewis' words], it is a serious thing to live in a society of possible gods and goddesses.[27]

It is not common for personality theories to trifle with human dignity. On the contrary, in the recent and lengthy heyday of behaviorism, personality theory was usually seen as the "poor country cousin" among psychological specialities, in part precisely because of its general refusal to espouse the biological and mechanical reductionisms then in vogue. The problem with personality theorizing has more often been the opposite, at least at the core level: it has tended (as Paul Vitz has graphically documented)[28] to promote the self-deifying impulse of human beings, especially in those theories of the fulfillment genre. Nevertheless, this does not justify throwing out the baby with the bathwater: human dignity *is* an irreducible aspect of the image of God, and is no respecter of race, sex, class, creed, or cleverness. Most current personality theorizing may indeed err on the side of self-deification, rather than reductionism—but the histories of Nazi Germany and South Africa serve as reminders that it does not take much to coopt both a society at large *and* its intelligentsia into agreeing that some human beings are less equal than others. So the assertion of human dignity as a core characteristic also functions as a criterion for evaluating the core statement of any personality theory.

---

[27]*Ibid.*, p. 11.
[28]Paul C. Vitz, *Psychology as Religion: The Cult of Self-Worship* (Grand Rapids, MI: Wm. B. Eerdmans Publishing Co., 1977).

Mary Stewart Van Leeuwen 193

The two core characteristics just mentioned—accountable dominion and dignity—would seem to focus on the image of God as merely *individual*. But Plantinga also leans heavily on the theme of *sociality*, *fellowship*, *mutuality* as another essential aspect of the image. This is suggested by the Genesis passage on men and women *jointly* (*i.e.*, in their interaction) imaging God (1:27), and in God's conclusion in 2:18 that it was not good for the first man to be alone without someone like himself to relate to. In the New Testament, the Johannine references to the Trinity itself as a fellowship of work, reciprocity, and even suffering (which the church on earth is to model) extend this theme even as they imply that basic, human sociality should show substantial healing under the sanctifying influence of the fruit of the spirit in believers. This too provides the Christian student with an essential control belief: any personality theory which views interpersonal attachments as mere "secondary reinforcers," acquired through association with basic biological necessities, or which sees human society only in grudging, social-contract terms, is a candidate for core revision, if not outright rejection.[29]

Finally, Plantinga intriguingly suggests that the need for *consistency* may even be part of the human core of personality—not as the single, contentless core *tendency* invoked by the consistency theories of personality previously mentioned, but rather as an essential core *characteristic* that can be used either with utmost effectiveness to rationalize rebellion against God, or conversely as an incentive toward progressive sanctification as the believer strives to bring his or her behavior more and more into line with the demands of New Testament living. The human core tendency, Plantinga agrees, is "incurably religious. [Human beings] want God even when they are not aware of it." But, he continues, "they hunger and thirst after righteousness so much that [as one core characteristic] they can seldom cease

---

[29]Plantinga also suggests that the very ability of humans to reproduce *other* images of God—*i.e.*, the capacity to procreate—also images God. See Plantinga, "Images," pp. 4–5.

rationalizing or scapegoating unrighteous behavior. . . . They strive for at least the *form* of godliness even in the midst of pathological wrongdoing. Human beings are incorrigibly concerned about their self-image."[30]

In summary, human core characteristics as reflected in Scripture seem to include *at least* accountable dominion, dignity, sociality, and a striving for consistency. With regard to the last of these, as long as the basic, intrapsychic conflict is tipped decisively against acknowledgement of God's lordship, human beings keep busy intellectually justifying (in ways most convincing to themselves, if not to others) the choices they make and the idols they choose to serve. And it seems that, more often than not, these idols are compulsive fixations on one or another of our own core characteristics, and as such not so much evil in themselves as a case of "worshipping the creation rather than the creator" (Romans 1:25). That is, we elevate what is merely a core *characteristic* to the status of a core *tendency* that dictates the shape of all other areas of our life, and which we follow at any cost. Thus, we "stand on our dignity" when it has long since ceased to be appropriate to do so; we reinterpret dominion as a mandate to ravage the earth, rather than to husband its resources in the process of discovering and applying its laws; we distort healthy sociality into mindless conformity or compulsive sexuality; we recognize our call to accountability, but in distorted ways, as when "honor among thieves" becomes a way of

---

[30]*Ibid.*, p. 3. Compare also David S. Myers's thesis in *The Inflated Self: Human Illusions and the Biblical Call to Hope* (New York: Seabury Press, 1980), in which he reviews the social psychological literature on attribution and concludes that people rationalize their own *misdeeds* as environmentally determined (and therefore nonaccountable) while crediting their positive achievements to their own self-generated effort and ability (and therefore deserving of praise). By contrast, their attributions concerning *other* persons' negative and positive accomplishments are *reversed*: they scapegoat others for their own misdeeds while tending to "explain away" their positive actions. All of which suggests a chronic inconsistency on the part of people's attempts to be consistent regarding attributions of virtue and sin. On the core concern of human beings to be perceived as doing the right thing—*i.e.*, to "advance their moral careers"—see Rom Harré, *Social Being: A Theory for Social Psychology* (Totowa, NJ: Rowman and Littlefield, 1980).

glossing over or even dignifying whatever counter-normative activities are being undertaken. But even in their distorted, parasitical forms, such human core characteristics can remind the Christian student of the centrality of the *imago Dei* in human personality.

Accounting for Conversion and Sanctification

Earlier I suggested the image of a balance scale to understand the universal, human core tendency as biblically understood — *i.e.*, the intrapsychic, "approach–avoidance" conflict that all persons experience with regard to God as an inevitable heritage from the Fall. I suggested that the balance of this conflict in all persons is so firmly tipped toward the avoidance of God's call that, without his direct intervention, whether early or late in life, none of our intermittent approach tendencies is ever sufficient to swing the balance the other way.

You can probably see that I am about to use the image of *reversed* weights to capture the idea of spiritual regeneration: it is through God's gracious intervention, and the person's acceptance of it, that the balance of the conflict is decisively reversed, and the core tendency changes from the impulse to worship idols to the desire to serve the God of the Scriptures. There are several advantages to this image of reversed weights as a way of talking about conversion. First of all, even prior to the reversal, it allows for the working of common grace in unbelievers: in them, although the felt weight of God's influence is insufficient to bring about the great reversal represented by conversion, that influence is still very real. Consequently, as Plantinga points out,

> all human beings are to be viewed not only seriously, but also hopefully. . . . All human beings are by creation children of God. Sin betrays and disrupts this relation, but it does not destroy it. Further, because Jesus Christ's redeeming work ranges universally across the human race (Romans 5:18), all humans are to be *seen* in Christ unless they give final and deci-

sive evidence to the contrary. They are to be regarded as brothers and sisters, as fellow children of God. They are to be called to the appropriate response of faith and obedience. And in any case we must try to find in them the signs, even the quirky and distorted ones, of *eros* for their maker, even when such signs are larded over with sin and self-deception.[31]

Second, this way of conceptualizing the changed core does not require alteration of the structure of human core *characteristics*, but only of the core *tendency*. In the person regenerated through salvation, accountable dominion, dignity, sociality, and the striving for consistency are now directed, however imperfectly, toward the service of God and his kingdom, rather than the service of idols. Third, the image of reversed weights allows room for progressive sanctification in the life of the Christian; the God-directed side of the balance may be only marginally (although decisively) heavier at conversion than the idolatrous side—but with time, the former will become heavier and heavier at the expense of the latter. By implication, this also allows room for the struggles with sin from which even mature Christians are not exempt; the idol-worshipping side, while in regression, continues to be influential as long as it has *any* degree of weight.

Finally, this conceptualization also allows for the occurrence of the "great reversal" at any point in a person's life span. This being the case, God's acceptance of our subsequent efforts is based not on the absolute amount of progress we make between conversion and death, but rather on the progress we make relative to the time of our conversion and the abilities with which we are endowed. This is a point strongly made by both the parable of the talents and the parable of the laborers in the vineyard (Matthew 20:1-16 and 25:14-30).

It can further be argued that, once conversion has occurred, this biblically based personality theory may be better understood as an *actualization* theory of the perfection variety, rather

---

[31]Plantinga, "Images," pp. 11-12. See also Neal Punt, *Unconditional Good News* (Grand Rapids, MI: Wm. B. Eerdmans Publishing Co., 1980).

than as a conflict theory. Perfection theories, Maddi writes, are "expressions of idealism."[32] The core tendencies they posit are always cast in terms of striving for the ideal expression of something. For Adler, it is the striving to overcome real or imagined inferiorities; for Allport and Fromm, it is the striving after an idealized expression of one's human nature. Likewise Paul, writing to the Philippian church, expressed his changed core tendency in terms of striving (however imperfectly) to be like Jesus Christ:

> I count everything as loss because of the surpassing worth of knowing Christ Jesus my Lord . . . [having] the righteousness from God that depends on faith; that I may know him and the power of his resurrection, and may share his sufferings, becoming like him in his death. . . . Not that I have already obtained this or am already perfect; but I press on to make it my own, because Christ Jesus had made me his own. . . . One thing I do: forgetting what lies behind and straining forward to what lies ahead, I press on toward the goal for the prize of the upward call of God in Christ Jesus (Philippians 3:8-14).

In the final analysis, I do not think it matters whether we use the "balance-scale" image or the "two-stage" image (*i.e.*, from a conflict theory before conversion to a perfection theory after it) to express a biblical "prototheory" of personality. Either way, what is finally important is that the theory does justice to: (1) the core *characteristics* by which all human beings image God; (2) the conflict-ridden, human core *tendency* (Will persons worship the living God, or substitute idols instead?); (3) the possibility of a very real change in this core tendency through conversion; and (4) the possibility of a progressive and substantial—but in this life never total—reorientation of our core characteristics toward the service of God during the Christian life.

Although the foregoing could be seen as the beginnings of a full-blown theory of personality, its primary purpose has been

---

[32]Maddi, *Personality Theories*, p. 118.

to show how Christian control beliefs can interact with existing concepts in personality theory in a way that does justice to the latter without compromising the former. In the course of this paper, it has been shown that it is possible to use many of the constructs suggested by personality theorists (*e.g.*, conflict, consistency, perfection) in developing a biblical view of personality, but that Christian control beliefs may lead us either to reinterpret the meaning of such constructs, or to assign them a different place in our own system than they have in others. Thus, personality theory gives us an expanded vocabulary with which to think about biblical anthropology and, conversely, a biblical understanding of the nature of personhood gives us insights with which to challenge, evaluate, adapt, or reject existing theories of personality. It is this kind of mutually influential dialogue that I have tried to exemplify at the level of personality theory's concern with the core tendency and core characteristics shared by all human beings.

A Christian Theory of Personality: Covenant Theory

Paul C. Vitz

Dr. Paul C. Vitz, professor of psychology at New York University, attended the University of Michigan where he earned Phi Beta Kappa honors. He received his Ph.D. from Stanford University. He is currently the director of New York University's newly established graduate program in the psychology of art. He is on the board of directors of the Fellowship of Catholic Scholars and the executive committee of the Catholic Commission on Intellectual and Cultural Affairs. Dr. Vitz is the author of *Psychology as Religion: The Cult of Self-Worship*, *Sigmund Freud's Christian Unconscious*, and many articles. His recent book, *Modern Art and Modern Science: The Parallel Analysis of Vision*, reflects his interest in the relationships between contemporary aesthetics and science. Other interests include Christian thought and the topics of personality theory, moral development, psychoanalysis, and counseling.

In my previous article some of the important context for a Christian theory of personality was described. Specifically, we saw that the major secular theories of personality are deeply imbedded in religious issues. Theorists like Freud, Jung, Adler, and Rogers were each personally involved in religion, especially Christianity, throughout their lives. Although most of these and other secular theorists have been hostile to Christianity, this does not mean that their thinking was not influenced by Christian theology. In fact, we saw that the Oedipus complex and much of Roger's humanistic psychology can be clearly understood as translations of Christian concepts from the transcendent world of theology into the natural world of psychology. We also noted some of the many ways in which psychology functions like a religion in people's lives; and, in addition, some of the antireligious consequences of the common philosophical assumptions of secular psychology were identified.

Before describing some of the major characteristics of a positive Christian psychology, I would like to begin with some important preliminary qualifications. I have often been a very hard critic of psychology,[1] but psychology is not entirely false by any means. It suffers primarily from a variety of contradictory, narrow, and usually false metaphysical assumptions, combined with similar weaknesses with respect to its moral and ethical positions. With these two major failings it is not surprising that much of psychology is antireligious. Nor is it surprising that no generally acceptable doctrine or theory of human psychology has developed. Instead psychology has fragmented into a complex mosaic of many different and conflicting psychologies. Into this confusion I believe Christianity can bring a major synthetic and integrating framework as well as quite specific theoretical concepts and important practical understanding.

More generally, I think that an appreciable amount of psychology (let's say one-quarter) is truly scientific. There is much that is relevant to psychotherapy in developmental and cognitive psychology that is obviously science. In the practice of psychotherapy there is some scientific knowledge as well. For example, separation anxiety (*e.g.*, Bowlby) exists, and it causes significant psychological pathology; also some families set up patterns of interpersonal behavior that are pathological, and that can be improved via psychotherapy. A Christian psychology should deal with this scientific knowledge about people.

In addition, much of the knowledge in psychology and in psychotherapy is not scientific, but nevertheless is true knowledge. The over-evaluation of traditional scientific understanding is a pathology of our culture, one that psychology has

---

[1]P. C. Vitz, *Psychology as Religion: The Cult of Self-Worship* (Grand Rapids, MI: Wm. B. Eerdmans Publishing Co., 1977).

traded on shamelessly, but nevertheless, our overemphasis on "scientific" knowledge is an intellectual sickness. Nonscientific knowledge needs to be appreciated and respected for its own sake. (Indeed, the great majority of our *true* knowledge is nonscientific.) Some of this knowledge is true in a permanent sense—like objective moral knowledge, and some of it is true only for our period of history and culture. (The latter is like knowledge about a game that exists only within culturally determined rules.) In both cases this knowledge is true in some important sense—and a Christian psychology must deal with it.

Of course, a large part (perhaps 50 percent) of so-called psychological knowledge in clinical psychology is not true, or very misleading in how it is understood. Here a Christian is in a very favorable critical position for cutting out much of the pseudo-understanding. In particular, much of this false knowledge is gnostic—but not all of it, of course. The real gnostic problem with psychology is not with what is claimed to be true but with what can be called the "gnostic impulse"—something that shows up mostly in metapsychology, or metascience. For example, the assumption that the self can save itself through knowledge is a central gnostic assumption. "If I can only gain insight into my problems then life will be fine." I call this the illusion of "self-salvation." It is important to keep in mind that this gnostic impulse and its slightly different expressions permeate much of today's physics and biology as well as psychology. It must be confronted—but we should not throw the baby of genuine knowledge out with the bathwater of the gnostic desire for self-salvation.

There is also a specifically Christian field of applied psychology. For example, forgiveness is a basic Christian concept and a duty (see below). Unfortunately many people want to forgive but don't know how. It is common in therapy to find people who say they have forgiven but haven't. Many of the barriers to forgiveness are psychological. There are probably stages in forgiveness that can be identified. The patient needs help in clearing the barriers. In this sense the Christian psychologist is called to use his knowledge to "make straight the way for the Lord."

Scripture identifies one of the gifts of the Spirit as the gift of counselling others.

As you see I claim there is a field of Christian psychology the purpose of which is to unpack the latent psychology found in Scripture and to coordinate that with valid psychological knowledge (of both the scientific and nonscientific kind). The gnostic danger of "salvation through knowledge" is always present—but that is true in *all* intellectual endeavors from theology to physics, yet we are called to use our minds. The best defense against gnosticism is prayer and humility. But, there will always be risk. Historically, intellectuals have been the chief heretics. With this frightening and humbling observation we turn to the task at hand.

The Origin of the Concept "Person"

To begin the rationale for a Christian concept of personality, let us consider some important historical background, taken largely from Müller and Halder.[2] As many psychologists know, the word "person" comes from the Latin "persona" which means mask, and also the theatrical role that went with the mask. (The Latin was probably first used as the best equivalent to a Greek word with the same meanings.) But the origin of the word "person" is not a significant thing: what *is* important is that the *concept* of a "person," which is unique to the Western world, was first introduced into Western thought as part of basic Christian theology. That is, the first use of the word for person in the modern sense arose out of the theology of the Trinity and of the Incarnation: God as three persons, and Christ as both the second person of the Trinity and as its perfect embodiment in human form. Now of course, in certain respects, the origin of the idea of a person is found in Judaism, where from the beginning God was understood as a person, and not merely as an abstraction. Yahweh was a personal God. But

---

[2]Mueller and Halder, "Person: Concept," in *Sacramentum mundi*, 4 (New York: Herder & Herder, 1969).

in any case, the concept of a person "remained unknown to ancient pagan philosophy and first appears as a technical term in early Christian theology. . . ." The concept of a "person" then continued to develop within the framework of Christian thought, for hundreds of years — and this concept of a person "still determines modern thinking to a great extent."[3]

More specifically, because we are made in the image of a trinitarian God, we are made to be *interpersonal*. The Trinity of Father, Son, and Holy Spirit is interpersonal and hence we are called to a loving, committed interpersonal relationship with God and others. That is, a covenant theory of personality claims that to an important extent we are created by our relationships with others. It is not by separation from others but by commitment to them that persons come into existence: to a large degree, we each are our interpersonal relationships.

It was after writing this that I was shown the same claim made by the theologian and historian of science, Thomas Torrance. In describing contemporary particle physics Torrance writes that particles are no longer thought of as separate elements, but ". . . we have come to think of particles as continuously connected together in dynamic fields of force where the interrelations between particles are part of what particles actually are."[4]

Torrance goes on to note explicitly that this kind of thinking first emerged in the early theology of the Trinity when the concept of person and God as three persons was being conceptualized. (Torrance also claims that the scientist and devout Christian James Clark Maxwell was able to propose his historic theory of the electromagnetic field because of the influence on his scientific thought of basic Trinitarian concepts.)

The notion of personality in its contemporary psychological and utterly secular sense is quite recent, being no more than fifty or sixty years old. In view of the antitheistic assumptions

---

[3]*Ibid.*, p. 404.
[4]T. Torrance, *The Mediation of Christ* (Grand Rapids, MI: Wm. B. Eerdmans Publishing Co., 1983), p. 58.

of modern personality theory, it is not surprising that these secular theories should end up by reducing the concept of a person to something like the pre-Christian pagan idea: that is, to an essentially naturalistic idea of the individual. As we shall see, the concept of a person and that of an individual are in many respects opposites. The pagan notion of an individual, for example, is lacking the dignity and spiritual dimension of the Judeo-Christian understanding of a person, which always implies, necessarily, that one is a person because he or she is made in the image of God. Indeed the widespread loss of respect for the person in recent decades—as in abortion, pornography, facism, etc.—can be attributed, in part, to the rise in prominence of the secular, modern pagan understanding of "personality" (really individuality)—which has no concept of our sacred nature.

A "Covenant Theory" of Personality

The point of this history is not just to identify the strongly Christian origin of the notion of person, but primarily to show its direct relevance to a concept of Christian personality which has yet to be explored by psychology—at least by modern psychology. The general situation can be summarized thus: Each human being is created in the image of God; true personality is the expression of this image, or divinely implanted "role," if you will; expression requires that the person attend to, and respond to, God—that is, each of us must love and cooperate with God. For the Christian this means loving and following—imitating—Jesus, who as the perfect incarnation of God gives us the model for expressing our latent, true personality. The fact that God was incarnate and dwelt among us gives the Christian the unique and enormously beneficial model of Jesus with whom to identify. The process of identifying with Jesus has both psychological and spiritual aspects to it.[5] The psychological aspects of this religious centering of personality are available for study. Many of the spiritual aspects, although intrinsically unavailable for study and experiment, have effects that can be readily observed—and can be contrasted with purely psychological characteristics. Psychology has learned to live with the mind-body problem, and it can learn to live with what might be called a mind-spirit problem as well.

The other, closely related, great interpersonal emphasis of a Christian theory of personality is the concern with, the love of, others; that is, the concern with committed or covenant relationships with others. The central psychological principle here is that personality is developed into its highest form through loving commitment to others. It is through *agape*: through serving others—even unto death—that the Christian personality grows and reaches its highest development. The very idea of commitment, of deep caring for another, of being bonded to another, is the exact opposite of so much of today's humanistic psychology. Today nothing must hinder the growth of the ego; nothing—no one—must restrict the autonomy of the individual. Perhaps James Bond of movie fame is the best example of this ideal—a man without any bonds with anyone. He appears to have no mother or father, no true friends; and certainly the whole idea of his relationship with women is to avoid commitment. Hugh Heffner is another familiar example of this kind of "personality." The idea that a man's personality is developed— "created," if you will—by bonds of commitment to others, is antithetical to all contemporary personality theory.[6]

---

[5] P. C. Vitz and J. Gartner, "Christianity and Psychoanalysis, Part 1: Jesus as the anti-Oedipus," *Journal of Psychology and Theology*, 12 (1984), 4-14; P. C. Vitz and J. Gartner, "Christianity and Psychoanalysis, Part 2: Jesus the Transformer of the Super Ego," *Journal of Psychology and Theology*, 12 (1984), 82-90.

[6] For a book-length documentation of psychology's widespread assumption of selfishness, see M. A. Wallach and L. Wallach, *Psychology's Sanction for Selfishness: The Error of Egoism in Theory and Therapy* (San Francisco: Freeman, 1983).

In creating a person, God initiates a covenant with each of us. The very bringing of a person into existence is a demonstration of God's covenant love; God begins the relationship of covenant and asks that we reciprocate: we are each to love God and to love others (the two great commandments). We are to love God because He loves us, and we are to love others because God loves them—even if they don't love us, *e.g.*, our enemies. The essence of covenant then is committed *agape* love, and it can be characterized by showing faithfulness, hope, loyalty, patience, courage, and related psychological characteristics. The presence of these "virtues" should be seen as evidence that a person has developed, that one is expressing the image of God—the person—implanted in us.

Now God gives each of us the choice to choose freely to covenant with Him. We are constantly offered the choice to reaffirm our commitment to God and others or to reject covenant. Since Adam we have reliably chosen to reject God and to choose ourselves, that is, various idols which are disguised projections of the self. This fundamental tendency based on pride creates the pervasive human expression of narcissism, that is, the choice of self-love over love of God and others. This is, of course, the familiar, fundamental motivation of Satan. The scandal of modern psychological theory is that it openly champions the narcissistic love of oneself and explicitly rejects love of God and of others. Some, like Fromm, deny this,[7] but in fact their denial is only superficial, since the proposed love of others is always dependent on a prior, total commitment to the self and its desires. The individual self is always the final, ultimate court of approval. Fromm, in spite of his occasional protests against selfishness and narcissism, proposed a theory that is thoroughly based on self-love with all its destructive consequences.[8]

Because human beings since Adam and Eve have chosen, in

---

[7] E. Fromm, *The Art of Loving* (New York: Harper, 1956).

[8] W. K. Kilpatrick, *Psychological Seduction* (Nashville, TN: Thomas Nelson Inc., 1983); Vitz, *Psychology as Religion*; Wallach and Wallach, *Psychology's Sanction*.

general, to break the covenant with God, the Jews were explicitly chosen to keep the covenant alive. And, the history of the Jews has been a constant struggle with the powerful tendency to break this covenant, to run after false gods, all "disguised" projections of the self. (Examples of the substitute for Yahweh range from Astarte and Baal to secular Zionism.) This covenant with the Jews is God's first explicit social covenant and by implication there is a Jewish covenant psychology—that is, a psychology of how a Jew is to express his or her internal image of God. This "old" or first covenant theory of personality would presumably derive from the history of the struggle to express, maintain, and develop the covenant that God made with the Jews, a story centered on the great Jewish figures such as Abraham, Moses, Joseph, David, and the prophets—all models for a covenant psychology.

However, our focus is on the New Testament or New Covenant, which is understood as completing and fulfilling the original covenent—but certainly not negating it. In this new covenant all people have been given Jesus as the model for a covenant relationship with God and with others. The image of God in us—the person in us—develops through a commitment to Jesus and others. It is through this loving commitment to others that each human being comes into a fuller existence as a person—that is how one "becomes a person."

When Carl Rogers titles his well-known book *On Becoming a Person*,[9] he is simply wrong. Instead he has written a book on becoming an *individual*, in particular, an autonomous, self-actualizing, independent individual. An individual is created by separating from others, by breaking, by concentrating psychological energy and effect on the self instead of on God and others. The founders of modern psychology clearly knew this. The first expression of the ideas Rogers made more widely known is in the earlier writings of Alfred Adler and Carl Jung. Adler called his psychology "Individual Psychology"; Jung called the central process of self-development "individuation."

---

[9]C. Rogers, *On Becoming a Person* (Boston: Houghton-Mifflin, 1961).

Hence, Rogers should have called his book *On Becoming an Individual*. But a person is in fundamental respects the opposite of an individual, for a person comes into existence by connecting with others—not by separating, by choosing covenant and connection, not by choosing autonomy and separation. That is, much of humanistic self-psychology is the antipsychology or antistructure of a Christian covenant psychology. (Philosophy has long maintained the difference between the individual and the person.)[10]

For example, in our relationship to others, Christians are called to love and to forgive, while secular psychology calls people to trust and to forget. Briefly, let us look at these relationships. First, one should ask whether it makes any sense to make trust in others the fundamental virtue. Certainly not—and Jesus never asks one to do it. (He was too much of a Jewish realist.) Jesus certainly never trusted others; in particular, he didn't trust the apostles and for good reason, since one would betray him, another deny him, and all abandon him. But he did love them! A mother may not always trust her child, a husband may not always trust his alcoholic wife, but both can always love. After one has been betrayed once, much less long before "seventy times seven," one would be a fool to trust the other person—but it is still possible to forgive. Secular psychology is being utterly foolish to ask to trust, much less to forget, under the circumstances. In short, to love and when hurt to forgive is realistic and possible (however difficult) but to trust and when hurt to forget is foolish and impossible. (It is impossible to truly forget that another has hurt you.)

One further major point that distinguishes a Christian and covenant theory of personality from a secular and self-theory of the individual: covenant theory is not just psychologically realistic, it is based on reality—on that which exists outside the self. To become a person is to be respectful of external realities. All secular theories of personality, by making the self the center of

---

[10] J. Maritain, *The Person and the Common Good* (Notre Dame: University of Notre Dame Press, 1966; first published in 1947).

personality, in contrast, withdraw one from reality, from the external world created by God and filled with real others. In short, secular theories of the individual are intrinsically subjective. This means that the secular psychology of a person is intrinsically atheistic and relativistic; it tends to gnosticism, solipsism, nihilism, and total subjectivism. A good example of this tendency is Carl Rogers's most recent book in which he argues for a thoroughgoing subjectivism: "there are as many realities as there are persons"; we must prepare for a world of "no solid basis, a world of process and change . . . in which the mind . . . creates, the new reality."[11] Other evidence for the subjectivity of much "personality" theory has been its reliable tendency to merge with Eastern religion, with subjective drug states and many kinds of occult world views that claim reality is the creation of each self. The ultimate narcissism is that you are the creator of the world.[12]

Actually, the essential logic of becoming an individual — that is, of separating and distancing the self from others — eventually gets carried to its logical extreme. First you break the "chains" that link you to society, then to others, then the chains that link you to self, and finally, the rejection of the self itself — that is, separation from the illusion of the ego. Finally you reject the ego and all its desires — something that culminates in an experience, or state of nothing. Radical autonomy ultimately means separation from everything, it means total or ultra-autonomy where the self is gone, hence, the affinity of self-psychology for transpersonal psychology and finally the subjective states of Eastern religions, *e.g.*, Buddhism.

The development of a person, being the antiprocess of the development of an autonomous individual, moves in an opposite direction. The person is created by union with God and others. It is love that brings this union — this enlargement. The person knows not the "peace of nothing" — but instead knows

---

[11]C. Rogers, *A Way of Being* (Boston: Houghton-Mifflin, 1980), p. 352.
[12]For a discussion of this tendency of self and individual-oriented psychology to turn into subjectivism, see Kilpatrick, *Psychological Seduction*.

the joy of union in love. We are one with Christ — and Christ and the Father are one.

To summarize:

A *Person* is created by God in the Image of God.
An *Individual* is created by the self in the image of the self.

A *Person* loves God and others and loves the self as others.
An *Individual* loves and trusts the self, may trust others, and rejects or ignores God.

A *Person* has the fundamental goal of a state of union with God.
An *Individual* has the fundamental goal of a process of separating from others, and eventually of separating from the self.

For a *Person* true freedom is complete dependence on God who is autonomous.
For an *Individual* true freedom is complete dependence on the autonomous self.

For a *Person*, God and others and the physical world are objective realities.
For an *Individual*, all outside the self is subjective — a nonreality.

Manhood and Fatherhood, Womanhood and Motherhood as Basic to a Person

Furthermore, each person is called to become a man or a woman: "male and female He created them." After our existence, our sex is the basic reality. Thus, a covenant psychology leads directly to the psychology of manhood and womanhood (something no secular self-psychology has ever mentioned). Almost all secular psychologies, however, call each self to a unisex or androgynous ideal.

As just one example of this sexual expression of covenant psychology we take the great and traditional interpersonal relationship of father to son or daughter. To my knowledge, there is no theory of personality or psychotherapy which has as a central or even as a peripheral premise that a man's personality is nourished and brought to richness, strength and deep significance, through being a father. This absence aside from being profoundly antisocial is intellectually inexcusable. One has only to look at the greatest works of literature to see how important to humanity the theme of fatherhood has been. We in the West have become a people, a society, with no concept of fatherhood. Our theories of what it means to be a man, a male person, contain no reference to fatherhood. Is it any wonder that we are also a nation of absent fathers? But Christianity has always known the importance of fatherhood — and I don't just mean the biological relationship. Christian history is full of men, from St. Paul to Chuck Colson, who developed as Christians, as distinctive "persons," in large part through their very functioning as *fathers* to others.

The same goes, of course, for motherhood. I began with a discussion of the importance of fathers, because it is that relationship which seems in such danger of collapse at present. But even that greatest of all human commitments, motherhood, the covenant between mother and child has been very much undermined in recent years. Again, one looks in vain, in our psychologies of personality, for theory which places *any* emphasis on being a mother as central to the development of a mature, deep personality in a woman. And again, the Christian emphasis on the relationship of mother to child is not restricted to marriage, or to biological motherhood. From Mary and Martha in the New Testament to Mother Teresa of Calcutta, Christian history is filled with great "mothers" who had no natural children.

Apparently, it is just beginning to dawn on people that the psychology of manhood is central to much of what is going on in our society today. We are starting to understand that we are in the midst of a crisis in what it means to be a man and, above all, in what it means to be a father — most particularly, in what it means to be a Christian man and father. This crisis has developed because the concepts of manhood and fatherhood have been under relentless attack throughout the modern period, an attack that has become acute in recent years.

Let me describe the situation in which the Christian father finds himself today. He is, if you will, the point man, leading his family as best he can like a small patrol through a hostile and anti-Christian society. He is being shot at from all sides. The world of business and the professions couldn't care less about a man's family or his function as father. They want one thing—commitment to the job, to the business, and the more time and energy you give to that the better. A family is a kind of luxury that shouldn't get in the way. To have three or more children is often seen as a statement of lack of full commitment to your job, your company, your career. It certainly takes time, and that will often cost the father promotions and raises. The result is that the man who needs more money gets less. There is certainly no longer any real status in our society to being a father. And, of course, for decades, corporations have assumed a father will move his family whenever his skills can be used elsewhere, or even leave his family on a few months of special assignment because of the corporate need. If he turns down the "opportunity," this is often seen as evidence of lack of full commitment.

Meanwhile, the new world of sexuality and pornography has placed another aggressive anti-family force in the corporate business world. Everywhere the Christian father gets the message: look out for yourself, forget fidelity, grab all the gusto you can. And now there are all the new sexual temptations and pressures from so many women working in the business and professional worlds. No wonder divorce is rampant. We care more about our individual rights and salaries, about our personal pleasures, than about anything else.

Then there is our pluralistic culture, a culture that increasingly mocks Christianity and very openly makes fun of Christian values. The net effect of all these pressures is to make the Christian father look like, and often feel like, some kind of chump, some kind of fool, even a drudge. Again no wonder so many fathers move on and cop out.

From a different side come the shots of the feminists, and the shooting has been pretty heavy from that direction for thirty years now. They have provided a constant, strident attack on men for being men—or for not being the men *they* want men to be. Above all, this movement has consistently expressed a hatred for the very concepts of manhood and fatherhood, and its adherents actively work for the suppression or removal of these important, distinctive realities.

This long-term, multifaceted attack from all sides on men, especially on fathers, has had enormous impact. American men increasingly seem to fall into two categories. Many remain men but cease caring much for others. They devote their energy, strength, and intelligence exclusively to their own individual well-being, to their careers, to looking out for "Number One." They distance themselves from women who are seen as sex partners, while marriage is understood as something to be avoided or as just a current arrangement to be temporarily maintained until something or someone better comes along.

However, many other men, often unconsciously, cease being men at all. They become nice androgynous creatures, but they are also indecisive, unreliable, and weak. Very briefly, men are opting for one of two ways of being: the strong man who leads and exploits, or the weak man who is ineffectual but nice. Recently, it seems like the latter is the fastest-growing category. We all know "the Great American Wimp." He feels uncomfortable among men, because men sense he is squishy. The wimp needs to be loved at all costs, and the typical cost of this need is the truth. In particular, the truth of manhood embarrasses him and therefore he acts as though it doesn't exist. This new type of American, "the wimp man," was at first welcomed by many women. But by now the complaints are coming in loud and strong. The wimp, like the macho, fundamentally avoids commitment to others, he can't be counted on, often he is still too dependent, too much like a child—a Peter Pan. Hence both the macho man and the wimp man avoid true commitment to women—and, of course, women know it. The final result is that a good man becomes even harder to find. All this only increases the disappointment, frustration, bitterness, and anger of many women, which only leads them to further attacks on men and manhood, which further pushes men away. What a vicious cycle.

The answer to all this — let me suggest — is the Christian man, the man who is fully a man in the natural sense: he leads, he has energy, zeal, but he puts his manhood in the service of God and of others — his family, employees, or community. Here is the man who truly enjoys his God-given masculinity, because he is using this gift for others. Thus does grace perfect nature. He is a man with true strength, without the macho's selfish insecurity, without the secret cringing and anxiety of the wimp.

One could go on at length about the crisis of manhood in our society, and about the Christian man devoted to servant leadership as the answer. Instead I will conclude this topic by pointing out that this concept of manhood is just beginning to be appreciated in psychology. Well-known recent, major contributions have documented the great importance of the father for the healthy psychological development of his children. Less known are the quite recent books that have focused on homosexuality as a form of arrested masculine or feminine development.[13] This is a problem that in recent years thousands of homosexuals have been able to surmount within the framework of various spiritual programs, most especially those governed by Christianity.[14]

Christian Concepts for Counseling: The Position of Stanley R. Strong

I turn now to some explicit practical concepts, applicable to counseling, that derive from a Christian theory of the person. I

---

[13] E. Moberly, *Homosexuality: A New Christian Ethic* (Cambridge: Clarke, 1983); E. Moberly, *The Psychology of Self and Others* (London: Methuen/Tavistock, 1985); Van den Aardweg, *On the Origins and Treatment of Homosexuality* (New York: Praeger Publishers, 1986).

[14] E. Moberly, *Psychogenesis* (London: Routledge & Kegan Paul, 1983); L. Payne, *The Broken Image* (Westchester, IL: Crossway, 1981); L. Payne, *Crisis in Masculinity* (Westchester, IL: Crossway, 1985); Van den Aardweg, *Homosexuality and Hope* (Ann Arbor, MI: Servant Publications, 1985); Van den Aardweg, *Origins*.

will focus on the problems of anger and forgiveness, and on the understanding of both proposed by the Christian psychologist Stanley R. Strong.[15] That is, much of this material will be quoted and summarized from the writings of Strong. I choose Strong's work because he articulates the issues especially well and, of course, because I generally agree with him. The kind of psychology exemplified by Strong, I like to call "Reconciliation Psychology" since that is what it is focused on. (In ways it has parallels to the newly emerging reconciliation theology, which is a response to liberation theology. In this respect it is interesting to note that humanistic or self-psychology has much in common with liberation theology.)

Strong observes that in his counseling experience

> . . . we definitely live in the post-Freudian era. That is to say, Freud found people who were repressed, who felt guilty about not carrying out their responsibilities, who needed confession and release from repression to gain health. We have not found anyone who feels guilty. The people I see are not guilty, they are angry. They feel that their individual rights have been violated. They are self-righteously angry and are seeking vengeance and retribution.[16]

No doubt Strong has somewhat overstated his case, since some older-style guilty clients are still to be found, but my own experience and that of countless other therapists overwhelmingly support Strong's claim. Strong continues:

> If we reflect a moment, we see that seeking individual rights is the password of the day. In all areas of our society individuals are encouraged to reach out for their "just" desserts, to stand up for their rights, to be assertive. This philosophy of social justice is creating a fallout of victims who are angry at the injustices others do to them and who are seeking vengeance or who turn

---

[15] S. Strong, "Christian Counseling in Action," *Counseling and Values* 21 (1977), 89–128.

[16] S. Strong, "Christian Counseling," *Counseling and Values* 20 (1976), 151–160.

that anger inward and are wallowing in self-pity and depression. Unfortunately, living with other individuals is quite impossible when everyone is seeking his individual rights. Insuring that we receive our just rights requires a vigilance of others' actions to make sure that they are not violating our rights. The inevitable violations and transgressions result in demands for redress and vengeance. The rights orientation within a group such as a marital pair results in a spiral of accelerating demands where one injustice leads to angry actions to correct that injustice which creates a greater injustice which leads to reciprocation which leads to divorce.[17]

Jesus was very clear about anger. In Matthew 5:20-23, Jesus describes the new standard he has brought for us:

For I tell you if your virtue goes no deeper than that of the scribes and Pharisees, you will never get into the kingdom of heaven. You have learnt how it was said to our ancestors: you must not kill; and if anyone does kill, he must answer for it before the court, but I say this to you: anyone who is angry with his brother will answer for it before the court; if a man calls his brother "Fool," he will answer for it before the Sanhedrin; and if a man calls him "Renegade," he will answer for it in hell fire.

Strong notes that this presents a progression of the seriousness of the consequences of anger to match the depth of the anger and the depth of the self-righteousness causing it. To call a transgressor a "fool" is to call him emptyheaded, an idiot lost of his senses. He is foolish but not intending to be evil. To call the transgressor "renegade" is to see him as intending to do evil. Since we are all familiar with anger in ourselves, we recognize that this progression follows naturally. The depth of insight in this is surprising to Strong, for murder is but a step away from deep anger. Like Strong, I have come to understand hell fire not only as possible eternal damnation but more compelling as the hell in which the person is now living. A person who burns in rage, whose entire existence is bent upon revenge and self-

---

[17]*Ibid.*

protection from unscrupulous tormentors, is truly living right now in hell.

Rights

Strong's analysis of individual rights is striking and insightful:

> Anger stems from a perception of rights. I do not become angry at a man unless I see him as transgressing my rights. Anger represents my concern for me. "Rights" is an interesting concept, one which I have not run into in the New Testament. It is an area in which I could use help from you. For example, I see the Ten Commandments as entailing responsibilities, not rights. "Thou shalt not kill" is not "Thou hath a right not to be killed" but rather "Thou hath a responsibility not to kill." The emphasis is on the responsibility I have with respect to my fellows, rather than on the rights I can expect my fellows to carry out for me. This is a very important concept. In God's order of things, I have no right not to be put upon, insulted, humiliated, beaten, even murdered. I rather have a responsibility not to so do.[18]

Perhaps in our own life each of us has felt the evil pleasure that accompanies the trouble that befalls an antagonist, particularly a spouse. In fact, rights get in the way, and indeed taking offense, being resentful, delighting in sin are self-righteous, hateful actions.

> The Old and New Testament advise Hebrews and Christians to avoid vengeance. God makes it clear that vengeance for wrongdoing is His domain and we are not to take His prerogatives (Deuteronomy 32:35; Job 36:13; Psalms 37; Matthew 5:21-23). We are to trust Him to punish wickedness and sin. Pride, or setting ourselves up as God, is the root of vengeance. The New Testament offers an explicit alternative to vengeance — forgiveness. Jesus warns us of the evils of anger (Matthew 5:22-24); the Lord's Prayer explicitly reminds us that we must

---
[18]*Ibid.*

forgive those who transgress our rights if we are to receive the forgiveness God freely gives us. Our punishment for not forgiving is the fire of anger, the poison of vindictiveness, and the rot of bitterness.[19]

Strong, like many psychotherapists, has often talked with people who believe they have a right to be loved. They are constantly on the vigilance to make sure that those who ought to love them do love them and they burn in jealousy and resentment because, in fact, these persons are not fully and perfectly loving. Strong urges them to accept responsibility to love, to seek to love rather than to seek to be loved. While no one can do anything to ensure that he will be loved, everyone can always be loving and his life will be rich, rewarding, and full.

Depression

Depression very often comes from a belief in a conditional, works-oriented personal worth. If to be worthy I must measure up to certain standards and achieve recognition from others, I will most certainly conclude that I am unworthy and will be filled with anger at my imperfections and filled with self-pity because I am not endowed as I should be and have a right to expect. Depression is closely related to anger at others.

> Depending on whether the person feels himself worthy and perfect or unworthy and imperfect, he or she will be full of self-hatred and self-pity for being so wretchedly inadequate or will be full of hate, bitterness, and anger at the others who do not pay tribute to perfection. Depression has a deep component of hatred for God: God is responsible for my imperfection; my self-hatred parallels my hatred of God.[20]

Of course, the self-hatred stems from pride, or more particularly, from self-worship. The person has created his own stan-

---

[19]Strong, "Christian Counseling in Action," p. 120.
[20]*Ibid.*, p. 121.

dards of self-worth (a function usurped from God) and then condemns himself from failing to meet the standards of self-significance he (or she) has set up. Thus the person condemns himself. In the extreme this logic of judging the self by one's own standards can lead to suicide. However, we must always remember that vengeance is the Lord's and *we have no right to condemn any self, our own or others*.

Forgiveness

Strong notes that to move from a position of self-righteousness and anger to a position of love and concern requires an ability to forgive others for their trespasses and to seek forgiveness from others for our anger. The very sharp teeth in the Lord's Prayer are often overlooked: " . . .and forgive us our trespasses as we forgive those who trespass against us . . ." How well do we forgive those who trespass against us? No doubt among those who read this are some who harbor resentments and unforgiveness. We are each in great moral danger to the extent that we are unforgiving of others' offenses against us. Jesus made many provisions for routing out anger and self-righteousness. He placed responsibility on those who receive the anger as well as on those who are angry. If we love one another, we have a responsibility and a deep concern for our brothers who are in such treacherous danger. If they are angry, they are in grave danger. If we love them, we are grieved by the danger and will take responsibility for helping them with that danger. In Matthew 5:23-24, Jesus said:

> . . . so then, if you are bringing your offering to the altar and remember that your brother has something against you, leave your offering there before the altar, go and be reconciled with your brother first and then come back and present your offering.

Strong's position is that, in love for my brother, each of us must take the step for reconciliation. In working with individuals and couples, a key and critical problem is to begin the process of forgiveness.

Forgiveness, however, is not always a simple or easy process. Indeed, there are probably stages of forgiveness, and what they are and how to facilitate them is one of the tasks of Christian psychology. For example, what is false or cheap forgiveness? How do you recognize it? Once recognized how is this to be communicated to the client? Is the first stage of forgiveness "denial" that one is even angry, much less that forgiveness is needed? What is the therapist's role as a model for forgiveness? In this respect Strong gives a striking and surprising example.

> An incident that taught me the power of the counselor as a model occurred when I was working with a family in which the husband had steadfastly avoided accepting his responsibility for many of the household difficulties. One night I was boring in on a small but illuminating incident of his failure when, much to my surprise, he exploded, "I am not going to sit here and be beaten over the head with this trivial, insignificant incident." He leapt to his feet and lunged for the door. He grasped the door unsteadily (or was my vision blurring?), turned to his wife, and said, "I'm going home. Are you coming with me"? . . . The way he said it chilled my bones: This was the critical point for their marriage. She quickly got up and left (thank God!).

> I was left shell-shocked. My vision tunneled and my heart pounded. My first thought was to retreat to the rationalizations of my profession: Obviously the husband is not ready for counseling, and I'll simply sign him off as a premature termination. But I remained troubled, and that night it became clear that I could not just sign him off. First, I was responsible for what happened. Although he had reacted wildly outside my expectations, I had failed to note his rising agitation. Was it loving of me to push him beyond his ability to control himself? Who was supposed to be clinically sensitive? Who was the counselor—and in Christ at that? Also, Christ taught that when our brother is angry with us we are to go to him and be reconciled, not necessarily for our sake but for his. Anger separates him from God,

and we, in love for him, are concerned for this grievous situation.

> In fear and trembling I called him. He did not seem happy to hear from me. I told him I had been wrong; I had been insensitive; I had been unloving; and I asked him to forgive me. To my relief and joy he readily did so. He asked forgiveness for his actions, which I in joy gave. Before long he asked to come back. He and his wife reported that the incident had turned their family life around. I had modeled what he needed to learn (he also taught me what I needed to learn). He was now less afraid to make wrong judgments as head of the household. He acknowledged when he was wrong and asked forgiveness. I saw them several times after that, worked out details in their family relationships, but they were equipped for handling the crises life has for us all and they now serve as an inspiration to the rest of us.[21]

Although forgiveness is a powerful force for healing, no major secular theory of psychology uses this idea. After all, in the secular world of the ego, to forgive is a sign of weakness. Indeed, learning to be *angry* at others, is what most of "consciousness-raising" is all about: one comes to an awareness of how badly one had been treated by others! Forgiveness has no role here. In secular therapy one is to *forget*—but not *forgive*. The irony is that it is not really possible to forget, but it is possible to forgive. In a word, forgiveness, with its many benefits for the psyche (and the soul) has no place in secular approaches to psychotherapy or counseling. Yet without forgiveness there is no reconciliation either between God and man, or between man and man. In short, the psychology of forgiveness is at the center of a covenant psychology or psychology of reconciliation.

In conclusion, as you reflect on such very basic and psychologically important concepts as "person" and "forgiveness" it should, I hope, be clear that a Christian understanding or theory of personality is not just a critique of the secular models but

---

[21]*Ibid.*, pp. 104–105.

a very important positive contribution. Furthermore, a Christian model is compatible with many of the genuine contributions of the secular theories, but one with a powerful transcendent and synthesizing character. Of course, much of this positive contribution remains to be articulated and tested. However, with God's grace Christian psychologists will continue developing this surprisingly new model of the person. After many decades when we Christians have been on the defensive, this shift should be most welcome. For such a shift has all the signs of being a major paradigm shift for all of psychology, the kind of paradigm shift so cogently advocated in the writing of Mary Stewart Van Leeuwen.[22] In any case, the best defense is a good offense—and it is much more fun besides.

---

[22] M. S. Van Leeuwen, *The Sorcerer's Apprentice* (Downers Grove, IL: InterVarsity Press, 1982); M. S. Van Leeuwen, *The Person in Psychology: A Contemporary Christian Appraisal* (Grand Rapids, MI: Wm. B. Eerdmans Publishing Co., 1985).

Index

A

Adams, Jay 91, 105
Adler, Alfred 77, 87, 176-177, 199, 207
    fulfillment model 184, 197
    individual psychology 207
agape 205, 206
agnosticism 66
Allport, Gordon 20, 23, 27, 29, 38, 177, 184, 197
analytic psychology 3, 72, 77-78, 85-86
    individuation 207
    personality types 175, 180
    self-realization 72-73, 87, 207
    also see Carl Jung
Angyal, Andras 177
Aquinas, Sir Thomas 13
Arendt, Hannah 112, 114
Aristotle
    essentialism 13-14
atheism 66, 74
    functional 66
attribution 194
Augustine, St. 13, 187

B

Bakan, David 62
Barth, Karl 164
behaviorism 16-17, 22, 99-100, 111-114, 192
    difficulties of 17, 111-116
    radical 191
    also see B. F. Skinner
Berger, Paul
    Introduction to Sociology 24-25
Berkhouwer, G. C. 188-189, 190
Bethge, Eberhard 153
Bible
    see Christian theory of personality—biblical perspectives
Binswanger, Ludwig 184
Bonhoeffer, Dietrich 153, 170
Boss, Médard 184
Brentano, Franz 63
Briggs, Stephen
    biography 19
    chapter summary viii-ix, 33-34
Bruke, Ernst 58, 59
Buber, Martin 126, 127
Burke, Thomas
    biography 1

chapter summary vii–viii
Buscaglia, Leo 108

C

Calvin, John 13, 188
- *Institutes* xiv
Cattell, R. B. 29
character, defined 38
Chesterton, G. K. 139
Christian
  defined 34–35
  Jungian 66
Christian theology 6–13,
  191–195
  fundamentals of 39–49
Christian theory of personality
  33–41, 149–170, 214–222
  atheism and 66
  biblical perspectives 11–17,
    114, 123, 162–168, 186–195
  biological considerations
    36–37
  conversion and sanctification
    195–198
  convenant theory 199–222
  gnosticism and 72–74
  individualism and 70
  naturalism and 67
  plurality of 171–173
  reconciliation psychology
    217–222
  reductionism and 67–70
  relativism and 70–71
  strengths of 104–105,
    142–143, 149
  subjectivism and 71
  also see personality theory
cognitive functioning 10–12
cognitive psychology 100–102

purpose of 202
Coles, Robert 152–153, 168–169
Comte, Auguste 159–160
consort, defined 45n5

D

Dawson, Christopher 138
Descartes, René
  anti-Cartesian tradition
    124–129
  self-knowledge 116–123
Du Bois-Reymond, Emil 58, 59
Dykstra, Craig
  Vision and Character 145
Dykstra, D. Ivan 109–110

E

Eastern religions 88, 209
Eberhart, Richard 154
Eddington, Sir Arthur 32
Einstein, Albert 15
Erhard Seminar Training (est)
  88
Erikson, Erik 23
  continuity view 142
Evans, Stephen 189, 190
existentialism xii
Eysenck, Hans 23, 29

F

family, assaults on 212–214
fatherhood and manhood
  210–214
Feuerbach, Ludwig 119, 159
Fichte, Johann 117–118
Fiske, Donald 177, 185
forgiveness 201, 219–222

Fosdick, Harry Emerson 73
Frankl, Victor 137, 169-170
Freud, Jakob 56, 57, 58
Freud, Sigmund 22, 23, 98, 103, 104, 109, 121, 177
   cult of 79
   The Interpretation of Dreams 113
   Jung and 86-87
   Moses study 61-63
   Moses and Monotheism 83
   on religious feelings 52, 66, 159, 199
   Sartre and 112-114
   spiritual odyssey of 55-63
   also see psychoanalysis
Fromm, Erich 76, 77, 87, 88-89, 177, 184, 197, 206
   The Dogma of Christ 89
   You Shall be as Gods 89

G

Glover, Willis B. 14
   Biblical Origins of Modern Secular Culture 13
gnosticism 72-74, 201
Goldstein, K. 87
Greene, Graham 155
Guilford, J. P. 29

H

Hall, A. R. 14
Hall, G. Stanley 63, 76
Hauerwas, Stanley 135
Hegel, Georg Wilhelm 116, 122, 124
   The Phenomenology of Spirit 118

Helmholtz, Hermann von 58
Herbsleb, Jim 96
Hogan, R. 68, 69
Howard, Tom
   Chance or the Dance? 136
humanism xii, 22
   vs science 3-5, 15-16
humanistic psychology 86-88, 104, 108, 199
   also see self-psychology; Carl Rogers; Abraham Maslow
Hume, David 2
Husserl, Edmund 116

I

Ichheiser, Gustav
   Appearance and Realities 27
Image of God 12, 159-168, 193, 203
individualism 70
intersubjectivity 116, 123-129, 129-131
intuition 96-97

J

Jacobi, Jolande 72
Jaki, Stanley 14-15
James, William 43, 44, 63, 76
   The Varieties of Religious Experience 43
Jesus Christ
   on anger 216, 219
   as anti-Oedipus 81-85
   identification with 204-210
Jones, E. E. 25
Journal of Personality and Social Psychology 22
Judaism

Reform 56
  assimilated Jews 56-57
Jung, Carl 23, 72, 77-78, 177
  Answer to Job 85
  Freud and 86-87
  religion and 199
  also see analytic psychology
Jungian Christians 66

K

Kant, Immanuel 117-118
Kelly, George 23, 177, 185
Kelsey, Morton 78
Kierkegaard, Soren 116, 119, 124
Kilpatrick, William Kirk 92, 93
  biography 133
  chapter summary xiii
knowledge, three types of 5
  propositional 6-10
knowledgism 72-74

L

Lasch, Christopher 76-77
Lewis, C. S. 105, 192
liberal arts education 18
liberation theology 215
logic 97-98
logical positivism 2
logos, Nicene-Chalcedonian doctrine of 14-15
Ludwig, Carl 58

M

MacIntyre, Alasdair
  After Virtue 142
MacKinnon, Donald 20

Maddi, Salvatore xiv-xv, 173-174, 177
  metatheory of personality 174-185
    core statements 176-180, 186-195
    developmental statements 181
    ideal personality types 181
    peripheral/concrete statements 180
    schematic representation 177
    tabular summary of 177
  typology of personality theories 183-185
    conflict models 183, 187-188
    consistency model 184-185
    from a biblical perspective 186-188
    fulfillment models 183-184, 197-198
Malony, H. Newton 101
Marcel, Gabriel 126, 127
Marx, Karl 116, 119, 122, 124
Maslow, Abraham 67, 87, 104, 131, 177, 178
  actualization model 184
  also see self-psychology
Masters and Johnson 67
  Human Sexual Response 68
Maxwell, James Clark 203
May, Rollo 76, 87
McClelland, David 177, 185
Menninger, Karl 76
  Whatever Happened to Sin 91
Moses
  Freud's study of 61-63, 83

motherhood and women 211
Mower, O. H. 91
Mueller, Johannes 58
Murphy, Gardner 76
Murphy, Michael 76
Murray, Henry 23, 174, 177
Myers, David 92-93, 97
mystery, defined 110

N

naturalism 67
Nietzsche, Friedrich 119
Nisbett, R. 25
nominalists 130

O

Olson, Elder 160-161
operationism 45

P

Packer, James 35
pagan concept of individual 204
Perl, Fritz 87
person
    defined 150, 202-204
    vs personage 21
personality
    defined 20-22, 28
    inner orientation 28-33
        personality characteristics acquisition 29-31
    outer orientation 24-27
    research 22
        social cognition (personal perception) 25-26, 27
        sociological approach to 24-25, 27
        summary-trait approach 26, 27, 29, 180-181
    also see behaviorism; humanistic psychology; psychoanalysis
personality theory
    narrative vs therapeutic 133-147
    pagan concept 204
    secular vs Christian 37-41, 73-74
    secular, shortcomings of 38-41, 135, 192-193
    truth and 156-157
    also see individual theories and theorists
perspectivalism 98
perspectivism 98-99
philosophy
    Christian psychology and 116-123
    scientific revolution and 3
physicalistic reductionism, failure of 17
Piaget, Jean x, 46
    cognitive development 51-52
    The Mission of the Idea 49
    Outlines of a Philosophy of Religion 48
    The Quest 50
    spiritual odyssey of 47-55
        hermeneutical shift in 53-55
        on religion and science 49-53
    Two Types of Religious Attitude 51
Plantinga, Neal 191-195
Plato 10-11

psychoanalysis xiii, 3, 18, 22, 33, 67, 76-77, 78-94, 130
  biological perspective 101-103, 153
  Cartesian assumptions of 118-119
  conflict/psychosocial model 183, 187
  core statements 186
  Oedipus complex x-xi, 79-85, 199
    Jesus as anti-Oedipus 81-85
  personality types 175, 180-182
  rationalization 122
psychology, secular
  antireligion assumptions of 66-74
  biological 36-37, 102-103
  limitations of 123-147, 208
  religion and 44-47, 74-76, 93, 153-154, 208-209
    Catholic-Protestant split 76-78
    Episcopalian mentality 77
    protestantized version of 77-78
  religious characteristics of
    general 74-78
    specific 78-93
  scientific methods and v-vi, 95, 200, 201
  also see individual theories and theorists

Q

Quine, W. V. 18

R

radical autonomy 209
radical materialism 58-59
Rank, Otto 177, 180
  conflict theory 183
Ransford, Charles
  biography 95
  chapter summary xi-xii
rationality
  and the Image of God 12
reason 97-98
reconciliation psychology 218-222
  depression 218-219
  forgiveness 219-222
  individual rights 217-218
reductionism 67-70, 192
  physicalistic 17
Reformation 189-190
Reist, John
  biography 149
  chapter summary xiii-xiv
relativism 70-71
religion
  Eastern 88, 209
  and psychology 44-47, 74-76, 93-94, 153-154, 208-209
  general characteristics 74-78
  secularized religion themes 46-47
  specific characteristics of 78-94
    of self-psychology 88-94
  also see Christian theory of personality
Rieff, Phillip 135
Robinson, Bishop J. A. T.

The Body: A Study in Pauline Theology 149-150
Rogers, Carl 22, 23, 33, 76, 77, 87-91, 104, 108, 131, 153, 177, 181, 182
  actualization model 184
  On Becoming a Person 207, 208
  A Way of Being 209
  also see self-psychology
Rousseau, Jean-Jacques 124
Runyon, W. M. 32

S

Sabatier, Auguste 48
Sanford, John A. 78
Sartre, Jean-Paul 89, 90, 124, 127
  Freud and 112-114
  on love 125, 126
Schleiermacher, F. D. E. 161-162
scholasticism 1
Schopenhauer, Arthur 119
Schroeder, D. 68, 69
science
  defined 2, 36
  vs humanism 3-5, 15-16
scientific revolution 1-5
  and psychological theory 1-2, 200, 201
self-deification 192-193
selfism 90
  also see self-psychology
self-knowledge 116-123, 129-131
  defined 116-117
self-psychology 86-88
  problems of 90
  religious aspects of 88-94
  also see humanistic psychology; Abraham Maslow; Carl Rogers; transactional analysis
Skinner, B. F. 22, 23, 33, 104, 130, 155
  behaviorism 99-100, 112, 114
Stevens, S. S. 44-45
Strong, Stanley R. 214-222
  also see reconciliation psychology
subjectivism 72

T

Ten Boom, Corrie 107-108
theory, defined 10, 20
  also see Christian theory; personality, secular
Tillich, Paul 161, 162
Torrance, Thomas 203
Tournier, Paul 21
transactional analysis 67, 88, 90
truth, defined 156

V

Vander Goot, Mary
  biography 43
  chapter summary x, 63-64
Van Leeuwen, Mary Stewart 96, 98, 222
  biography 171
  chapter summary xiv-xv, 198
vitalism 58-59
Vitz, Paul 33, 40, 90, 192
  biography 65, 199
  chapter summaries x, xv-xvi

W

Watson, J. B. 63
Westminster Confession of
 Faith 35
Westphal, Merold
 biography 111
 chapter summary xii, 129–131
White, Robert 23
Wolterstorff, Nicholas 186
world view
 as self-explanatory causal
  system 6
Wundt, Wilhelm 63